An Upper Great Lakes Archaeological Odyssey

An Upper Great Lakes Archaeological Odyssey

Essays in Honor of Charles E. Cleland

Edited by William A. Lovis

With a Dedication by Jim Harrison

Library of Congress Cataloging-in-Publication Data

An Upper Great Lakes archaeological odyssey : essays in honor of Charles E.
Cleland / edited by William A. Lovis ; with a dedication by Jim Harrison.
        p. cm.
Includes bibliographical references.
    ISBN 0-87737-045-1
    1. Lake States—Antiquities. 2. Great Lakes Region—Antiquities. 3. Excavations
(Archaeology)—Lake States. 4. Excavations (Archaeology)—Great Lakes Region.
5. Lake States—History. 6. Great Lakes Region—History. 7. Indians of North
America—Lake States—Antiquities. 8. Indians of North America—Great Lakes
Region—Antiquities. 9. Cleland, Charles E., 1936–   I. Lovis, William A.
II. Cleland, Charles E., 1936–

    F551.U67 2004
    977–dc22
                                                                    2003027598

Contents

Figures

Tables

Charles Cleland

. . . on the occasion of his retirement

A NUMBER of years ago I had the idea of making a Ken Starr-type investigation of the behavior of archeologists and anthropologists out in the field. I mean way out in the field, far from the comforts of home and the behavior modification process known as marriage. I have run into these esteemed academics in Africa, France, Russia, Costa Rica, Ecuador, and also the American West. Frankly, I have frequently been amazed at their behavior because it reminded me of that of poets and novelists.

Far be it from me to be critical. America, including academia, is fast becoming a fascist Disneyland, and I don't intend to cooperate one bit. And I'm proud to have observed that the anthropologists and archeologists I've observed aren't cooperating either. The paths of knowledge are as broad as life herself, and these folks don't wear draft-horse blinders. And where is the soul and nature of humankind laid more revealingly bare than in taverns? A few drinks and our receptors are altered in the direction of knowledge and wisdom. Even a truly immense barmaid can become Nefertiti, queen of Egypt, and worthy of some scholarly attention.

Of course no one in this room is guilty of anything, just very lucky that they are members of a discipline that is allowed outdoors rather than having to stay indoors all the time. They even know that the very concept of "indoors" is a more recent invention and one that has been overindulged.

I was amazed when I met Charles Cleland and equally amazed when I read him. I don't blame him for retiring and seeking his own counsel. I retired from Hollywood three years ago and have found it quite wonderful, though there are only nominal similarities between Hollywood and Michigan State University. Nominal but nonetheless real. Cleland's very large mind will continue to allow him to find the grace that he has so nobly earned.

Jim Harrison

Preface

THIS TRIBUTE has been a long time in the making. The construction of a volume that attempts to do justice to an anthropological polymath such as Charles E. Cleland is no mean feat. Cleland's career has both covered and contributed to the arenas of zooarchaeology, ethnozoology, paleoecology, prehistoric and historic archaeology, professional standards and ethics, Native American history, and contemporary treaty rights. These scholarly contributions and his continued involvement in professional organizations such as the Society of Professional Archaeologists (until 2001), the Register of Professional Archaeologists, the Society for Historical Archaeology, and other national, state, and local organizations create a potential palette of paper topics that taxes the imagination. His almost forty M.A. and Ph.D. students, moreover, explored an even wider range of topics and created a pool of potential contributors beyond the scope of this modest tribute.

This volume, therefore, does not pretend to address all of the directions that Chuck Cleland's work has taken. Rather, the contributors are a broad sample of Chuck's friends, colleagues, and former students, sometimes all three, who bring a wide range of perspectives to a diversity of topics in Upper Great Lakes archaeology, many of which Cleland has been directly or indirectly involved with. Aside from the Upper Great Lakes focus, the common thread is the cross- or multidisciplinary perspective that has characterized much of Chuck Cleland's work during the course of his career. Consequently, the various essays included here present ecological, zoological, historical, and taphonomic foci, employing data from the Upper Great Lakes in an attempt to answer archaeological questions both large and small.

The links with Cleland's cumulative research are quite evident, and the contribution by Vergil Noble and me (Chapter 1) places the linkages in historical perspective. For example, Carol Mason's work (Chapter 6) presents new insights into the late prehistoric cultural changes at the

Heins Creek site, a site with a faunal assemblage that Cleland used for his doctoral dissertation. Furthermore, it employs a set of data collected by a dedicated avocational archaeologist, an approach that Cleland was fond of employing in his own work. The essays by Janet Brashler and Margaret Holman (Chapter 2) and Marla Buckmaster (Chapter 3) revisit a pair of research topics that launched Chuck Cleland on his several-decades-long engagement with northern Michigan. These are the settlement and subsistence systems of the so-called transition zone between the Canadian and Carolinian Biotic Provinces, and the role of maize agriculture in the region, although the case study presented here by Buckmaster is further north than Chuck initially imagined. One of the outcomes of this fascination with the late prehistoric economics of the Upper Great Lakes was the development of a model of the Inland Shore Fishery, predicated on the development of the gill net, a topic here reassessed by Beverley Smith (Chapter 5) from the hindsight of twenty years of additional research.

Cleland's early contributions to zooarchaeology made him a leader in this specialty (see the quote from Cleland on this topic in Chapter 1). His leadership is reflected in this volume not only by the insightful work of Smith, but also through the contribution of Terrance Martin (Chapter 9), who applies zooarchaeological analysis to the remains of a historic Mesquakie fort. Martin thereby combines two of Cleland's primary interests: the historic archaeology of forts, and the analysis of animal remains. In fact, Cleland may be responsible for the excavation of more historic forts than anyone, not the least of which was his multiyear oversight of the work conducted at Fort Michilimackinac. James Brown (Chapter 8) capitalizes on this work at Michilimackinac by applying recent formulations of distance-based trade to the structure and assemblage of this important eighteenth century entrepôt. The entrée of Euro-Americans onto the nineteenth-century frontier of the Great Lakes likewise occupied segments of Cleland's career, both in terms of the political machinations of nation states as well as those of Europeans and Indians at the local level. Goldstein and Buikstra (Chapter 4) address this issue by assessing a small ethnic cemetery to gain insights into life on the rural nineteenth-century frontier.

Cleland's fascination with the cultural development of landscapes is partially reflected in my own contribution (Chapter 7), which seeks to understand how taphonomy and site preservation play a role in the integration of urban areas into regional prehistoric research. Notably, much of the data for this essay was drawn from compliance-related projects, an arena for which Cleland is an advocate and with which he is both familiar and adept. Neal Ferris (Chapter 10), brings us into the present with an insightful perspective on archaeologist–Native American relationships both legislative and pragmatic. These relationships are a topic near to the heart of Chuck Cleland and pervade his current work.

Those who know Chuck Cleland, and know archaeology and archaeologists, will of course appreciate the thoughts of Jim Harrison in his dedication to this volume. Harrison is clearly an admirer. He is in good company with the other contributors and may have missed his true calling.

Finally, I would like to thank all of those who contributed to this work both substantively and otherwise. In particular, I appreciate the continuing support of Dr. Michael Stafford, former Acting Director of the Cranbrook Institute of Science, without whose assistance this volume would have been much longer in the making. Likewise, I am indebted to the Consortium for Archaeological Research at Michigan State University, including the MSU Museum and the Department of Anthropology, for my incessant use of their facilities in the production of this volume, and particularly the forbearance of my colleagues while I occupied critical computers and peripherals during peak times.

As always, my partner Libby Bogdan-Lovis supported me throughout this at times frustrating and time-consuming enterprise. I tremendously appreciate both her understanding and forbearance.

William A. Lovis

1

Charles E. Cleland
A Retrospective

William A. Lovis and Vergil E. Noble

THE ARCHAEOLOGICAL world in which Charles Cleland (Figure 1.1) matured during the 1960s and the one in which he retired at the turn of the millennium are hardly recognizable as the same place. It would not be an understatement to say that he contributed both force and direction to the compelling winds of change that radically reshaped the discipline of anthropological archaeology. Environmental and evolutionary approaches underwent substantial critique and made way for more inclusive and action-oriented approaches that attended to gender, ethnicity, and class as major problem foci. The voice of American archaeology was altered from that of a single organization, the Society for American Archaeology, to include organizations such as the Society for Historical Archaeology and the Society of Professional Archaeologists (reborn phoenixlike as the Register of Professional Archaeologists), all of which he helped establish. Archaeology changed from a discipline primarily housed in museums and institutions of higher education to one also deeply entrenched in private enterprise and various levels of government. The weak legislation that protected the archaeological heritage of the United States was cumulatively supplanted by a comprehensive suite of laws allowing for the continued monitoring and protection of significant archaeological sites for the benefit of present and future generations. And, finally, the Native American peoples often the subjects of archaeological study, but rarely participants in the process, were afforded more prominent roles in the conduct of archaeology, the disposition of their ancestral human remains, and the protection of their heritage.

Chuck Cleland's influence on these changes in the archaeological milieu has been ongoing, prominent, and recognizable. His creativity and foresight have been instrumental in directing archaeological growth at

Figure 1.1 Charles E. Cleland, Emeritus Professor and Curator of Anthropology, Michigan State University; Montana, 1997. Photo courtesy of the Cleland family.

both the national and institutional levels, while many of the students he trained during his thirty-five-year tenure at Michigan State University today build upon his legacy of focused archaeopolitics and professional service.

While Chuck Cleland's most notable contributions are in the specific arena of archaeology, his training at the University of Michigan during the 1960s left him adamant in the view that archaeology was anthropology, and upon his retirement he insisted that his students, graduate and undergraduate alike, recognize this as an indisputable fact. Perhaps the most egregious sin an archaeology graduate student at Michigan State University could commit was to try to convince Chuck that archaeology should break with anthropology and become a separate discipline. Woe be to the student who naively argued that it would be of little value to take courses in linguistics, ethnography, or sociocultural anthropological theory! At such a prompt Chuck would launch into an exposition of the way in which Ann Arbor luminaries such as Leslie White, Kenneth Pike, Harold Hickerson, and Eric Wolf contributed to his own views of human behavior, the theory of social science, and the role of archaeology within the larger discipline. He would then conclude by telling the chastened student, who had been imparted perhaps more oral history than anticipated or desired, that he expected *his* students not only to be well-trained archaeologists, but well-trained sociocultural anthropologists to boot. Similarly, Chuck's many students who aspired to careers focused on the temporal confines of historical archaeology were summarily advised that they would instead prepare themselves to be North Americanists, first and foremost, familiar with the entire span of the continent's human occupation but emphasizing the most recent centuries. Those who worked with Chuck Cleland soon learned that neither his opinions nor his priorities were often left vague.

His students also soon learned, however, that Chuck was generous with his time and genuinely concerned about their progress. Further, he made sure that they had the opportunity to attend professional meetings and make connections with colleagues that would serve them well throughout their careers. Indeed, Chuck made a special effort to introduce his students to senior archaeological practitioners of his acquaintance, often in conference hotel rooms at informal gatherings that he dubbed "The Late Afternoon Drinking Society," thus bridging the generations and integrating his academic progeny into the profession. But this is getting ahead of our story.

In a recent bout of reflection Charles the Elder gave voice to the path taken by Charles the Younger in his steady ascent to professional archaeologist, thereby inadvertently (we think) making our joint task in this introduction to his festschrift somewhat easier. Titled "And One Thing Led to Another," Chuck presented his unique perspective on his own career as part of an invitational symposium at the Society for Historical Archaeology's Conference on Historical and Underwater Archaeology held in Québec City only a few days after the Y2K crossing.

What might seem a well-planned route was instead, by his own assessment, a convergence of serendipity and blind luck, with an ample dose of familial preadaptation. Chuck Cleland's initial exposure to archaeology came during his tenure as a master's student in zoology at the University of Arkansas in Fayetteville, where his task was to monitor populations of wild turkeys as the basis for his thesis titled "The Re-introduction of the Wild Turkey into the Ozark Highlands." His growing disenchantment with a potential career in wildlife management, coupled with being unemployed due to a conservative backlash as a consequence of his membership in purported subversive organizations, left him especially receptive to any new opportunity that might come his way. In that frame of mind, he happened into a chance encounter with Charles Robert McGimsey III, then a recent Harvard Ph.D. and new arrival on the Fayetteville campus. Bob McGimsey, too, was faced with a dilemma that needed to be solved: the identification of animal remains in the archaeological collections of the university museum. McGimsey inquired whether Cleland might be able to assist him, in which case he could use the data for a master's thesis in anthropology. Chuck's own words aptly capture the situation:

> Here, I confess to a bald faced lie. I told him I had extensive training in the topic and the minute we parted I hurried to the zoology library where I checked out all the books I could find on the osteology of various mammal and bird species. In my defense I had studied vertebrate taxonomy, mammalian anatomy, ecology and a variety of related subjects. By the time McGimsey and I met again a few days later, I was probably the fourth most knowledgeable archaeozoologist in the country after Barbara Lawrence of Harvard, Paul Parmalee at the Illinois State Museum, and Stanley Olson at Arizona. Of course that highfalutin title wasn't invented yet. (Cleland 2000)

It was through his fateful meeting with Bob McGimsey in Arkansas's small campus museum that the archaeological world opened up to Chuck Cleland. While engaged in writing his new thesis titled "Animal Remains of the Ozark Bluff Shelters" (published in 1964 as an article), he met and began a long-standing friendship with Hester "Rusty" Davis, later to be named the first state archaeologist of Arkansas. It was also through Mc-Gimsey that Chuck was eventually wooed by James Bennett Griffin of the University of Michigan to come to Ann Arbor on a four-year assistantship to study anthropology and analyze animal remains derived from archaeological sites around the Lake Huron basin for his dissertation. Thus, during a very short period at the end of the 1950s, Cleland made the drastic shift from turkey management to archaeology; he came under the lasting influence of two remarkable people, McGimsey and Davis, who were to become paramount forces in the development of archaeological legislation and professionalization; and he found himself entering the doctoral program at the University of Michigan to embark on a long career in Great Lakes archaeology under the tutelage of its most renowned practitioner.

Chuck's spontaneous choice of graduate schools, to say nothing of careers, placed him at the nexus of many important changes taking place in archaeology at the time, and he became an integral part of the process. Aside from the teachings of J. B. Griffin, he also took anthropology courses from such leaders in the field as Art Jelinek, Elman Service, Eric Wolf, Mervin Meggitt, Leslie White, Marshall Sahlins, and Frank Livingstone. Moreover, Chuck's residence at the Museum of Anthropology put him in close contact with Al Spaulding, Emerson Greenman, Volney Jones, and Kamer Aga-Oglu. He was then part of a cadre of bright young students hell-bent on changing the nature of archaeology as it was then practiced—students such as Lewis Binford, Mark Papworth, Richard Peske, James Fitting, Al McPherron, Anta White, Dick Flanders, and Earl Prahl. It was also during this period that Chuck expanded his horizons beyond the traditional prehistoric archaeological forte of Ann Arbor to include historical archaeology and ethnohistory, primarily catalyzed through his association with George I. Quimby, curator of North American Archaeology at the Field Museum and a close friend of Griffin. Further, he was soon introduced to the field research Moreau S. Maxwell of Michigan State University had recently begun at Fort Michilimackinac, initially with Chuck's fellow Michigan graduate student Lewis Binford serving as Maxwell's field assistant.

In 1964, Maxwell contacted Cleland about taking a temporary position at Michigan State University while Maxwell, a noted authority on Arctic archaeology, was off in Denmark on a Fulbright fellowship. Now, some readers might recognize that there is something of a rivalry between Ann Arbor and East Lansing. Further, that rivalry is manifested, in part, by the view held in Ann Arbor that MSU is a "cow college," referring of course to its origins as the pioneer land grant university and its incarnation as Michigan Agricultural College. With this in mind, Chuck still takes great glee in relating details of his interview visit to MSU, when he drove down Farm Lane behind a group of students trying desperately to rope an escaped Holstein! This vindicating experience behind him, he subsequently accepted a position as temporary instructor and curator of anthropology for the 1964–1965 academic year, in advance of sitting for his comprehensive exams at Ann Arbor and completing his dissertation. Upon Maxwell's return to campus and assumption of the position as chair of what was then the Sociology and Anthropology Department, Cleland's position became permanent. Thus, Chuck Cleland began his thirty-five-year association with Michigan State University.

The enormous amount of fieldwork being conducted by the University of Michigan during the 1960s left an indelible philosophical imprint on Cleland: archaeologists engage in long-term, field-oriented research focused on clear problems. Through such active fieldwork, he soon came to understand, academic programs are recognized and thrive, prosper, and attract top quality students. Chuck brought this philosophy with him to MSU where he found a kindred spirit in Moreau S. Maxwell, himself a devoted field archaeologist, and worked tirelessly to ingrain the philosophy in his students. Chuck consequently set for himself the mission of developing an archaeological field program in Michigan that would complement that of his alma mater.

In this process Chuck Cleland found a welcome ally in his newly hired colleague at Western Michigan University, Elizabeth Baldwin Garland, who was confronted with a similar challenge. Pooling their limited resources to buy field equipment, rent vehicles, and arrange for housing, they developed a joint MSU-WMU field school in northern Michigan during the summers of 1965 and 1966. The logical choice of a fieldwork location for Chuck was northern Michigan, an area he had grown to know and enjoy during his peregrinations as a student to various U of M field projects, and about which he had learned at the knee of George I. Quimby. The broad focus of this work was to explore in greater depth the concept of adaptations to the so-called Edge Area in Michigan; to comprehend the nature of the origins of food production, if any, in the region; and to refine our understanding of circular earthworks largely concentrated in the ecological transition zone. During those two seasons of work, Garland and Cleland excavated at the Skegemog Point and Samel's Field sites in

Grand Traverse County, and also at the Aetna and Boven Earthworks in Lake County. The task of overseeing the archaeological work being conducted at Fort Michilimackinac in those years by MSU through its association with the Mackinac Island State Park Commission simultaneously fell to Cleland, which further stimulated his interest in the historic period and led to his participation in the founding of the Society for Historical Archaeology at Dallas in 1967. Those field programs also assisted in the building of a small cohort of graduate students for the nascent program, including Lyle Stone, Shu Wu How, Val Canouts, Marla Buckmaster, Dick Clute, Peter Murray, and others, who were housed in a small room in the basement of what was then known as The Museum Department, or simply The Museum, at MSU.

From these inauspicious beginnings both the MSU and WMU programs were able to achieve programmatic autonomy and move forward in their own directions. In 1968, MSU hired two additional archaeologists, Larry Robbins, an Africanist, and James Brown, who specialized in eastern North America and who, before moving on to Northwestern University, would take primary responsibility for the ongoing work at Fort Michilimackinac for three summers. This was a period of tremendous growth for American higher education, and MSU was clearly one of the beneficiaries. Furthermore, those growing programs had access to relatively abundant funding from programs such as the National Science Foundation, thereby assisting in their financial stabilization. Ever the entrepreneur, Cleland took full advantage of the funding opportunities available to lay a solid foundation for MSU's archaeological presence in northern Michigan. From 1967 through 1975, he and his students focused primarily on problems related to the adaptations of the area he called "The Traverse Corridor" in northwest lower Michigan, between the Straits of Mackinac to the north and the southern reaches of Grand Traverse Bay to the south, although he occasionally strayed from these boundaries. During this period he and his students, particularly Bill Lovis, Margaret Holman, and Susan Martin, performed major excavations at the Wycamp Creek, Lasanen, O'Neil, Ponshewaing Point, Pine River Channel, Portage, Johnson, and Screaming Loon sites, while they also did major site surveys on North Manitou Island, the Leelanau Peninsula, the Inland Waterway, the upper Grand River, the Upper Peninsula, and the Pere Marquette River.

Toward the latter part of this period, Cleland's long-standing interest in the ethnographic consequences of contact between Euro-Americans and the indigenous populations of the Great Lakes began to dominate his research interests. No doubt this interest was fueled by his work at Fort Michilimackinac and across the Straits of Mackinac at the Lasanen site. More importantly, Chuck essentially abandoned archaeological fieldwork on prehistoric sites for fifteen years, until a brief period between 1990 and 1992 when he performed work along the St. Mary's River and on Drummond Island. Much of his work on major seventeenth-, eighteenth-, and nineteenth-century sites involved multiyear activities by the many graduate students he attracted to the MSU program in historical archaeology. These included work at Mill Creek by Pat Martin, at Fort Ouiatenon by Judy Tordoff and Vergil Noble, at Fort Brady by Lee Minnerly, at Marquette Mission by Sue Schacher, at Fort Gratiot by Mark Esarey, at Fort Drummond by Paul Demers, and at Indian Village by Eric Perkins. It was only during the brief period from 1979 to 1982, when he engaged in work at the nineteenth-century Mississippi town sites of Colbert, Barton, and Vinton as part of the massive Tennessee-Tombigbee Waterway Project, that Cleland strayed from the Great Lakes.

To put this field career in perspective, if one includes his years as a graduate student at the University of Michigan, Chuck Cleland was engaged in fieldwork every year but one from 1960 to 1998—almost continuously for thirty-eight field seasons! Furthermore, the work he directed formed the basis of theses and dissertations for almost fifty graduate students over that period.

While Cleland's reputation rests largely on his archaeological activities, his academic alter ego lay in ethnohistory. In some respects Cleland never saw a distinction between the use of archaeology and ethnohistory as academic enterprises and as a means to rectify contemporary social problems. As his experience in Arkansas revealed, his interest in social justice had deep roots. His membership in the NAACP and CORE (Congress of Racial Equality) resulted in his being fired from his job at a state institution, but also suggests that his awareness and willingness to act on social issues was well developed even as a graduate student. The juncture of archaeology and ethnohistory provided a vehicle for Cleland to address social issues as an anthropologist concerned with the plight of contemporary Native Americans. His course on North American Indians, ANP 419, incorporated these views so fully that he would often receive standing ovations for his summary lectures. To our knowledge, Cleland was also the first archaeologist in the state to recognize Native American interests in archaeology and, at the Ponshewaing Point site in 1970, to make a concerted effort at incorporating local Indian students into his archaeological fieldwork (Figure 1.2). These views also led to a parallel career as an expert witness on treaty rights cases across the Great Lakes region—an activity that occupied him for the last fifteen years of his MSU career. In those years, he worked for more than sixteen bands of Chippewa and Ottawa in Minnesota, Wisconsin, Michigan, and Ontario, and continues to do so. The results of this work are several. Noteworthy among them is his citation in a recent Supreme Court decision; his 1997 publication of *Rites of Conquest* (University of Michigan Press), detailing the Native American ethnography and ethnohistory of Michigan; and his recent book on the history of the Bay Mills Reservation community (Cleland 2001).

As we intimated earlier, Chuck Cleland's early career contacts with Bob McGimsey and Hester Davis at Arkansas provided him with exposure to activist political archaeology. Both of his early mentors were central in state- and national-level efforts to protect the archaeological heritage of the United States. His family background, too, with multiple generations of physicians and attorneys, provided him with further insights into the nature of professions and what it means to conduct oneself as an ethical professional. Cleland carried lessons learned in both contexts to his role in the development of archaeological organizations designed to enhance the status of archaeology, and to professionalize the discipline through codes of ethics and standards for practice and performance.

At the state level, he was a founding member of the Conference on Michigan Archaeology (COMA), where he served in several capacities including president. His abiding interest in the anthropological nature of historical archaeology as a research specialty (see Fitting and Cleland 1968), catalyzed by the work of Stanley South and Bob Schuyler, among others, led him to coordinate his efforts with those working toward establishment of the Society for Historical Archaeology (SHA). He served that organization in several important capacities, most notably three times as a member of the board of directors and as its president in 1973. And though it has been nearly twenty years since he last held an elected office in the SHA, he continues to be a dominant figure in that international society and the disciplinary specialty it represents. Recognition of the role he has played in both the establishment and maintenance of the SHA and historical archaeology at large has most recently been manifested by his nomination for the prestigious Harrington Medal, conferred at the SHA Annual Meeting in Mobile in 2002.

Without doubt, however, the majority of Cleland's efforts on behalf of professional societies was invested in the development of codes of ethics

Figure 1.2 Ponshewaing Point site field crew, 1970. Back row, left to right, Charles Cleland, Nancy Nowak Cleland, William Lovis, David Massey, Russell Menafee. Front row, left to right, Billy Massey, Patricia Fisher, Rebecca Drake, Joseph DeGuvara.

and professional standards, focused through the Society of Professional Archaeologists (Figure 1.3). With the advent of major national-level archaeological and historic preservation legislation during the 1960s and 1970s, archaeology saw an expansion beyond the traditional venues of the field in academic institutions and museums. Private archaeological firms were cropping up, and the archaeological bureaucracies at the state and national levels were expanding. This was a new arena for archaeology, and Cleland, as well as others, was concerned that the quality of work performed by archaeologists needed to be assured as those new niches expanded. He was convinced that whatever constituted professionalism in archaeology should be determined by archaeologists, much in the way that the American Medical Association and the American Bar Association monitor the performance of their respective memberships. This issue was also an increasing concern on the part of the Society for American Archaeology (SAA). To address the potential problems that might arise out of this disciplinary change, the SAA formed a committee to explore the issue and provide recommendations to the board of directors. Cleland was a member of that committee, which he would later often jokingly refer to as "The Dirty Dozen."

Chuck takes delight in relating how the committee, after considering the issues of archaeological expansion, professionalism, and representation, essentially seceded from the SAA and, in a revolutionary document infor-

Figure 1.3 SOPA organizational meeting, Fayetteville, Arkansas, 1976. Left to right, Charles McGimsey, Charles Cleland, Jane Buikstra, William McDonald.

mally known as the Monk's Mound Manifesto, founded the Society of Professional Archaeologists (SOPA). SOPA sought to enhance professionalism in archaeology through defining qualifications for a series of specialties to which archaeologists could apply for certification upon formal review. Members had to adhere to strict requirements for ethics and research standards, and if they appeared to be in violation of those standards they could be subject to grievances and disciplinary actions. While Cleland's hopes that SOPA would function in the same fashion as other professional associations never came to fruition, the larger impact of SOPA on the profession and professionalism was substantial.

Chuck Cleland served SOPA in a variety of elected positions: as an at-large member of the board of directors, as SHA representative to the board, and as president. Perhaps his most lasting impact, however, was through the role he played for two years as SOPA's grievance coordinator, upholding the codified standards and disciplinary procedures through investigation of grievances and formal hearings. His intensive interaction with the attorneys for SOPA during his tenure led him to state on more than one occasion that he was practicing law without a license. The diligence with which he tackled grievances did much to strengthen both SOPA and the profession of archaeology. His efforts on behalf of the profession were later recognized through conferral of SOPA's Distinguished Service Award in 1991.

Six years later, SOPA, with explicit endorsement and financial sponsorship by the SAA and SHA, became reincarnated as the Register of Professional Archaeologists (RPA), an organization that Chuck supported with the same fervor that he brought to the creation of SOPA some twenty years earlier. Indeed, his vigorous advocacy for this reformation resulted in his earning, along with his inspirational mentor, Bob McGimsey, the last SOPA Presidential Recognition Award in 1997. One year later, the Archaeological Institute of America joined the SAA and SHA as a sponsor of the RPA, representing the first time that all three of the major scholarly archaeological organizations in North America formally banded together to support the ideal of professionalism. And by the end of 1999, the number of archeologists voluntarily subject to explicit standards of performance and formal disciplinary procedures under the RPA had more than doubled the peak membership of SOPA. The dream Chuck shared with the other founders of SOPA in 1976 was at long last approaching its realization. His central role in this long process is best certified by RPA's resurrection in 2003 of SOPA's Distinguished Service Award, conferred on Chuck and his mentor Hester Davis. The wording on the award reads: "In Recognition of Significant Contributions to Professionalism in Archaeology."

Chuck has set an example in professional service that, in turn, has instilled an abiding dedication to professional service among his students that will continue to shape American archaeology in the coming decades. Many of his former students have selflessly contributed their time and talent to the SAA, the SHA, SOPA (and its successor, the RPA), COMA, and many others, including the Society for Industrial Archaeology, the Society for Archaeological Science, and the American Cultural Resources Association. Further, the colleagues, students, and employees of those students will likely carry Chuck's tradition of service to the profession forward through the end of the twenty-first century.

Chuck Cleland's research contributions in prehistoric and historical archaeology, his selfless investment in professional archaeological societies, his undaunted entrepreneurial prowess in the development of research programs at MSU, and the dozens of professionals who earned their degrees under his guidance perhaps represent a legacy more appropriate to several individuals. It should be no surprise, then, that the institution with which he has been affiliated for his entire teaching career should recognize those contributions with a Distinguished Faculty Award. That this high honor was conferred in 1978, when Cleland was in the middle years of his career, is particularly noteworthy. It is an award of which Chuck is singularly proud. Even as one of us (Lovis) sits writing this career summary, in close view there is a copy of a letter signed "Charles E. Cleland, Distinguished Professor of Anthropology." Truly, one can say that Chuck's career has, indeed, been distinguished.

2

Middle Woodland Adaptation in the Carolinian/Canadian Transition Zone of Western Lower Michigan

Janet G. Brashler and Margaret B. Holman

In his enduring work on ethnozoology in the Upper Great Lakes, Charles Cleland (1966) analyzed the differing adaptive strategies of Middle Woodland peoples living in the Carolinian and Canadian Biotic Provinces. Subsequent studies by Cleland and others focused on how people at various times used the transition zone between these biotic provinces. The models of Havana/Hopewell subsistence and settlement in western lower Michigan are evaluated with a view toward understanding how groups living at the northern limits of the Carolinian Biotic Province used the transition zone, which was also part of their local environment. Data from key habitation sites along the Grand River where Havana/Hopewell mound and village complexes are located is coupled with information as to site placement, environmental setting, and archaeological evidence from sites throughout the transition zone to address this problem.

SINCE THE RECOGNITION of a relationship between the Illinois heartland of the Havana Tradition and the St. Joseph, Grand, Muskegon, and Saginaw drainages of Michigan was noted more than half a century ago (Quimby 1941), Illinois models of Havana Hopewellian subsistence have been applied to sites of this time period in west Michigan. Thus, Cleland (1966) observed that west Michigan sites were in floodplain locations similar to those of Middle Woodland sites in the central and lower Illinois Valley where Struever (1964) had suggested that people practiced "mud flats" horticulture. The predominance of large game mammals at sites including Spoonville and Norton Mounds was considered by Cleland (1966) to be evidence of a similar horticultural adaptation supplemented by large mammal hunting. Cleland (1966, 67) further reasoned that Middle Woodland faunal assemblages with high usable meat percentages of large game animals were possibly associated with a shift in subsistence strategy toward significant dependence on plant food production. In such situations, hunting was thought to become a secondary seasonal activity emphasizing larger species such as deer and elk.

More recently, Kingsley (1981) addressed the question of Middle Woodland subsistence in Michigan by using Roper's (1979) application of the Illinois model of Intensive Harvest Collecting to less mature Illinois river systems, such as the Sangamon, and by use of analogy between the Sangamon and the Michigan rivers. Attempting to account for the relative absence of Middle Woodland sites in the Kalamazoo River valley, Kingsley reasoned that Middle Woodland populations in west Michigan favored environmental settings along the St. Joseph, Grand, and Muskegon Rivers, which were similar to those selected by Middle Woodland groups in the Illinois River valley, because of the inhabitants' dependence on a particular suite of resources present in some valley floodplains but absent in the Kalamazoo.

As research in Illinois and Ohio began to reveal a reliance on Eastern Agricultural plants by Middle Woodland groups (Asch, Farnsworth, and Asch 1979; Smith 1987), Michigan researchers renewed their efforts to document the introduction and role of these plants and other cultigens in Middle Woodland contexts in Michigan (Lovis et al. 1994; Parker 1992, 1996; Smith et al. 1994).

Studies of west Michigan Hopewellian subsistence have not only applied Illinois models but also assumed that subsistence procurement activities were essentially confined to the Carolinian Biotic Province (Figure 2.1). This assumption is based on the fact that the major Hopewellian Middle Woodland mound and occupation sites are on the Grand River of west Michigan at the northern edge of the Carolinian Biotic Province. It was recognized that the mound and occupation sites on the Muskegon River were in the transition zone between the Carolinian and Canadian biotic provinces (Prahl 1991), but these were not considered to be major sites, nor were they thought to be situated where site location characteristics were conducive to Intensive Harvest Collecting (Kingsley 1981).

Here, we test the applicability of the Illinois-derived subsistence and settlement models of Intensive Harvest Collecting and Eastern Agricultural Complex gardening to Havana-Hopewellian subsistence in west

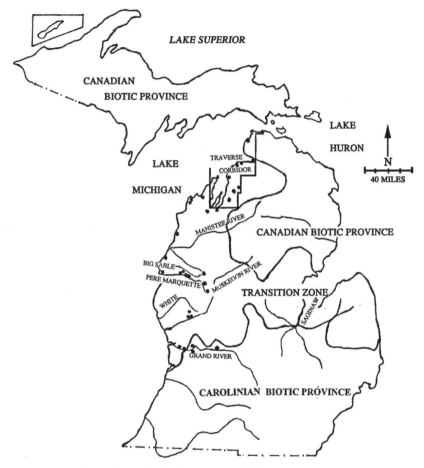

Figure 2.1 Biotic Provinces and Sites in Western Michigan

Michigan based on new information from sites in the Grand River basin at the northern edge of the Carolinian Biotic Province. Additionally, we examine the growing evidence concerning the use of the Carolinian-Canadian transition zone by Havana Middle Woodland groups along the Muskegon River and northward to discover whether systematic use of the transition zone was an essential part of their subsistence system.

According to Struever's (1964) original model, Illinois Hopewellians had an extremely successful subsistence strategy involving Intensive Harvest Collecting of a variety of key resources specific to the Carolinian and Illinoian biotic provinces, most notably hickory, acorn and other nuts,

Table 2.1

Attributes of Havana Middle Woodland Settlement in West Michigan (after Kingsley 1981)

1. Village (camp) sites located on a levee adjacent to the river
2. Village sites located near large areas of floodplain with oxbows and backwater lakes, floodplain areas suitable for cultivation
3. Sites occurring on well-drained land that is rarely flooded
4. Most sites located close to nut-bearing trees
5. All sites situated close to major resource zones, including riverine lowland areas and forested uplands

white tailed deer, migratory waterfowl, various species of fish, and various seed plants, at least some of which were probably cultivated. Kingsley's (1981) analysis of Middle Woodland settlement and subsistence in Michigan shows that environmental conditions present in the upper Sangamon Havana occupations (Roper 1979) are present in four of five of the Michigan drainages where Havana occupations are found, that is, all except the Kalamazoo (Table 2.1).

Kingsley (1981, 143–144) concludes that Havana Middle Woodland sites in Michigan are situated in locations with a "necessary configuration of environmental associations" similar to Roper's (1979) Strategy 2 base settlements in the Sangamon, and that it "would not be unexpected" that base settlements in Michigan might be year round occupations. He further suggests that "Hopewell Middle Woodland in west Michigan must be seen as a distinct mode of socioeconomic adaptation" (Kingsley 1981, 162) and that the Intensive Harvest Collecting system was "sufficiently flexible to be able to adapt to less ideal environments" than those found in the Illinois heartland (136).

Northern Carolinian Settlement and Adaptation in Western Michigan

Habitation and mortuary sites in the middle and lower Grand River valley (Figure 2.2) are situated close to the river on either high terraces or levees adjacent to the river and, thus, conform to the model Kingsley (1981) proposed for Intensive Harvest Collecting in west Michigan. In addition, many of these sites are located on alluvial soils in environments similar to those in Illinois that would have been conducive to gardening. Compared to the Illinois River valley, there are few mound groups and fewer habitation sites, which may or may not be related to carrying capacity of the regional environment. Most sites with Middle Woodland components are mixed with Early and Late Woodland occupations, and the Middle Woodland is frequently represented by a handful of diagnostics in an assemblage that is overwhelmingly Late Woodland.

Documented Middle Woodland sites with more than a few sherds and points include Spoonville (20OT1), which has associated mounds; Prison Farm (20IA58), a habitation with no mounds; and the recently excavated Converse site (20KT2), a habitation area associated with destroyed

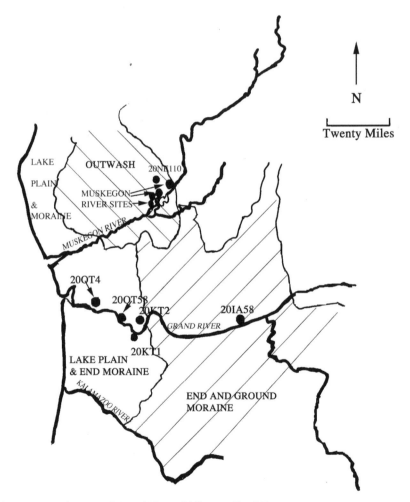

Figure 2.2 Muskegon and Grand River Middle Woodland Sites

mounds (see Figure 2.2). These three sites provide the best subsistence data for Middle Woodland adaptation in western Michigan.

The multicomponent Spoonville site is situated on a low terrace between the Grand River and Crockery Creek. Data from Spoonville suggests dependence on large game animals (Cleland 1966; Martin 1975). Relatively small samples of floated material from the site provide little evidence of intensive plant collecting and no evidence of Middle Woodland horticulture.

The Prison Farm site, excavated in 1996, 1997, and 1999, is an early Middle Woodland occupation in the central Grand River drainage. Calibrated dates from the site place initial occupation perhaps as early as the late second century B.C., but more likely in the first century B.C., with the latest Middle Woodland dates in the late first or perhaps early second century A.D. (Brashler 1998). The site is located in a setting congruent with Kingsley's (1981) proposed settlement model on a levee immediately adjacent to the Grand River, which is approximately 1km wide at the site. At this point, the river floods and produces temporary backwater lakes during the spring and summer, and a variety of seed, nut, fish, and mammal foodstuffs would have been available within 2–3km of the site.

Features from the site include primarily hearths, with three possible pit features. No post molds or any structural remains suggesting year-round or longer term occupation were observed in approximately 325m^2 of excavation. Nonetheless, this was clearly an intensively occupied site based on the number of features, artifacts, and faunal remains in a dense midden deposit.

Faunal remains indicate concentration on "big package" meat resources including sturgeon, deer, elk, black bear, beaver, and a variety of smaller mammals (Meekhof and Martin 1998). Thus, Prison Farm shows the pattern of emphasis on both fish and large mammals found by Cleland (1966) and Martin (1975) at other west Michigan Middle Woodland sites. There are remarkably few avian remains at Prison Farm.

Kathryn Parker's (2000) analysis of approximately thirty-five hundred liters of flotation from more than fifty features and associated midden deposits identifies the presence of relatively few seeds and nuts and a diverse wood charcoal assemblage. Taphonomic issues of trampling and exposure aside, botanical remains at Prison Farm, like those from Spoonville, do not suggest reliance on intensive plant collecting, nor do they indicate the practice of horticulture. In addition, the lithic assemblage lacks the hoes commonly found at Illinois sites. Thus, there are no agricultural tools evident at Prison Farm.

All things considered, Prison Farm has the site location requirements of Kingsley (1981) but lacks the floral and faunal data that indicates intensive plant collecting, much less a dependence on Eastern Agricultural complex seeds. All evidence so far points to a warm season occupation (no post molds, few seeds and nuts, abundant fish, mussels, and few migratory birds) with an emphasis on intensive hunting and fishing, including a sturgeon fishery (Meekhof and Martin 1998). If gardening or intensive plant collecting were practiced, they are not evident at Prison Farm or Spoonville.

Numerous other habitation sites along the Grand River with Middle Woodland materials were either destroyed or occur in mixed multicomponent contexts, such as the Zemaitis site with its two predominant Late Woodland components and an ephemeral Middle Woodland occupation (Brashler and Garland 1993). Many of these sites probably represent small seasonal occupations and occur in a variety of settings, including inland lakeshores along the Grand River and on tributary creeks (Brashler and Mead 1996). Though few of these sites have been systematically excavated, they appear to be small seasonal fishing and hunting stations. The commingling of many of these assemblages makes it difficult to identify discrete components.

The recently excavated Converse Village (20KT2) located in downtown Grand Rapids may provide subsistence information regarding the Middle Woodland in the area. Converse has long been thought to represent a later Middle Woodland occupation in this portion of Michigan, but most of the site was destroyed in the nineteenth century (Flanders 1977; Griffin, Flanders, and Titterington 1970). While the recent excavations produced a prodigious quantity of faunal material, it is not clear whether these remains are associated with the Middle or Late Woodland occupations at the site (Hambacher and Robertson 2000; Brashler et al. 2000). Early results from analysis of the flotation samples suggest a pattern similar to that seen at Prison Farm. That is, no gardening or intensive plant collecting appears to have been relied upon by any of the occupants of this site (Kathryn Egan-Bruhy, personal communication, 2000), until the eighteenth- or nineteenth-century occupation of the area by historic Ottawa.

It seems that people used various locations along the Grand River and its tributaries for various purposes throughout the year and that while many of the site locations are in settings congruent with the Intensive Harvest Collecting model, the evidence for that subsistence strategy is still not visible. Likewise, no evidence is available from any Middle Woodland site of any dependence on Eastern Agricultural Complex plants. In spite of this, it seems that maintaining flexibility in settlement systems practiced by Hopewellian populations, a key criterion in Kingsley's formula, is intentional in Middle Woodland subsistence and settlement at the northern edge of the Carolinian Biotic Province.

At the northern edge of the Carolinian Biotic Province, Middle Woodland groups appear to adapt to a variety of local situations in different ways. In the Saginaw River valley, there appears to be at least some knowledge of and reliance on starchy and oily seed plants (Lovis et al. 1994; Smith et al. 1994) supplemented by resources available in the diverse habitats present in the area including fish, tubers, and other marsh resources. The pattern on the Grand River seems different with no evidence of Eastern Agricultural plants and an emphasis on harvesting large animals, both terrestrial and aquatic.

Settlement and Adaptation in the Carolinian-Canadian Transition Zone
The Muskegon River Valley

The Muskegon River valley, like the Grand River valley, contains clearly Hopewell-related materials. Unlike the Grand River, however, it is not in the Carolinian Biotic Province (see Figure 2.1). Rather, the Muskegon has its headwaters in the high plains of the Canadian Biotic Province and flows south and west through the transition zone to Lake Michigan. Prahl (1991), working in this area, described a number of Havana-related Middle Woodland mounds (Brooks, Parsons, Palmiteer, Schumacher, Hardy Dam) and several habitation sites, most notably the Jancarich site (see Figure 2.2). Because these sites conform to the settlement location expectations that Kingsley (1981) articulates with mounds located on high bluffs and the Jancarich "village" site located lower and closer to the river, and because these sites also have associated prairie soils (Prahl 1991, 97), both Kingsley and Prahl conclude that intensive plant collecting was practiced here. Unfortunately, subsistence data from the Muskegon River sites are rare, with a few mammal, turtle, and fish remains from the Jancarich site (Prahl 1991) and no subsistence remains documented for the Toft Lake site (20NE110) (Losey 1967), which lies four miles north of the Muskegon River main channel (see Figure 2.2). Thus, it is not possible to say conclusively whether Intensive Harvest Collecting or gardening subsistence strategies were employed along the Muskegon River at this time.

The Transition Zone North of the Muskegon River Valley

The Grand and Muskegon drainages of western Michigan provide evidence of Havana–Hopewellian-related settlement and mortuary customs in locations congruent with Havana settlements elsewhere. While adaptive strategies in the northern Carolinian Biotic Province and the southern transition zone seem similar to those seen in the Havana-Hopewell heartland, no evidence of dependence on Intensive Harvest Collecting or Eastern Agricultural Complex cultivation has emerged over the last three decades of research. It appears that in this area, away from the Illinois "core," groups identifying with Havana-Hopewell modified their subsistence practices to a greater degree and maintained flexibility in their

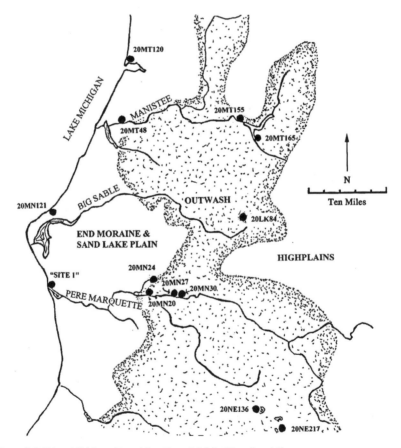

Figure 2.3 West Michigan Transition Zone Middle Woodland Sites

adaptations to a greater extent than Kingsley (1981) suggested. One such modification may have been to venture northward into the transition zone (Figure 2.3).

The reasons for this northern use are not obvious. There was no compelling need to seek an abundant or stable resource peculiar to the northern areas, such as seasonally spawning fish, migrating animals, or the like. In fact, the transition zone is characterized by biological diversity rather than abundance of one food source (Albert, Denton, and Barnes 1986). Similarly, the transition zone with its fewer frost-free days, sandy soils, and earlier spring frosts would not have offered better opportunities for reliable horticulture.

It is possible that people were going north to obtain something other than food, such as Norwood chert at the Pi-wan-go-ning quarry (20CX20) south of Charlevoix (Cleland 1973) or copper from northern neighbors. Norwood chert is found at sites in the Lower Peninsula but seems to have been available to anyone and was apparently not prominent in any system of long-distance trade. Indeed, Norwood chert occurs in several Middle Woodland sites along the Grand and Muskegon Rivers, including as caches in mortuary contexts.

Securing copper is another possible reason that southern groups ventured into the transition zone, as it certainly was widely traded during the Middle Woodland, but there is no abundant evidence of copper in transition zone sites. Rather, copper was usually moved south from its Lake Superior sources through Wisconsin (Martin 1999). If Havana-Hopewell peoples went north to trade, the items exchanged are not visible in the archaeological record.

Middle Woodland sites in the transition zone north of the Muskegon River reflect temporary occupations with the exception of one reported mound (20NE217) at the southeast edge of the Pere Marquette drainage basin. Sites here reflect an ancillary use of the transition zone by Havana-related peoples from west Michigan and the Saginaw Valley (Table 2.2). This common use of the transition zone is evidenced by Havana- and Hopewell-related pottery stylistically similar to ceramics found along the Grand and Muskegon Rivers (Griffin, Flanders, and Titterington 1970; Prahl 1991) or to Tittabawassee and Green Point wares found in the Saginaw Valley (Fischer 1972).

Lithic styles in the transition zone also indicate west Michigan and Saginaw Valley connections (see Table 2.2), as they include west Michigan projectile point styles such as Norton corner-notched (Griffin, Flanders,

Table 2.2   Attributes of Middle Woodland Sites in the Transition Zone

Site Number/Name	Location	Prehistoric Components	Middle Woodland Diagnostics	Key References *= from State of Michigan Site Files
Site 1 (CEC)	Mouth, Pere Marquette River	Middle Woodland	Havana pot in collection	Cleland, Report on file at Michigan State University
20MN121 Ox Yoke 4	Big Sable River, Lake Michigan	Middle Woodland	Present-Collector Report	*Branstner 1987
20 MT48 Airport 3	Manistee River	Middle Woodland, Late Woodland	Havana Pot	Mead 1979
20MT120 Point Arcadia	Point Arcadia, Lake Michigan	Archaic-Contact	5 Green Point Rocker Stamped	Hambacher 1988
20BZ16 Platte River Campground	Platte River	Middle Woodland, Late Woodland A.D. 260 +/−80 calib	Green Point Rocker Stamped, Bayport Preform Laurel	Weir et. al. 1986; Richner Richner, pers. comm. 1999, email to Holman
20BZ53	Platte River	Middle Woodland, Late Woodland	Laurel, Hopewell-like Rocker Stamped	Richner, pers. comm. 1999, email to Holman
20 LU21 Fisher Lake	Fisher Lake, Crystal River	Middle Woodland, Late Woodland	Corner-removed point on Bayport, North Bay, Sister Creeks/Goodwin Gresham, Laurel	Brose 1975
20LU22 Dunn Farm	Glen Lake, Crystal River	Early Woodland, Middle Woodland	Wild rice @ 1500 +/- 60 B.P. uncalibrated	Brose and Hambacher 1999
20GT89 Green Lake	Green Lake, Betsie River	Late Paleo-Indian; Early Archaic; Late Archaic; Early, Middle, and Late Woodland	Norton point on Hornstone, Schultz points, on Bayport and Zaleski chert preform	Douglass et al. 1998
20GT58 East Bay	East Arm Grand Traverse Bay	Middle Woodland, Early Late Woodland	Laurel plus one Havana/ Hopewellianderived pot, Norton-like point	Hambacher et al. 1994
20AN25 Round Lake (aka Szabo)	Torch Lake, Rapid River	Middle Woodland, Late Woodland	Present-Collector Report	Gillis 1964
20AN26 Holtz	Lake Bellaire, Intermediate River	Late Middle Woodland	Greenpoint and Havana pots, Schultz/Jancarich-like points	Lovis 1971
20CX19 Pine River Channel	Pine River Channel from Round Lake/Lake Charlevoix	Archaic, Middle Woodland, Late Woodland	Laurel, 2 Havana Pots, Norton Point of Norwood, corner-notched Burlington	Holman 1978
20CX20 Piwangoning Quarry 1998	Lake Michigan	Multiple components, Quarry site		Cleland 1973
20EM22 Portage	Little Traverse Bay	Middle Woodland, Late Woodland	Laurel, one Havana related	Martin 1985; Lovis et al.
20EM4 Wycamp Creek	Wycamp Creek	Middle Woodland, Late Woodland	Laurel	Lovis and Holman 1976
20EM1 Fort Michilimackinac	Straits of Mackinac	Middle Woodland, Late Woodland	Laurel	Lovis and Holman 1976

and Titterington 1970) and Jancarich-like expanding stem (Prahl 1991) as well as Saginaw Valley Schultz expanding stem points (Fitting 1972). The west Michigan types may be made of local Norwood chert (Holman 1978; Lovis 1971) or of chert from distant sources, such as Indiana Hornstone (Douglass, Holman, and Stephenson 1998). The Middle Woodland Schultz points in the transition zone, however, are made of Bayport chert, which outcrops in the Saginaw Valley (Brose 1975; Douglass, Holman, and Stephenson 1998), or of Norwood chert (Lovis 1971).

In addition to use by Havana-related people, the transition zone was used by Laurel Initial Woodland groups, who were in the region from the Grand Traverse Bay area in the south to the Straits of Mackinac in the north. There is no evidence that these northerners ventured south into the major river systems crossing the transition zone.

Transition Zone Site Location and Subsistence

The natural settings of Havana-related sites along the Lake Michigan coast north of the Muskegon River and in the Grand Traverse Bay region exhibit highly consistent characteristics. These consistencies reflect a situation where numerous microenvironments with their variety of resources occur in the immediate vicinity of a site. Every site is near a small lake, open marsh, and variously mixed upland and lowland forests.

While resource diversity characterizes the transition zone, resource density is not necessarily high, resource distribution is not necessarily uniform, and edge communities are relatively unstable (Cleland 1966). Havana-related sites were situated to maximize resource diversity by locating where microenvironments were contiguous. Such settings would have compensated for the lower carrying capacity and lessened resource density of the transition zone in comparison to the Carolinian Biotic Province (Fitting 1966, 147). Seasonally, there would always be something available at these sites, and in some seasons different members or subsets of the group could simultaneously exploit different resources. The fact that ten of the eleven predominantly Havana-related Middle Woodland sites were occupied repeatedly during the Late Woodland is indicative of the fact that these remained good locations for obtaining food.

Archaeological evidence for subsistence suggests season of occupation but is far from conclusive. Grape, cranberry, and nannyberry seeds were identified at the Platte River Campground site (20BZ16) along with remains of turtles and fish, with the implications of a warm season exploitation of the varied habitats near the site (Richner 1991, 59; Weir et al. 1986).

Clam shells plus a charred elk rib and vertebra at the Holtz site (20AN26) indicate hunting cervids (Lovis 1971, 61). Evidence that people could have been at Fisher Lake from spring through fall can be seen in the remains of mollusks, porcupine, deer, sturgeon, and bass found at the Fisher Lake site (20LU21) (Brose 1975). The nearby Dunn Farm site (20LU22) at Glen Lake yielded wild rice with a Middle Woodland date, thus suggesting a late summer to fall use of the site (Brose and Hambacher 1999, 176). Because the food remains from the sites in the Fisher Lake/Glen Lake locale could have been left by either Laurel or Havana groups, it is unclear who obtained this food.

Nine sites in the narrow outwash plain (Albert, Denton, and Barnes 1986) along the rivers north of the Muskegon River are not well dated, and we know little about them. In any case, limited tool kits, the absence of Havana pottery, and little evidence for reoccupation suggest transient use of the riverbanks, probably for hunting.

Cultural Interaction in the Traverse Corridor

The distribution of Middle Woodland sites confirms Cleland's (1967) observation that the transition zone's northernmost extension, termed the Traverse Corridor and ranging in width from fifty yards to twelve miles, was a continuous avenue of north-south interaction. Havana-related sites occur not only in the Traverse Corridor, but throughout the transition zone to the south. Sites attributable to northern Laurel groups and sites with mixed Laurel and Havana materials occur only in the Traverse Corridor and on the Leelanau Peninsula, that is, from Grand Traverse Bay north. The entire Traverse region was, therefore, a potential meeting place for southern and northern Middle Woodland peoples.

Site location characteristics in the Traverse Bay region reflect use by peoples with differing subsistence practices (Figure 2.4). Sites containing only Laurel materials were small seasonal fishing camps clearly oriented toward the Lake Michigan coast at the northern end of the transition zone in the Traverse Corridor (Martin 1985). Laurel peoples were fishers, hunters, and gatherers of the Canadian Biotic Province, and fish was a critical food during the spring spawning periods (Cleland 1982; Martin 1985). The Traverse Corridor, as part of the transition zone, was a rather unusual habitat for Laurel groups, and this area was not used by them as frequently as were other coastal regions, for example, the north shore of Lake Michigan (Martin 1985, 179). As the transition zone is very narrow at the northern end where Laurel fishing camps are located, it does not appear to have been a focus of subsistence. Similarly, predominantly Laurel sites, with some Havana remains, are confined to the Traverse Corridor and are coast-focused sites—that is, the East Bay site, 20GT58 (Hambacher, Dunham, and Branstner 1994), and the Pine River Channel site, 20CX19 (Holman 1978). The Portage site, 20EM22, on Little Traverse Bay is somewhat anomalous as it probably really did serve as a portage for moving to the interior via the Inland Waterway rather than as a fishing site (Lovis, Rajnovich, and Bartley 1998; Martin 1985).

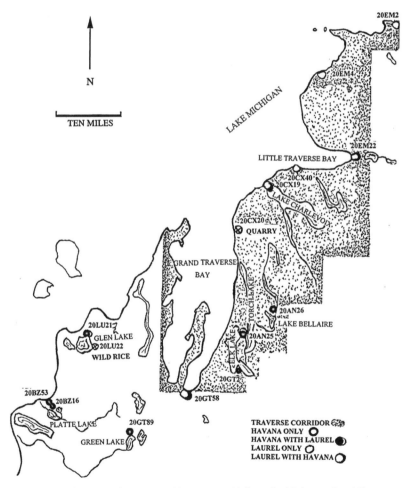

Figure 2.4 Northwest Michigan Transition Zone Middle and Initial Woodland Sites

Havana Middle Woodland sites in the Traverse region are located in consistent contrast to Laurel sites because, although they are near the lakeshore, they are not oriented toward the lake (Platte River Campground/20BZ16, Green Lake/20GT89, Skegemog Point/20GT2, and Holtz/20AN26) (see Figure 2.4). Sites are on small lakes (Platte Lake, Green Lake, Lake Skegemog, and Lake Bellaire) with open marshes, near mixed lowland and upland forests, and near berries, wild rice, and the like. Again, these sites are situated where several habitats supported a variety of foods in the immediate vicinity of the site. Rivers that occur at these sites are not avenues to the interior, but rather relatively small streams with relatively bounded drainage basins. Predominantly Havana sites with some Laurel remains are also varied habitat sites (Platte River/20BZ53, Fisher Lake/20LU21, Round Lake/20AN25).

Ceramic evidence coupled with environmental setting shows that people with two differing cultural traditions were using the northwest portion of the transition zone just as Cleland (1967) observed, but they were using it in different ways. This joint use offered the clear possibility of interaction.

It is not clear, however, whether interaction took place on a regular basis, and if so whether it involved deliberate or fortuitous contact, or whether it took place rarely if at all. At this point there is no obvious evidence for purposeful exchange. If meetings did occur, some gift giving would have been involved, perhaps of perishables not preserved in the archaeological record or of items that we might not recognize as having value as gifts.

Use of the northwest transition zone for subsistence was not a necessity for either group. Laurel peoples were most likely to have been in the Traverse Corridor during the spring fishing season, while limited evidence suggests that Havana-related peoples were in the region later during the warm season. Neither group was confined to being in the Traverse Corridor only during those times, however, so seasonal schedules could have been modified to allow a meeting. The choice of diverse habitat sites would have increased scheduling flexibility, so it appears that people kept open both their subsistence and their social options.

Conclusion

Intensively occupied Middle Woodland base camps along the Grand and Muskegon Rivers conform to the expectations of the Intensive Harvest Collecting model of subsistence in terms of both natural setting and evidence for an emphasis on large game. Even though these sites are located within reach of a wide range of plant resources, botanical remains do not suggest intensive collecting of wild plants or a reliance on seed plant cultivation. This absence of plants may reflect a differential preservation, but this alternative seems less likely given the redundant patterns of plant use that appear to be emerging. Certainly, it does not mean that plants were ignored, but it may mean that there were modifications in the selection, collection, and use of plants at the northern edge of the Carolinian Biotic Province. The presence of habitation sites along the Grand River in varying natural settings suggests a strategy of using different locations along the river for different purposes. It has been posited that there are nonceramic specialized sites that may have been used during the Middle Woodland, although these are difficult to recognize and their relationship to the settlement and subsistence system is not understood at present (Brashler and Mead 1996, 220). It seems fairly clear, however, that the Illinois model of Middle Woodland subsistence in this area was modified to allow people to live on the abundant resources of the Grand River, and as Kingsley (1981) asserted, this subsistence strategy was very flexible.

Our brief review of the Middle Woodland occupation of the transition zone in the Traverse Corridor indicates use by groups from both the north and south. No one group was resident full-time. Of particular interest to us is the evidence that Havana-related groups appear to have pushed into the northwestern part of the transition zone to occupy temporary camps situated to take advantage of available biodiversity. It may be that Havana- Hopewell groups were drawn to the area because it offered a diverse array of resources, many of which were already familiar and significant in their more southern subsistence strategy and at the same time allowed the possibility of social contact with northern neighbors. The Carolinian/ Canadian transition zone was used in very flexible ways both socially and economically in this most interesting period of cultural adaptation and interaction. By understanding Middle Woodland subsistence and settlement in areas such as the northern Carolinian Biotic Province and in the Carolinian/Canadian transition zone, we can perhaps eventually better understand the complexities of Hopewellian adaptations in their apparently diverse and flexible configurations.

3

The Northern Limits of Ridge Field Agriculture

An Example from Menominee County

Marla M. Buckmaster

The discovery of ridged gardens in Menominee County, Michigan, in the fall of 1996 extended the northern limits of ridge field agriculture in the Upper Midwest. Identified as 20ME61, these garden ridges provided an unusual opportunity to map extensive and relatively complete ridged agricultural fields. Limited testing exposed a unique feature, suggesting that these prehistoric gardeners were not only ridging their fields, but were experimenting with other ways to modify the microenvironment of their crops to combat the rigorous northern climate. Phytolith and flotation samples were taken to identify cultigens. Corn cupules were recovered. An Accelerator Mass Spectrometer (AMS) date indicates that these garden ridges are chronologically similar to many of the late prehistoric ridged gardens reported in Wisconsin.

SITE 20ME61 IS AN agricultural locale in Lake Township, Menominee County, Michigan. The site, identified by discontinuous clusters of parallel ridges arranged in a perpendicular checkerboard pattern, extends a considerable distance along the southeastern bank of the Menominee River approximately fifteen miles north/northwest of the river mouth.

Although this area has been the focus of several archaeological investigations, the garden ridges had not previously been reported. Obscured by summer vegetation, the garden beds escaped detection during the more than four decades of archaeological research along the Menominee River.

Figure 3.1 Winter Photo of Site 20ME61 Showing Ridges. Photo by James Voss.

A local resident brought the ridges to my attention in the fall of 1996. Although obscured by vegetation much of the year, the ridges can be easily seen under a fresh blanket of snow (Figure 3.1) or early in the spring just after the snow melts but prior to the new spring growth. The extent of the ridging is impressive. The approximate boundaries of the garden beds are shown in Figure 3.2. Fortunately, most of the site appears undisturbed. A two-lane paved road, an abandoned historic logging or supply trail, and a dirt road dissect the site, and a small grassy parking area for a boat ramp used by local fishermen has been constructed along the riverbank near one end of the ridge clusters. Only one owner of the occasional house or camp in the area remembers leveling the "inconvenient bumps" found in his yard. Except for these activities the garden ridges appear undisturbed. Historic logging in the area, documented by the presence of an early logging camp near a ridge cluster, appears to have had little impact on the raised beds. In fact, several of the raised beds cross the supply trail that passes the logging camp, which creates a corrugated trail and must have puzzled many wagon drivers. Site 20ME61, therefore, offers an unusual opportunity to map and document the extent of prehistoric raised bed gardens in the Upper Midwest.

A small group of enthusiastic Menominee County Historical Society members volunteered their time during the early spring of 1997 to begin mapping 20ME61. They have continued to provide their support and labor

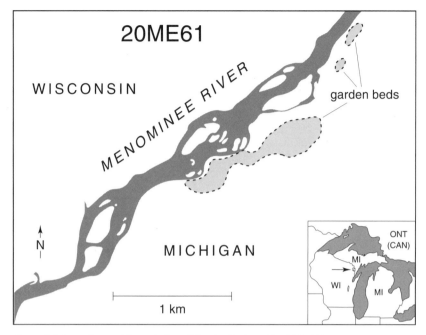

Figure 3.2 Location and Boundaries of Garden Beds at Site 20ME61

during the three years of intermittent fieldwork at the site and were not discouraged by rain, sleet, snow, ticks, or temperatures exceeding 100%F. With their help, an impressive 95,000m², or approximately 60 percent of the site, has been mapped (Figure 3.3). During the summer of 1999, Dr. Janet Brashler and many of the students who participated in Grand Valley State University's field school volunteered to excavate three 1×3-m test trenches as well as undertake flotation of much of the excavated soil.

Background

Prehistoric garden beds, also referred to as ridge fields, planting grounds, aboriginal clearings, ridges, or cornfields, are not unknown or new to Michigan prehistory. Henry Rowe Schoolcraft (1860) provided an early description of garden beds in western Michigan and the adjacent portions of Indiana:

> They are of various sizes, covering, generally, from twenty to one
> hundred acres. Some of them are reported to embrace even three

hundred acres. . . . They certainly offer new and unique traits in our antiquities, denoting a species of cultivation in older times of an unusual kind, but which has been abandoned for centuries. They are called "garden beds," in common parlance, from the difficulty of assimilating them to anything else; though it would be more proper, perhaps, to consider them as the vestiges of ancient field labor. The areas are too large to admit the assumption of their being required for the purposes of ordinary horticulture. . . . The beds are of various sizes. Nearly all the lines of each area or sub-area of beds, are rectangular and parallel. Others admit of half-circles, and variously curved beds with avenues, and are differently grouped and disposed. (55–56)

The agricultural features Schoolcraft was describing consisted of sets of elongated ridges raised 10–40cm above the intervening paths or furrows. These ridges varied from 40cm to approximately 2m in breadth. Hinsdale (1931) identifies thirty of these agricultural sites in Kalamazoo County alone and makes special note of an exceptionally large garden in St. Joseph County. These gardens were identified using historical references and accounts of early settlers. Peters (1980) uses these same sources to document the gardens' clear association with the climax prairies or dry prairies in St. Joseph, Cass, and Kalamazoo Counties in the southwest

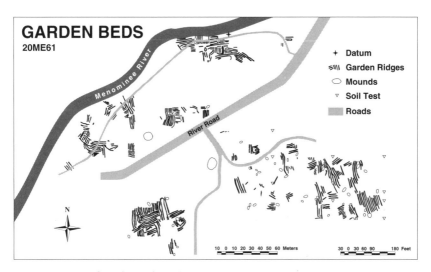

Figure 3.3 Map of Garden Beds at Site 20ME61

corner of Michigan's Lower Peninsula. The current state site file lists twenty-eight garden bed sites. Five of these sites are identified as historic Native American gardens. Four of these five historic gardens are located in the Upper Peninsula. The remaining twenty-two sites are prehistoric. Based on the location information provided by Hinsdale (1931), Peters (1980), and the state site files, the primary distribution of these prehistoric agricultural features lies in the southwestern portion of the state with occasional or sporadic occurrences elsewhere in the state south of a line from Berrien and Van Buren Counties in the west to Sanilac County in the east. Site 20ME61 is noteworthy in Michigan prehistory since it is located more than three hundred miles north of any other prehistoric garden site in the state.

Garden bed sites have also been reported in Wisconsin, where the state site file lists nearly three hundred agricultural sites, more than half of which are the remains of ridged gardens. Fox (1959) describes the distribution of these sites as south of a line from Brunett County east to Marinette County. Although located in Michigan, 20ME61 is geographically and presumably culturally closer to these Wisconsin agricultural sites than those reported in Michigan.

Information regarding the antiquity, cultural affiliation, and function of these sites is very limited. This is particularly true of southwestern Michigan, where prairie soils attracted prehistoric horticulturalists as well as early European settlers who plowed the soil, obliterating most of the earlier ridge and furrow gardens. This destruction occurred before accurate information on the size, distribution, and antiquity of these gardens was recorded. As a result, Michigan prehistory is left with only historical descriptions and the early work of individuals such as Bela Hubbard, who in 1878 identified eight types of raised beds found in Michigan. Hinsdale (1931) later consolidated these into four types. As late as 1957, Greenman suggested that these surface features had been constructed to slow the speed of pursued bison herds by historic tribes. We may never know if these features functioned as historic speed bumps; however, there is no doubt that most if not all of these features were constructed for agricultural purposes.

Early attempts to determine the age of particular garden bed sites were based on an examination of trees or tree stumps located on these features. In some cases, the minimal age of these trees was determined using a primitive system of dendrochronology, while in other cases estimates were based simply on measurement of tree girth. Such efforts, however, simply provide an estimated date for the abandonment of a garden site. More recently, Elizabeth Garland (personal communication, 1998), while working on archaeological survey projects in southwestern Michigan, has shovel-tested several reported garden bed sites. Her efforts failed to locate any associated cultural material. At present, there is no direct association between these surface features and cultural materials in the lower peninsula of Michigan. It appears likely that we may never know their antiquity and cultural affiliation.

Fortunately, somewhat more is known about Wisconsin's garden bed sites. A tentative relationship between Lake Winnebago Phase Oneota settlements and adjacent ridge and furrow surface features was established by Peske's (1966) work at the Lasleys Point and Eulrich sites. He dated these gardens circa A.D. 1000–1300. Overstreet (1976, 1981) has suggested a somewhat later date for these gardens as well as an association of garden bed sites with Oneota villages of varying phases in eastern Wisconsin and argues for later (ca. A.D. 1300–1650) utilization of these features. More recent work at the Sand Point site in southwestern Wisconsin has documented an association between ridge field agriculture and a prehistoric Oneota occupation (Gallagher et al. 1985). A series of radiocarbon samples obtained from both primary ridge contexts and rebuilt ridges place their use between A.D. 1400 and A.D. 1450 (Sasso et al. 1985). The Sand Point fields, however, were constructed to help with moisture control in floodplain settings and differ from the garden beds located on the well-drained sandy soils of eastern Wisconsin (Gallagher and Sasso 1987).

Recently, Gartner (1999) has suggested that effigy mounds and ridged fields in Wisconsin represent territorial markers. Using ethnographic data, he argues that these landscape modifications embody concepts of area, boundary, and control. Although he makes a strong case for effigy mounds having political and territorial importance, his argument is somewhat weaker when including ridged fields, which appear to have specific agricultural functions such as improving soil and ameliorating the microclimates for crops grown in marginal climates.

The Garden Beds

Since few garden bed sites have been excavated or even tested, and little is known regarding their age and cultural affiliation, site 20ME61 provides an opportunity to add to this relatively small body of data on ridged field agriculture in the Upper Midwest. The site extends in discontinuous clus-

Wall profile from garden beds

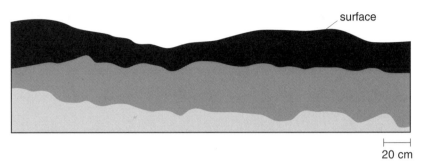

20 cm

South wall profile from
non-ridged area

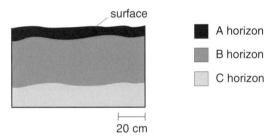

20 cm

Figure 3.4 Variation in A Zone Depth between Test Trench 1 (East Profile) and
Exploratory Test Pit

ters of ridges and furrows punctuated by mounds of varying sizes, slightly
less than two miles along the banks of the Menominee River. These raised
beds extend inland or south from the riverbank as much as 500m, or
1,500 feet. Located in an area that is variously listed as having 110 to
130 frost-free days, 20ME61 is clearly situated at the northern limits of
effective maize agriculture (Yarnell 1964). In fact, its location in an area
that remains agriculturally marginal is in great part responsible for the
site's preservation. Located outside the area typically associated with economically successful farming has meant that 20ME61's system of raised
beds escaped obliteration by plow.

The soil at 20ME61 is best described as a deep, well to moderately
drained sandy loam. The A horizon soils are neutral with a pH of 7.0.
The soil becomes somewhat more acidic with depth, reaching a pH of 6.0
thirty centimeters below the surface. A comparison of soil profiles within
a ridge and furrow cluster with a soil profile from an area exhibiting no

signs of having been part of the gardens suggests that the soil within the gardens was enriched. Within the ridge clusters the A horizon varied from twenty to thirty-five centimeters in depth, while an area outside the ridge clusters but adjacent to the garden beds had an A horizon less than ten centimeters in depth. A comparison of the east wall profile of Test Trench 1, which cross-sectioned two ridges, with a wall profile from an exploratory test pit clearly illustrates the variation in A zone depth (Figure 3.4).

Currently, this soil supports a mixed deciduous forest of bitter nut hickory, red maple, sugar maple, black ash, white ash, aspen, white oak, red oak, basswood, blue beech, ironwood, and alternate leaf dogwood. An occasional hemlock and white pine can be found among these deciduous trees.

One of the most important questions concerning 20ME61 relates to the origins and antiquity of the ridges. The garden beds appear to be associated with the Backlund site. Raised beds are located both up and down stream as well as behind the site. The Backlund site was first investigated in 1956 by Albert Spaulding and Robert Hruska, who incorrectly assumed that the garden beds were historic and focused their attention on the excavation of three mounds located slightly southeast of the village. Their excavations recovered a mixed Oneota and Woodland ceramic assemblage. Brose (1968) reporting on this work suggested a date of A.D. 1000–1300 for the mounds. During the early 1970s, the Backlund site was revisited (Buckmaster 1979). At that time, fifteen 2×2-m test pits were excavated within the perimeter of the Backlund village using a stratified unaligned sampling strategy. The excavation of these fifteen units recovered cultural materials from an area approximately 70×90m, or roughly two hundred by three hundred feet. The excavated ceramic assemblage consisted of five hundred sherds. Seventy-five percent of these sherds were shell tempered with a smooth exterior surface. The remaining sherds were grit tempered. Eighty percent of these grit-tempered sherds exhibited a smooth exterior surface. Slightly less than 5 percent of the village ceramic assemblage consisted of grit-tempered cord-marked sherds. A limited lithic assemblage included one small triangular projectile point, three scrapers, and a relatively small number of flakes and cores. These thinly scattered materials suggest an Oneota occupation of limited size and duration, which is surprising given the extent of the raised beds.

The association of the garden beds with the Backlund site is complicated by the fact that limited shovel testing and the excavation of four 1×3-m units recovered only grit-tempered cord-marked sherds. The total number of sherds recovered from the garden beds is small and contains no rim sherds, and except for a single dime-size sherd recovered in a soil probe that exhibited incised lines, the sherds are remarkable only in their total lack of any decorative characteristics. The absence of shell-tempered smooth sherds, which dominated the ceramic assemblage at the Backlund site, at best confuses the relationship between the raised beds and the Backlund site. The distribution of the grit-tempered sherds in the garden beds, however, may be an important clue to this association. Based on limited shovel testing and the excavation of only four test units, the distribution of the grit-tempered sherds and an occasional small flake was limited to a small area near the riverbank. It is possible, if not likely, that these grit-tempered sherds recovered in the garden beds may be the result of an earlier utilization of the site. Additional shovel testing and excavation will be necessary to fully confirm this.

Why did the prehistoric occupants of this area construct raised garden beds? Riley and Freimuth (1979) cite numerous ethnographic examples of raised field agriculture for frost retardation. Their experimental work in northern Illinois, although hardly a marginal area for agriculture by Upper Peninsula standards, documents the importance of raised beds in extending the growing season as cold air from late spring or early fall frosts

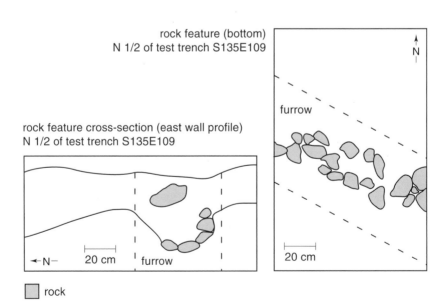

Figure 3.5 Rock Lining of Furrow from 1999 Test Unit at 20ME61

is drained off the ridges into the furrows. Site 20ME61 is clearly at the northern limits for prehistoric agriculture. The closest weather station, located in Stephenson, Michigan, reports that 32%F or 0%C is reached five out of ten years by September 18. In the spring, freezing temperatures are reached 50 percent of the time after May 30. Considering that the time between spring and fall temperatures of 32%F could be as short as 110 days, construction of raised beds may have been the only way to ensure more regular agricultural success.

Of particular note when discussing temperature control is a rock feature located in one of the 1×3-m units excavated during the summer of 1999. The feature consisted of rock used to line and partially fill the furrow. This rock lining was clearly visible in both the floor of the unit and the wall profile (Figure 3.5). Since rock was rarely encountered in these loamy, water-laid soils during the excavation, this may have been a purposeful attempt at thermal manipulation with heat accumulating and being stored in the rock during the day, then released at night when the air temperature dropped.

While thermal manipulation appears to have been the primary benefit derived from the construction of raised beds, there were secondary benefits. Riley and Freimuth (1979) note the role of garden beds in controlling weeds. Other benefits may have been soil aeration, ease of mixing organic matter into the soil, insect control, harvest facilitation, and increased moisture within the ridge. In addition, the wall profile in Figure 3.6, from a 1×3-m test trench located in the southern section of the site, indicates that the buried A horizon was removed from the furrows and deposited on the ridges, thus increasing soil fertility on the ridge tops where crops were planted.

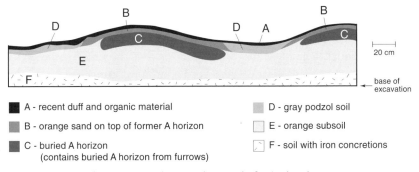

Figure 3.6 Profile from Test Trench at Southern End of Raised Beds

The final question the research at 20ME61 addressed was, what was being grown in this northern marginal environment? To answer this question, twenty-five soil samples were collected for phytolith analysis. Samples were collected from a variety of locations: on ridges, in the furrows, locations within the garden area not exhibiting ridges and furrows, and off-site. The samples were dried, and after careful evaluation twelve were selected and sent to the University of Minnesota, Duluth, for processing and analysis. A quick scan to determine the presence or absence of phytoliths and, if present, the condition of the phytoliths was completed. The results of this initial quick scan look promising. All twelve samples contained significant amounts of phytoliths. In addition, the phytoliths appeared to be in a good state of preservation, suggesting that they could be identified. Several important cultigens including maize, sunflower, squash, and beans produce phytoliths. Additional analysis, however, failed to identify any of these cultigens, the phytolith assemblages being generally dominated by grasses. The nongrass phytoliths were from other herbaceous plants. No pattern in phytolith abundance, grass amount, or grass type was observed between samples taken from ridges, furrows, or outside the ridge and furrow clusters. The phytolith assemblage contrasts with the present mixed deciduous and coniferous forest or that associated with an agricultural field. Grasses and other herbaceous species, however, would have been the first colonizers of abandoned fields, which may explain their abundance.

In addition to the soil samples for phytolith analysis, one hundred liters of soil were collected and saved for flotation from each 10-cm level in the three 1×3-m units excavated during the 1999 field season. More than one thousand liters of soil were floated. The resulting floats were sent to Lake States Archaeological and Ecological Consulting for analysis. The analysis on a representative sample of these materials has been completed. Identification of the wood charcoal in these samples suggests that the climate during the era when the gardens were in use was not significantly different than it is today. The identified taxa indicates that the forest community could be characterized as a northern hardwood community dominated by red oak, red maple, sugar maple, aspen, white birch, and white pine.

Also identified in the botanical analysis were a variety of nutshell fragments and charred seeds. While the nut species and many of the seeds are from edible taxa such as raspberry, elderberry, blackberry, hazelnut, and cherry, the vertical distribution of these remains and their context suggest that they are probably forest detritus that was burned following the white pine logging era. In addition, many of these species are characteristic of disturbed habitats, which suggests they may have invaded the area following the Native American use of the area and before the logging era. Therefore, it is unlikely that any of these species were cultivated by the prehistoric gardeners who worked so diligently to construct the system of ridges and furrows at 20ME61.

Fortunately, the flotation samples also contained three corn cupules. Two cupules were recovered from level 3, or between 20 and 30cm below surface. The third cupule was associated with level 2. The presence of the cupules in levels 2 and 3 clearly identifies maize as a cultigen at 20ME61.

Finally, two small shell-tempered sherds were recovered from the flotation samples. Their presence is notable given the recovery of only grit-tempered sherds in the shovel tests and test excavations.

A date of 480±40 B.P. (Beta-140450; charred corn; $\delta^{13}C= -10.9$ ‰) was obtained from one of the recovered corn cupules. The calibrated date is 1410–1460 cal A.D. (calibrated at 1 sigma with 68 percent probability). This date is consistent with dates associated with the buried ridges at Sand Lake as well as other Oneota sites in southwestern Wisconsin and Overstreet's (1976, 1981) placement of the Lasley Point and Eulrich sites in eastern Wisconsin.

Conclusion

Site 20ME61 adds to a growing body of data on prehistoric ridge fields in the Upper Midwest. Like the ridge fields in eastern Wisconsin, 20ME61 is located near a significant water body on loamy well-drained soil. The site's location in Michigan's Upper Peninsula expands the northern limits of prehistoric agriculture and adds to an already convincing case that these northerly ridged fields functioned as microclimatic frost-control devices. The recovery of corn cupules further demonstrates their use as agricultural fields.

Although the ridge fields at Sand Lake have been accurately dated (Gallagher et al. 1985) in southwestern Wisconsin where they are unequivocally associated with an Oneota occupation, similar association is less well documented for eastern Wisconsin. A date of A.D. 1435 is consistent with an Oneota occupation. However, a definite association with the Backlund site Oneota occupation remains somewhat elusive given the recovery of grit-tempered cord-marked pottery in the shovel tests and test trenches. Two very small shell-tempered sherds, however, were recovered and reported from the macrobotanical samples. Additional research will be required to fully confirm a direct association between the Backlund site and these nearby ridged fields.

Acknowledgments

This research would not have been possible without the volunteer efforts of many people, including Menominee County Historical Society Volunteers, students, and colleagues. While it is not possible to individually recognize everyone's efforts, several people deserve mention. Beverly and Bruce Johnson and Janet and James Voss opened their homes and housed numerous groups of student volunteers. James Voss, John Helfert, and Bob Brisson spent many hours staking grid lines in preparation for the student volunteers who mapped thousands of square meters of garden ridges. I would like to extend my thanks to these individuals as well as all the other members of the Menominee County Historical Society who provided field labor, support, encouragement, and friendship during the several years needed to map the site.

Dr. Robert F. Sasso provided initial guidance as we approached work at 20ME61. His encouragement and enthusiasm for the project were greatly appreciated.

Of special note were the efforts of Dr. Janet Brashler and a group of her 1999 field school students who extended their field season and drove five hundred miles north to excavate three 1×3-m test trenches and then enthusiastically floated almost half of the excavated soil. Without their help we would not have documented the presence of corn at 20ME61 or have a reliable date.

4

A Nineteenth-Century Rural Irish Cemetery in McDonough County, Illinois

Lynne G. Goldstein and Jane E. Buikstra

The Irish Cemetery is a historic rural family cemetery site located south of the city of Macomb, Illinois. The cemetery was in use from 1848 through 1871 and was then abandoned. When strip-mining operations began in the area in 1981, the site was rediscovered and the graves had to be moved. Because of vandalism, tombstones were out of place and there was no obvious way to identify where individuals were buried or to know which tombstone represented which burial. The authors were called in to locate, excavate, and identify the graves so that they could be removed to other cemeteries. Although archaeological and osteological evidence was critical to identification, it was impossible to put together the life stories of these people without the additional use of historical, archival, and genealogical data. The integration of multiple lines of evidence is key in outlining the story and interrelationships of this area's settlers from Ireland via Pennsylvania and Ohio and the War of 1812.

IN SOME RESPECTS, this is an unusual contribution to a volume honoring Charles E. Cleland. Cleland has certainly long been interested in the historic period in the Upper Midwest, but his focus has been on Native American historic sites and Native American–European interactions, rather than on European settler sites. Further, Cleland has not usually focused on cemeteries. Nonetheless, this essay is a fitting inclusion for this volume because its focus is on what can be learned from small sites that one excavates as a result of contract relationships or other circumstances.

Cleland's own work has consistently and elegantly drawn from a number of such projects, putting together overall pictures of a region, a time, or a place. This is not an essay of grand conclusions and well-developed theory; it is a modest contribution that focuses on the integration of several lines of evidence from a small rural nineteenth-century cemetery. We move between these lines of evidence as we pull together the overall story; no one set of data was sufficient or complete enough to provide a picture of the whole. In this approach, we follow the kind of interplay between data sources advocated by scholars such as Feinman (1997) and Leone and Potter (1988), and also followed by Buikstra, O'Gorman, and Sutton (2000) in their analysis of a larger nineteenth-century cemetery in Illinois.

Between November 12 and November 15, 1981, a crew comprised of University of Wisconsin–Milwaukee (UWM) staff and students located, mapped, and excavated a series of burials within an area known as the Old Irish Cemetery near Macomb, Illinois, outside the town of Industry. This work was done under a contract with the Clugston Funeral Home of Macomb. Principal investigator for the project was Lynne Goldstein, then of UWM. Jane Buikstra, a bioanthropologist at Northwestern University at that time, served as a special consultant for the project; she was responsible for the human osteological analysis.

The Old Irish Cemetery, or Irish Cemetery, is located about ten miles due south of Macomb. The cemetery was in use for a limited period of time—from 1848 to 1871. The quarter-acre parcel of land is in McDonough County, Bethel Township, in the northwest quarter of the southwest quarter of the northwest quarter of Section 25 (T4N, R3W). The site is located on the summit of a ridge in the dissected uplands south of Grindstone Creek; it is at the northern edge of the area locally known as Gin Ridge.

The property was part of a larger plot purchased by the United Electric Coal Companies in 1953. United Electric Coal Companies merged with Freeman United Coal Company and is now known as Freeman United Coal Mining Company. Freeman United wanted to develop a strip-mining operation at this locale. When the parcel was purchased, there was no exception or reference in the deed to a cemetery, and a title search indicated that the land had been conveyed without any such exception or reservation since 1877. Discussions with area residents suggested that the cemetery was abandoned and its presence largely unknown even within the local community.

Freeman United discovered the cemetery during a survey of the land in preparation for strip-mining activities. The cemetery was so overgrown that most of the gravestones were not immediately visible. Upon closer inspection and clearing of underbrush, portions of thirteen different gravestones were found. Few of the stones appeared to be in their original location; most were overturned, and many had been scattered. Freeman United mapped all the stones as they were found and began a search to locate the descendants of the individuals. Upon completion of this partially successful genealogical search, Freeman United petitioned the courts to have the cemetery declared legally closed and requested permission to move the graves to a different location. All known next of kin agreed to the relocation, and the court granted Freeman United's request.

In 1981, Illinois law required a permit for disinterment and reinterment. Such a permit could only be granted to a licensed funeral director. Freeman United contracted with the Clugston Funeral Home, Macomb, for both disinterment and reinterment of these burials.

Duane Clugston, director of the Clugston Funeral Home, discovered that because the gravestones were scattered, it was impossible, from the surface, to determine the precise location of any single grave. Further, he could find no one with the expertise or willingness to locate the graves. Lawrence Conrad, archaeologist at Western Illinois University in Macomb, heard about the problem and suggested that the situation was ideally suited to the expertise of archaeologists; further, he noted that archaeologists/physical anthropologists might be able to provide detailed information about the individuals in addition to their age and sex. Conrad called Goldstein at UWM and initiated the discussions between Clugston and the university.

Freeman United wanted to proceed with its operations as quickly as possible, and the work had to be done under less than ideal conditions. The situation was further complicated by delays in receiving court permission to move the cemetery. Although the work had been tentatively scheduled for July or August 1981, the second week in November was the earliest date the necessary court procedures would allow. Further difficulties, including the possibility of frost, were apparent in November. In the end, there was a period of only four days to complete all fieldwork.

The Historic Context

The following general history of the county is taken from several sources, including Clarke (1878) and Chenoweth and Semonis (1992, 2). According to Clarke (1878), in 1821 the area now known as McDonough County was placed within the boundaries of Pike County. It was removed from Pike County in 1825, and its present boundaries were determined in 1826 when it was attached to Schuyler County. By 1830, there were a sufficient number of residents to justify the organization of a separate county. The county is named for Commodore Thomas McDonough, who led a successful campaign against the British in the War of 1812. As of 1830, the county had a population of 350 residents, of which it is believed that 200 were "white" and the rest "Indian" (Chenoweth and Semonis 1992). Chenoweth and Semonis (1992) indicate that the Indians were gone by the mid-1830s, and by 1835 the European pioneer population of the county had grown to more than 2,000.

Bethel Township is in the southern portion of the county. The southern portion of Bethel Township is principally timberland and is also the home of large coal beds and extensive quantities of limestone and sandstone. The northern part of the township is primarily prairie, which became excellent farms with European settlement. The township contains many creeks and streams. The Irish Cemetery is located in the southern portion of the township. Examination of federal census records from 1850 and 1870 (U.S. Bureau of the Census 1850, 1870) indicates that farming and blacksmithing were the primary occupations in Bethel Township, and that the population of the township was never large. In 1870, Bethel Township had a population of 1,040, with 186 dwellings and 134 farms (U.S. Bureau of the Census 1870).

People who settled this part of Illinois came from a variety of places to the east. The 1850 federal census (U.S. Bureau of the Census 1850) indicates that the most common birthplaces outside Illinois for residents of McDonough County were Indiana, Kentucky, Ohio, Pennsylvania, Tennessee, England, Ireland, and Scotland. Few, if any, of the residents were wealthy; most were poor farmers trying to create a new life in Illinois. The fact that McDonough County is named after a War of 1812 officer is probably not a coincidence. A number of people who settled in this portion of Illinois were soldiers in the War of 1812. After the war, much of McDonough County was part of what was termed military bounty land, and bounty land grants of exactly 160 acres were made to veterans. In Bethel Township, much of the 1812 bounty land was settled from the late 1830s through the mid-1840s (McDonough County Genealogical Society 1996). It is likely that the availability of land to veterans was the process by which many settlers acquired their land.

Chenoweth and Semonis (1992) and Peter and Hotchkiss (1996) report that about sixteen historic cemeteries have been recorded in the township. Most of these are family cemeteries, although a few churches also created cemeteries. Most of the formal early churches in the township were Baptist or Methodist. What we now call the Irish Cemetery was a multifamily cemetery that had been forgotten over the years; the last mention of the cemetery in land records was in 1867 when Frederick and Jane Bowman transferred the land to George Calvin with an exception for the quarter-acre on which the cemetery is located.

Nineteenth-Century Funerals and Cemeteries

Haberstein and Lamers (1962) outline a history of American funerary practices, noting the different cycles or trends in funerary customs. Mueller (1976), focusing specifically on tombstones, also outlines some of these trends, moving from early Puritan memorials to elaborate Victorian monuments to modern twentieth-century horizontal (rather than vertical) forms. Similarly, Buikstra (2000, 17–20) summarizes the changing trends in American mortuary customs from a social, as well as a material, perspective. Not surprisingly, most of these trends began in eastern cities and eventually spread west. If one went solely by date, the Irish Cemetery would fall squarely within the Victorian traditions of beautification of death and ostentatious funerary. Archaeologists have interpreted the meaning of these Victorian customs differently. Cannon (1989, 437–438) has criticized archaeologists' interpretations of status differentiation, arguing that rather than explaining specific examples of elaboration, it is necessary to examine changes over time; there are regular cycles of ostentation and leveling effects. Bell (1990) sees the presence of elaborate coffin hardware as representing availability of mass-produced items and chronological changes, rather than status distinctions. McGuire (1988) emphasizes the dynamic role of cemeteries in social negotiations and cultural change, rather than as representative of status differentiation. Little, Lanphear, and Owsley (1992), in the investigation of a family cemetery in Virginia, see the cemetery as a reflection of the general Victorian trends, mass-production of coffins and coffin hardware, and the need of the family to maintain visible symbols of status. The important lesson here is that there is seldom a simple, one-to-one correlation between elaboration and status, particularly in these historic cemeteries.

The Irish Cemetery is a small family cemetery that we believe should reflect the attitudes and way of life practiced on the Illinois prairie in the mid-1800s. All of the people were from farm families of similar circumstances and backgrounds; there should be little differentiation between individuals. The cemetery predates the professionalization of the funeral business; family and friends are responsible for death rituals. As Buikstra (2000, 29–30) notes, coffin construction at this time was often undertaken by local cabinetmakers, but this trend is more apparent in the second half of the nineteenth century and is more likely to have taken place in cities than in rural areas; there were few merchants in rural McDonough County and even fewer cabinetmakers. Coffin shape in the first half of the nineteenth century was hexagonal or octagonal, with tapering to the toe. Later, rectangular forms were dominant. In the case of the Irish Cemetery, the shape may be dependent on who made the coffin as much as any particular trend. It is our guess that expediency was as likely a determining factor as what was considered to be proper. As for tombstones, forms or pattern books were likely used in their manufacture if they were made locally. There was ample limestone and sandstone available for use. We would not expect the stones to represent the latest fashion, but instead be a lagged or delayed representation of what was popular in the east—people on the frontier would not have any means of or interest in knowing the latest trends.

Our expectations for the Irish Cemetery thus included the following: (1) a site dominated by one or more related families who lived immediately adjacent to the cemetery; (2) a site with little status differentiation between individuals; (3) some evidence of Victorian representation in tombstones, but with a local perspective; (4) coffins, coffin hardware, and grave goods that are local and/or expedient in manufacture; and (5) spatial patterning that reflects family relationships. While we originally had great hopes for analyses and interpretations based on what we could learn from the bones themselves, the poor preservation at the site severely limited this avenue of investigation.

Strategy and Methods of Excavation

By the time the UWM crew arrived at the cemetery site, the trees and brush had been cleared and all of the tombstones had been removed. Freeman United provided a map indicating the location of each tombstone, and our map was completed using the same datum as that used by the coal company. UWM did not produce a detailed topographic map of the site—the ground had already been disturbed by the clearing activities, and only a generalized topographic map (based on U.S. Geological Survey quadrangle maps) could be produced.

The soil beneath the topsoil (A horizon) was a weathered loess that was extremely hard and compact. This soil appeared to be a well-developed illuvial B horizon formed in loess. No graves or grave outlines were clearly discernible on the surface, so it was necessary to strip the surface in order to expose grave outlines. Freeman United provided a large "paddle-wheel" or "pan" machine (and an operator) to strip the surface. The equipment was able to remove a fairly even layer of about 10cm of soil with each pass. After each pass, we checked for grave outlines or other features. After the removal of about 0.4m of soil, the grave outlines were generally discernible.

Unexpectedly, the graves were not clear and distinct; the grave fill was only slightly darker and slightly more mottled than surrounding soil. The graves and other possible features were photographed, incised, photographed again, and then mapped by transit. Each grave was assigned a number, and each feature that was not clearly a grave was assigned a letter.

Prior to excavation, there was no clear indication of the average depth of a grave. General histories of the period and discussions with local residents and Duane Clugston indicate that variability was all one could reliably expect. At the time the cemetery was used (1848–1871), it was common to dig "six-foot" graves, but that was a variable six feet; in addition, infants and children were often placed in shallower graves. Weather conditions, time of year, and the soil itself would also affect the depth of the grave for a given individual.

Given the problems of unknown depth, unknown preservation of materials, and compactness and lack of clear color distinction of the grave fill, the strategy for the excavation of the graves can be summarized as follows.

After defining, photographing, and mapping the grave, a line bisecting the long axis of the grave was incised. We then excavated the west half of the grave down to the point at which the coffin (or coffin remnants) was present. This approach allowed us to carefully discover the depth of grave with a minimum amount of disturbance. We could also examine the profile of the grave and determine whether or not the limits of the grave as seen in plan view matched the limits as seen in vertical perspective. Given the problems of grave visibility, this process of checking limits was important.

The graves were excavated in the same manner as any other feature:

the grave fill was carefully excavated from the surrounding matrix. The compactness of the soil necessitated the use of shovels, but we attempted to remove the fill in levels. Careful notes were taken throughout the excavations—each excavator recorded all pertinent information in a notebook. Forms were used for recording osteological information. Each grave was mapped at several levels, and we piece-plotted all items recovered.

Once the coffin (or coffin remnants) was reached, the entire grave was exposed and trowels were used to outline the coffin and excavate down to the human remains. From the point of reaching the coffin, all materials recovered were carefully mapped in three dimensions, and all soil was screened through ⅛-inch hardware cloth.

Buikstra examined the human remains as they were uncovered, and again when the bones were removed from the ground. After removal from the grave, the skeletal materials were cleaned and analyzed in the field. We continued excavation until it was certain that we had reached the bottom of the grave.

All materials recovered were inventoried, and grave identification (i.e., who was likely to be the individual in the grave) was done upon completion of the grave excavation and the osteological analysis. The remains of the individuals were placed in wooden boxes provided by the Clugston Funeral Home, and each box was labeled with the name of the individual represented.

Unfortunately, bone preservation was extremely poor throughout the cemetery, and it was not possible to determine as much information about each individual as we had hoped. Because we knew the soil was loess, we had hoped for excellent preservation. Unfortunately, the soil is a weathered loess that was extremely acidic.

Other features besides burials were also discovered in the cemetery. Each of these features was mapped and photographed, and each feature was then cross-sectioned, excavated, and examined.

The Cemetery

The Irish Cemetery was a small family cemetery, and several different lines of evidence were used to trace individuals and families: tombstones, land records, genealogical records, census data, archaeological data, and osteological data. No one line of evidence could be used to identify the individuals in the cemetery; identification required integration of all data available. Some of the archival work was conducted by the Freeman

United Coal Company in its quest to have the court allow removal of the cemetery, some was conducted as a result of genealogical searches by family members, and some was directed by Goldstein. Buikstra conducted all of the osteological analysis, and Goldstein integrated the archaeological and tombstone data.

While the immediate purpose of the project was to identify individuals so that they could be properly reburied, the longer-term goals, outlined earlier, include a desire to create life histories for these individuals in an attempt to better understand the settlement of this area and the culture of the settlers.

Osteologically, the investigatory challenge presented by this type of cemetery project is similar to that found in contemporary forensic situations. Given the fact that the gravestones were not in place, the burials represent an assemblage—as with mass disasters—in which certain attributes of individuals are known but matching of individuals (graves) with the attributes is subject to interpretation. While the remains are not commingled, the marginal preservation and the limited information about the individuals result in a significant challenge.

Determination of cause of death in a preservation situation such as this is impossible; the best one can do is examine records of the time and see how causes of death have been recorded. Lowell Volkel (1980) prepared a transcription of the 1860 Mortality Schedule for the State of Illinois. Although none of the people in the Irish Cemetery died within the months covered by the report, one can get a sense of what diseases and problems were most prevalent for McDonough County. For adults, common causes of death include brain fever, consumption, typhoid fever, dropsy, flux, poison, delirium tremens, lung congestion, and old age. For children, common causes of death are typhoid fever, brain fever, croup, quinzy, consumption, dysentery, and "unknown."

Figure 4.1 represents the layout of the cemetery, after individuals had been identified. Archaeologically, there were three types of features identified at the Irish Cemetery: graves, features, and posts. The posts were apparently part of a fence that at one time encompassed at least a portion of the cemetery; at least two of the three nonpost features appear to have been corner markers. Fourteen graves were found in the cemetery area, creating an identification problem since only thirteen gravestones were recovered. It is possible that this fourteenth individual had no gravestone, but it is more likely that the gravestone was vandalized and/or removed by person(s) unknown.

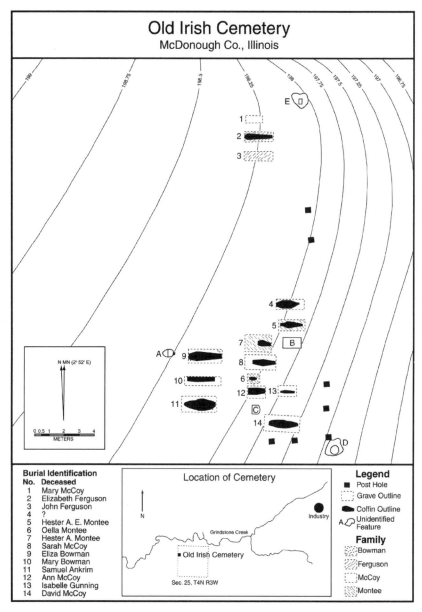

Old Irish Cemetery
McDonough Co., Illinois

Burial Identification

No.	Deceased
1	Mary McCoy
2	Elizabeth Ferguson
3	John Ferguson
4	?
5	Hester A. E. Montee
6	Oella Montee
7	Hester A. Montee
8	Sarah McCoy
9	Eliza Bowman
10	Mary Bowman
11	Samuel Ankrim
12	Ann McCoy
13	Isabelle Gunning
14	David McCoy

Location of Cemetery

Industry

Grindstone Creek

■ Old Irish Cemetery

Sec. 25, T4N R3W

Legend

■ Post Hole
Grave Outline
Coffin Outline
A Unidentified Feature

Family
Bowman
Ferguson
McCoy
Montee

Figure 4.1 Map of the Irish Cemetery with Generalized Topography Indicated and Graves Identified By Individual and Family

There are five infants, one adolescent, three young adults, two middle-aged adults, and two old adults represented by gravestones. Normally, in a situation with well-preserved remains, the identification of these individuals would present little challenge. The only instances of possible confusion would involve Mary Bowman with Elizabeth Ferguson and David McCoy with John Ferguson. However, given the fact that these represent the earliest and most recent male and female remains, and that we expect John and Elizabeth Ferguson to be buried together due to affinal relationship, it is probable that little confusion should ensue—*if* the remains were well preserved. Since the remains are not well preserved, and in some cases no skeletal or dental evidence is present, individual identification becomes more of a challenge. Identifications were made using as many lines of evidence as could be found; these include osteological evidence as well as grave size, placement, and goods.

Table 4.1 is a summary of information recorded from each gravestone and correlated with the identification of the contents of each grave. The list is arranged by date of death. All but four of the known deaths occurred between 1854 and 1862. The thirteen known individuals are primarily members of four families: the Fergusons, the Montees, the McCoys, and the Bowmans. Also present in the cemetery were the remains of Isabelle Gunning and Samuel Ankrim.

The Fergusons

John Ferguson was born in 1785 in Washington County, Pennsylvania (Chenoweth and Semonis 1992, 244). In the 1790s, the family moved to Scioto County, Ohio. In April 1817, in the first marriage officially recorded in Lawrence County, Ohio, Ferguson married Elizabeth McCoy, a native of Ireland. Since Elizabeth Ferguson's maiden name was McCoy, there is likely to be a relationship between at least two of the four families discussed here. According to the 1830 federal census (Ohio Family Historians 1964, 397), John Ferguson owned land in Scioto County, Ohio. The Fergusons moved to Bethel Township in 1836 with their five living children. They purchased 120 acres of land, selected because of the availability of wood for fuel and game for food. Family history notes that John Ferguson's nickname was "Tip" because he fought in the battle of Tippecanoe and went to an Indian powwow to help arrange a peace treaty (Anonymous n.d., 5).

Elizabeth died in 1844 and was the first individual interred in the cemetery. John died in 1848 and was also buried in the cemetery. None of the

Table 4.1 Individuals Recovered from the Irish Cemetery

Name	Date of Death	Age at Death	Grave No.	Relationship
Elizabeth Ferguson	December 14, 1844	48 years	2	Wife of John; nee McCoy
John Ferguson	May 26, 1848	62 years, 6 months, 27 days	3	Husband of Elizabeth
Sarah McCoy	October 30, 1848	27 years	8	Wife of David
Ann McCoy	September 25, 1850	12 days	12	Sister of Mary, niece of David
Oella Montee	June 5, 1854	neonate	6	Niece of Hester A. E., cousin of Hester A.
Hester A. Montee	October 13, 1855	1 year, 6 months, 13 days	7	Niece of Hester A. E., cousin of Oella
Isabelle Gunning	October 19, 1856	2 years, 4 months	13	No known relationship to others in cemetery
Mary McCoy	September 16, 1858	9 months, 16 days	1	Niece of David, sister of Ann
Hester A. E. Montee	December 8, 1858	13 years, 1 month, 1 day	5	Aunt of Oella and Hester A.
Samuel Ankrim	March 22, 1860	26 years, 6 months, 5 days	11	Possibly related to McCoys
Eliza Bowman	May 11, 1861	21 years, 7 months	9	Daughter of Mary
Mary Bowman	September 9, 1862	42 years	10	Mother of Eliza
David McCoy	January 19, 1871	56 years	14	Husband of Sarah, uncle of Ann and Mary
Unknown female	Unknown	Old	4	May be related to McCoys?

Ferguson children were buried in the cemetery; they either died prior to the Fergusons moving to McDonough County, or they moved away or died after 1871, the last date the cemetery was used.

Elizabeth Ferguson's grave had the most elaborate stone—a large rectangular, simple-carved stone slab with no writing was placed along the length of the grave, and a footstone indicated the specific information. Likely because of the size and weight of the stone, her tombstone was the only one that was not moved out of place. Her grave was approximately 190cm long and 55cm wide. The coffin itself was rectangular and very narrow—it was only 25cm wide. A total of three different types of fasteners were used for the coffin: large screws (4–5cm long) were used to attach boards together, copper tacks were apparently used to decorate the coffin, and small iron tacks were used to attach the cloth coffin lining. In her hand were remnants of a netted, coarse fabric; we believe it may have been the binding of a bible. The bones were poorly preserved, but Elizabeth was placed in the coffin extended and on her back, with her arms crossed across her body. Elizabeth may have had the most elaborate grave because she was the first buried in the cemetery or because of her husband's grief over her death.

While John Ferguson did not have as elaborate a grave marker, his tombstone clearly identified him as a head of a family. Figure 4.2A is a photograph of Ferguson's stone; it is a large broken column surrounded by a simple banner or festoon. In 1947, the American Monument Association published a guide for memorial dealers; the book depicts common and historical memorial symbols and their meanings. The broken column is a common theme for sorrow, particularly for the head of a family. Both copper rivets and square nails were found in his grave, along with some evidence of planking from the coffin. He was also placed on his back with his arms crossed across his body.

The McCoys

Sarah and David McCoy were husband and wife, and David purchased land just east of the cemetery in 1842 (State of Illinois 1842). Sarah was David's first wife; she died in 1848 at the age of twenty-seven. Although David moved away and remarried Ann Stanley seven years later (State of Illinois n.d.), his body was returned to this cemetery for burial when he died in 1871 at the age of fifty-six. David McCoy was the last known burial in the cemetery. The other McCoys in the cemetery represent extended family rather than children. Ann and Mary McCoy were sisters; they were both nieces of David McCoy.

There is one feature of inherited dental morphology observable in the remains of the Irish Cemetery: Carabelli's Cusp. This is an accessory cusp located on the mesiolingual aspect of upper molars and is characteristically found in whites and blacks, but not in Mongoloid peoples (cf. Buikstra and Ubelaker 1994). This trait was expressed in six remains from the site: those tentatively identified as David McCoy, Isabelle Gunning, Sarah McCoy, Elizabeth Ferguson, and the unknown female in Grave 4. To some extent, this strengthens the argument that Elizabeth Ferguson (nee McCoy) was related to the McCoys. The apparent co-expression of the trait in affines David and Sarah McCoy is either fortuitous or possible evidence of cousin marriage. Perhaps the elder female in Grave 4 was also related to the McCoy lineage. The presence of the trait in the single deciduous tooth from Grave 13 makes one wish to identify this burial as one of the McCoys

Figure 4.2 Examples of tombstones in the Irish Cemetery. (A) John Ferguson's stone. (B) Sarah McCoy's stone. (C) Hester A. Montee's stone.

rather than as Isabelle Gunning. However, it is possible that the trait in the Gunning girl indicates a distant blood relationship not discovered in the genealogy search. That the trait is absent in John Ferguson, Samuel Ankrim, and Hester A. E. Montee is not unexpected.

David McCoy also had a tombstone that indicated his role as family head; it had a finger pointing to heaven, signaling that he had "gone home" (American Monument Association 1947). Some of the coffin in this grave was preserved, and there is evidence that the lid had slumped in, pushing the sidewalls inward. Bones were present but were poorly preserved. Based on dental wear patterns, McCoy apparently smoked a pipe; he also still had a mulberry seed stuck in his teeth.

Sarah McCoy's stone is seen in Figure 4.2B; a weeping willow is carved at the top of the stone. Willows, and especially weeping willows, are a common Victorian memorial symbol (American Monument Association 1947; Mueller 1976). There was some evidence of a coffin and bone in the grave, but preservation was variable with some long bones and some teeth present.

The grave identified as that of Mary McCoy (death in 1858 at nine months old) had no remaining evidence of a coffin but did include a few beads and some teeth. The identification of this individual as Mary

McCoy was based largely on a comparison of the estimated age based on teeth with age represented on tombstones.

Ann McCoy died in 1850 at the age of twelve days. It is unlikely that much of the body would remain, particularly given the overall poor preservation at the site. We identified Grave 12 as that of Ann McCoy, largely based on a process of elimination and the pattern of bone meal present. There were no grave goods, although some square nails, small hinges, and hinge pins were recovered.

The Montees

Marge Harris has outlined the Montee family history (1984, 73–74). The Montees represented in the Irish Cemetery are all members of the Francis Abraham and Hester Ann (Wilson) Montee family. Francis Abraham was known as Abram. Abram Montee was born near Plattsburg, New York, in April 1800; he served in the War of 1812. He and Hester Ann Wilson were married in Plattsburg. She was born there in 1804. They moved to Ohio, where he was a farmer and a lumberman, then on to Illinois, probably in 1852. Abram died in 1877 at the age of seventy-six, and Hester Ann died in 1882 at the age of seventy-eight.

Abram and Hester Ann had a total of twelve children. There are three Montee children, who died between 1854 and 1858, buried in the cemetery. Hester A. E. Montee died in 1858 at the age of thirteen; she was the daughter of Abram and Hester Ann. Oella and Hester A. were grandchildren of Abram and Hester Ann. Oella died as a neonate in 1854, and Hester A. died at the age of eighteen months in 1855. Oella's parents were William and Lydia Montee, who later moved to Ohio; Hester A.'s mother was Nancy Montee, who was seventeen when Hester A. was born.

A Montee son, Charles, died at the age of twenty-seven and was buried at Macomb. According to Harris (1984, 74), Abram, Hester, and Nancy all appear in the 1860 census, listed as living in Chalmers Township.

Figure 4.2C is a photograph of Hester A. Montee's tombstone. It has a lamb carved in it, which, according to the American Monument Association (1947, 27), has long been a favorite for commemorating little children. With the exception of the children who were under the age of one month at death, all children in the cemetery had lambs or angels on their tombstones. Hester A.'s grave also contained remnants of some fabric around the shoulders that seemed to represent a linen-backed wool blanket. A belt buckle and white glass buttons were also found in the grave.

Hester A. E. Montee's grave also had some remnants of a coffin, some teeth, and some bone meal. Thirteen buttons (five white, eight pink) were located in an area from neck to waist. The buttons were four-holed and were 11mm in diameter.

Oella Montee's tombstone had no symbolic carvings—it merely stated the fact of her birth and death on June 5, 1854. Not unexpectedly, very little was found in her grave. Some evidence of a coffin was visible, and fourteen nails were recovered. The grave was very shallow.

The Bowmans

From the title search done by Freeman United as part of its petition to move the cemetery, we know that in 1867 Frederick and Jane Bowman transferred the land on which the cemetery was located to another individual. That was also the last time mention was made of the cemetery in land records, even though the last burial was in 1871. We assume that Frederick and Jane Bowman were related to the Bowmans buried in the cemetery, but we have not been able to verify this. We do not know if Mary was a first wife of Frederick or if they are related in some other way. We do know that Mary Bowman was the mother of Eliza Bowman—we do not know if they have a relationship to anyone else in the cemetery.

Mary Bowman died in 1862 at the age of forty-two; her daughter Eliza preceded her in death by one year. Eliza was twenty-one when she died. Preservation in both graves was poor; some wood, nails, and bone were found in each grave. Mary Bowman's grave was in slightly better condition, but no grave goods were recovered.

Others Buried in the Cemetery

There were three other individuals buried in the cemetery: an unknown old adult female, Isabelle Gunning, and Samuel Ankrim.

The unknown adult female was the only individual we could not associate with a tombstone. We assume that the tombstone was vandalized or stolen, rather than never present. The grave had evidence of a coffin and contained a glass button. In addition, some cloth was found under the shoulder and the left forearm. The body was extended, with the head turned on its right side. Both arms were folded across the body. Ironically, this individual was likely the best preserved in the cemetery. We know it was not anyone listed above because the individual was too old to be any of those women for whom we had tombstones. As noted earlier, the presence of a Carabelli's Cusp suggests that this individual might be related to the McCoys.

The presence of a Carabelli's Cusp also suggests that Isabelle Gunning was related to the McCoys. Isabelle died in 1856 at two years of age. Her grave was small, with a coffin represented by nails all around it but no grave goods. Isabelle was the daughter of William and Lydia Gunning (Lester n.d., 14). According to the 1880 federal census (U.S. Bureau of the Census 1880), William Gunning was from Pennsylvania and Lydia was from Ohio; William's parents were both from Ireland. The Gunnings remained in the area, although Isabelle was the only member of the family to be buried in this cemetery.

The most puzzling inclusion in the cemetery is Samuel Ankrim. His tombstone indicates that he died in 1860 at the age of twenty-six; a carved open book is at the top of the stone. No one was able to find any record of Samuel Ankrim living in McDonough County, but several separate lines of evidence suggest a possible explanation. First, we know that the Irish Cemetery is not a Catholic cemetery; Catholic cemeteries have crosses and other specific symbols of faith (cf. American Monument Association 1947), and there were no Catholic churches in the area at that time. Second, an open-book symbol carved on a tombstone often signified a particularly learned individual, a very religious individual, or a preacher (American Monument Association 1947; Mueller 1976). Our initial thought was that perhaps Ankrim was a traveling preacher or a preacher new to the area. We also thought it possible that his placement in the cemetery and near the Bowmans might represent a relationship with Eliza Bowman; he died a year before her. While this interpretation would account for his presence in the cemetery and his absence in the archival records, we decided to investigate further.

Most of the individuals in the Irish Cemetery came either directly from Ireland or indirectly from Ireland via a generation in Ohio or Pennsylvania. Using genealogical sources, we tried to trace Samuel Ankrim in Ohio. We found evidence of a Samuel Ankrum who was a sergeant in the War of 1812 (U.S. Government n.d.) and who (listed as Ankrim) bought land in Lawrence County, Ohio, the same place John Ferguson was from, at various times from 1828 through 1856 (Lawrence County, Ohio, n.d.). Even more interestingly, Ankrim married a Sarah McCoy in 1828 (Murnahan 1987, 9). Given that the Samuel Ankrim in the Irish Cemetery was born in 1834, the Ohio Samuel Ankrim could be his father. While McCoy is not an uncommon name, it is tempting to link Ankrim to the McCoys and Fergusons in the cemetery through Ankrim's mother and the fact that his parents lived in Lawrence County, Ohio. Whether or not Samuel Ankrim was a preacher who was a distant relation to the McCoys and Fergusons as well as a significant other to Eliza Bowman may never be known. However, at least some of these possibilities are likely to be true and further substantiate the family character of this cemetery.

General Observations and Interpretations

Table 4.1 summarizes the demographic data for the cemetery. There are a number of ways to use these data to form predictions concerning cemetery structure and osteological characteristics. For example, there are a series of individuals with consanguineous relationships (e.g., the McCoy and the Montee children). In addition, there are affines present: John and Elizabeth Ferguson, David and Sarah McCoy. In most cases, we would expect affinal relationships to assume priority in structuring the cemetery. However, there are exceptions: David McCoy moved from the region and remarried. His remains were returned to the area and interred much later (twenty-three years) than those of his first wife. It is likely that affinal relationship as a structuring mechanism would be tempered by time lapsed since the death of Sarah, and perhaps more pragmatically by crowding at the cemetery. In sum, we might expect that consanguineous relationship would structure burial clusters when they are not preempted by affinal relationship. Time can also be an intervening variable.

It is interesting to note that although the spatial organization of the cemetery appears to be structured by affinal/consanguineous relationships, there is also an important impact of order-of-death/interment. It appears that the initial burials were the Fergusons, located at the high point of the ridge and removed from most of the others. After the Fergusons, Sarah McCoy initiated the McCoy precinct a distance away from the Fergusons. With a few exceptions, a centrifugal patterning persists; David McCoy, as the most recent addition to the cemetery, occupies a decidedly peripheral location.

The type of limestone and sandstone gravestones used in the cemetery are common for the period and were apparently introduced in the eastern United States about twenty years before their use here (cf. Mueller 1976). Some minor differences can be seen between the styles of gravestones for the earliest interments and the most recent. Because innovation and change in gravestones happened first in the East where large centers of population were located, the pattern of diffusion of styles went from east to west. What is interesting is that this diffusion took approximately twenty years to reach rural Illinois. The tombstones also allow us to make several other observations and conclusions:

1. The types of symbols used on the stones (especially the absence of crosses) indicate that this was *not* an Irish Catholic cemetery, but an Irish Protestant cemetery.

2. The symbols used on the gravestones represent widely used sentiments of expression by the living for the dead. Thus, the children who died before the age of one month had no symbols on their stones. The other children generally had either an angel or a lamb, and this symbol was not used for anyone other than a child or adolescent. Women had either a vine or a willow, and the males who were head of the family had symbols so indicating. John Ferguson had an impressive stone with a broken pillar, and David McCoy had a finger pointing to heaven indicating that he had "gone home."

3. There is little evidence for status differentiation and elaboration between individuals. Stones tend to mark individuals by age, sex, and status within the family (cf. McGuire's [1988] discussion of marking male dominance at the household level).

4. Analysis of the stones allows some mysteries of the cemetery to be resolved, or the stones at least present some alternative explanations. In particular, identification of Samuel Ankrim presented many problems. Who was he and why was he not with family? His gravestone had an open book surrounded by leaves. This symbol was generally used for individuals who were either very religious or who were preachers. Given that this was not a Catholic cemetery, it is likely that Ankrim was a preacher. A preacher would commonly be found away from family and friends. This evidence, taken with his placement next to Eliza Bowman, suggests that perhaps Ankrim was engaged to Bowman but died before they could be wed. The genealogical research possibly linking Ankrim with the McCoys does not dispute this finding but suggests that he may have had some kin relationship to the families in the cemetery.

Conclusion

The Irish Cemetery project is an excellent example of why such cemeteries should be excavated by qualified archaeologists and physical anthropologists. Although the initial goal of the project was to locate and identify individuals and to move the cemetery prior to construction, this goal was best served by using multiple lines of evidence and expertise. However, the project also demonstrates that archaeological and osteological data alone were insufficient to answer the questions of identification and relationship; many other lines of evidence were also required. In other words, it is the integration of multiple lines of evidence that can best address complex questions of relationship in this kind of historic context. No one kind of data has precedence or status over others.

The Irish Cemetery represents a group of pioneers who moved west from Ireland to Pennsylvania and Ohio, and eventually to Illinois. Understanding these people requires understanding their movement west. They were hard-working farmers and hunters who settled in this area because the resources were plentiful, and here they could make a home. Most of the pioneers were able to settle here because of benefits they received as a result of being veterans of the War of 1812. These people were not the prominent or wealthy folks of McDonough County; they did not have many material possessions, but they were not necessarily poor. They were a group linked together by their relationships with their own and their spouses' extended families; they were together in life and in death. Their graves reflect the structure of the family at that time, and the relative absence of grave goods may signal their practical nature as much as their apparent lack of wealth.

As a sparsely populated rural area with few merchants or craftsmen, McDonough County will not represent the most current and fashionable styles in tombstones—the stones and symbols used here lag behind what is in vogue further east. However, the tombstone styles are well within the range for the Victorian period, and anyone viewing these stones would easily classify them as early Victorian. What is troubling, however, is the notion that one might also then interpret the symbols used as a reflection of the Victorian beautification and ostentation of death. As discussed earlier, the Victorians tried to fit the symbolism of their monuments to the deceased, and they expressed their deep feeling for nature. They were sentimental. While the people at the Irish Cemetery likely had an understanding of nature and likely grieved at the death of a loved one and especially of a child, it is hard to characterize these people as Victorian in sentiment. Life on the rural frontier was too hard for us to believe that these folks were deeply sentimental and saw death as "sleep." While the general symbolic associations hold (e.g., lambs for children, broken columns for heads of households), and the focus is on family relationship and structure, one questions how far this can be taken, and whether this would be properly described as a Victorian view. More likely is the perspective (somewhat similar to Bell 1990) that because of the popularity of pattern books, a certain uniformity in stones resulted, and while these symbols allow the identification of broad status differences (child, head of family, etc.), beyond these broad distinctions the displays are more representative of time and availability than of worldview.

In addition to what we were able to learn from the site, the project allowed the descendants of the individuals buried at the cemetery to visit the site and see that the remains of their ancestors were treated with care and respect. They learned something about their relatives as well, ranging from incidental information such as the fact that David McCoy smoked a pipe and had a mulberry seed stuck in his teeth, to information about genetic relationships. They also learned something about the potential of archaeology and osteology to assist in such circumstances, and they felt much better about having to move their ancestors' graves.

This project did not result in earth-shattering conclusions about life in rural Illinois in the mid-1800s. It did not address larger regional issues concerning the European settlement of the Great Lakes region. What it did do was provide some insight into life on the rural frontier as well as how symbols are applied and used at the local level and how a single data source cannot provide a sufficiently rich or complete perspective on a complex cultural situation. We think that all of these things are well within the spirit of the kind of work regularly done by Charles E. Cleland.

Acknowledgments

We would like to thank the following people for their cooperation and assistance: Duane Clugston of the Clugston Funeral Home, Dale Anderson of the Freeman United Coal Mining Company, and especially the descendants of the individuals who were buried in the Irish Cemetery. We also wish to thank the volunteers who helped us excavate the cemetery on a number of very cold November days. They did a terrific job under stressful circumstances. Goldstein would like to thank Maureen Gaff and Donald Gaff for their expertise and assistance in researching historical, archival, and genealogical records. Donald Gaff also helped prepare the figures for this paper. Finally, this project would never have been possible without the assistance, coordination, and vision of Larry Conrad, archaeologist at Western Illinois University. It was Conrad who believed that archaeologists were the right people to do this project, and he convinced both Freeman United and Clugston that this was the right way to get it done properly. We are indebted to him.

5

The Gill Net's "Native Country"

The Inland Shore Fishery in the Northern Lake Michigan Basin

Beverley A. Smith

Archaeologists have long recognized the importance of fish in the subsistence strategies of Upper Great Lakes native peoples during the Middle Woodland through Late Woodland periods. Changes in both technology and target species as an explanation for social change has been the subject, however, of controversy in archaeological modeling. The evidence for archaeological fish remains in the northern Lake Michigan basin is examined to address the problem of alleged differences between Middle and Late Woodland fishing strategies and also to address the power of current models as explanatory devices in delineating these two major cultural periods. The data supports Cleland's (1982) thesis that the transition between Middle and Late Woodland fishing strategies was profound and that evidence for the fall gill net fishery finds its earliest manifestation in the Straits of Mackinac at A.D. 800. However, Martin's (1985) analysis of site location indicates that traditional Middle Woodland fishing localities are not abandoned in the Late Woodland period with the appearance of gill net technology.

THE DRAMATIC AND PROVOCATIVE ethnohistoric accounts of the productive late seventeenth-century fisheries in the Straits of Mackinac and St. Mary's Rapids in the central Upper Great Lakes have justifiably intrigued archaeologists interested in reconstructing the lives of precontact period people. To what extent can the traditional native fishing activities, described by seventeenth- and early-eighteenth-century Europeans, be extended back in time? Surely if the scale of fishing documented historically was practiced with the same skill and intensity in the Late Woodland period (A.D. 600–1650) or even the Middle Woodland period (250 B.C.–A.D. 600), economic and technological data substantiating the development and importance of the fishery should be evident in the archaeological record.

This essay seeks to review the evidence for fish remains excavated from archaeological sites in the northern Lake Michigan basin with the goal of reassessing the disparate models presented by Cleland (1982, 1989) and Martin (1985, 1989) regarding the development of the fall fishery for spawning Lake Whitefish and Lake Trout using gill net technology. The debate is important because an understanding of this intensive fishery has been implicated in efforts to explain regional settlement patterns, population changes, relations of production, and social organization during the Late Woodland period in the region.

The important 1982 essay by Charles E. Cleland titled "The Inland Shore Fishery of the Northern Great Lakes: Its Development and Importance In Prehistory" presents an evolutionary model of technological changes in fishing strategies from the Late Archaic through the Late Woodland periods. In Cleland's model, the Late Woodland period heralded a substantial change in settlement pattern and social relations due, in large part, to the development of the gill net, which was essential for exploiting concentrations of Lake Whitefish and Lake Trout during their fall spawns. In this model, the invention of the gill net in the Late Woodland period resulted in the need for large labor parties to harvest and process the abundant quantities of fall-spawning fish, which in turn provided a storable resource that allowed for larger human populations, stronger delineations of group identity and boundaries, and increased exchange of ideas across the region.

Cleland's model was subsequently scrutinized by Susan R. Martin in her 1985 dissertation titled "Models of Change in the Woodland Settlement of the Northern Great Lakes Region." Her work was summarized in a 1989 *American Antiquity* article (Martin 1989). Martin analyzed site locational data and conducted a statistical analysis of the environmental variables at Middle and Late Woodland sites in the northeastern Lake Michigan and southeastern Lake Superior regions. She found little evidence to support Cleland's model of the sudden appearance of gill net technology in the Late Woodland period, because she found no substantive changes in site location between the Middle and Late Woodland periods. Furthermore, her analysis does not support the long-standing view of increasing human populations from Middle Woodland to Late Woodland times, whether the result of increased intensity of fishing (Cleland 1982; Lovis and Holman 1976), migration (Fitting 1979), or other nonspecified reasons (Mason 1981). For Martin, Middle Woodland sites in Northern Michigan have near-shore and offshore physiographic characteristics that overlap with Late Woodland site locations, and site locations from both periods are proximal to both fall-spawner habitats as well as prime spring and summer fish habitats. She contends that the faunal assemblages and ubiquitous net weights support the hypothesis that "the gill net was not a technology exclusive to the Late Woodland period, but may predate it" (1989, 596).

In his rejoinder to Martin (1989), Cleland states that "Martin's suggestion that there is great continuity in subsistence strategy through the Middle and Late Woodland periods of the Northern Great Lakes is rejected. She fails to produce convincing evidence for the use of gill nets during Middle Woodland times and to account for the difference in fish fauna on sites of these two periods" (1989, 605).

Indeed, both models suffer to "produce convincing evidence" since they each fail to present a systematic review of the empirical evidence of fish remains from any of the archaeological sites in the region. In fact, Cleland refers vaguely and only to the Juntunen (20MK1), Scott Point (20MK22), and P-Flat (47AS47) sites, "as well as some others" as "containing thick deposits of whitefish and lake trout bones and scales" (1989, 605). With only 298 whitefish and Lake Trout elements identified from all cultural components at the stratified Juntunen site (Cleland 1966), and only 35 identified from the Scott Point site (Martin 1982), the only site that comes close to this description is the P-Flat site where 3,948 salmonid elements were identified (Colburn and Martin 1989; Smith and Cleland 1987). However, the P-Flat site, located at the southwestern end of Lake Superior, is a historic site dating to between 1650 and 1800 and replicates the ethnohistoric descriptions rather than addresses the precontact evolution of the gill net fishery. If this fishery was so important prior to contact, why could Cleland only cite two specific precontact sites in support of his thesis?

Martin did consider the fish remains from Woodland period sites in her study area but reported only the presence/absence of species identified at these sites (1985, 98–100). She contends that sampling error and taphonomic variables were primarily responsible for the sparse faunal evidence, especially evidence that would indicate a fall-season gill net fishery for salmonids (101–102). Her contention that the transition to the Late Woodland was a gradual one and not marked by major changes in either site location or the invention of the gill net relied primarily on a simulation modeling.

Where then is the empirical evidence of the gill net in the Middle Woodland period or, for that matter, the Late Woodland period? Twenty years have passed since Cleland first proposed his evolutionary model, and since then additional sites have been excavated with more refined recovery techniques and a greater understanding of the taphonomic processes affecting fish bone.

This essay summarizes the fish faunal evidence of the northern Lake Michigan basin in an arc extending from south of Traverse Bay to the Straits of Mackinac and along the north shore of Lake Michigan to Green Bay in Wisconsin. Culturally, the sites represent the Lake Forest Middle Woodland period (ca. 250 B.C.–A.D. 600) (Brose and Hambacher 1999, 173), the transitional Middle to Late Woodland period (ca. A.D. 600–800), and the Late Woodland period (ca. A.D. 800–1650)(Holman and Brashler 1999, 212). The location of the sites is presented in Figure 5.1.

Taphonomy, Recovery Techniques, and Sample Size in Woodland Sites Fish Fauna

There are significant sources of bias in the fish component of faunal assemblages from the study region that influence interpretations of capture technique, seasonality, or subsistence reconstruction derived from the data. These biases include taphonomic variables, identification of fish vertebrae, archaeological recovery technique, reporting of data, and sample size.

Destructive forces for bone in the region generally include acidic soil, slow soil development, turbative processes, perthotaxic factors, and, of course, time (Micozzi 1991). While the literature is complex, the most important factor in survivability of fish remains is bone density (Micozzi 1991, 55; Wheeler and Jones 1989, 62–63) and, to a lesser extent, element shape and size (Nicholson 1992). Vertebrae generally preserve better than cranial elements due to their bulky shape. The high density of the bone and readily recognizable texture of the dermal plates of the Lake Sturgeon, for example, enhances both preservation and identification of this species in the region's archaeological record.

On the other extreme, salmonid bones are considered to be particularly vulnerable, especially, it appears, the cranial bones of whitefish spe-

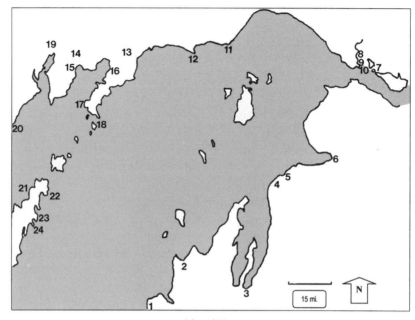

List of Sites

1.	Point Arcadia (20MT120)	13.	Thunder Lake (20ST109)
2.	Fisher Lake (20LU21)	14.	Ten Mile Rapids (20DE188)
3.	East Bay (20GT58)	15.	Ogontz Bay (20DE296)
4.	O'Neill (20CX18)	16.	Winter (20DE17)
5.	Pine River Channel (20CX19)	17.	Fayette Cliffs
6.	Portage (20EM22)	18.	Summer Island (20DE4)
7.	Juntunen (20MK1)	19.	Sturgeon River (20DE75)
8.	Carp River Mouth (20MK261)	20.	Menoninee River Sites
9.	Beyer (20MK45)	21.	Shanty Bay
10.	Gyftakis (20MK51)	22.	Mero
11.	Scott Point (20MK22)	23.	Heins Creek
12.	Ekdahl-Goodreau (20ST1)	24.	Whitefish Bay View (47DR167)

Figure 5.1 Location of Upper Great Lakes Sites with Fish Remains Used in the Analysis

cies. Lubinski (1996) variously boiled, burned, baked, and then bathed samples of Lake Whitefish cranial elements and vertebrae in a solution of potassium acid pthalate and an alkalide solution of borax and sodium hydroxide. Not surprisingly, the bones did not fare well. There is no doubt that fish bone, especially whitefish bone, is highly susceptible to agents of destruction. However, without tests that subject other species of fish to similar treatments in controlled experiments, it remains unclear just how much more fragile the bone of freshwater salmonids are than, for example, species of the Bass/Sunfish/Bluegill family (Centrarchidae). In support of other studies, Lubinski (1996, 180) also concluded that cranial elements are destroyed more quickly than vertebrae.

The identification of fish vertebrae to zoological family has only recently become a standard practice in the analysis of faunal assemblages from the region's sites. From Middle Woodland sites, only the Ekdahl-Goodreau (20ST1) (Smith 1983) and Fayette Cliffs (Martin 1995) site fish assemblage analyses attempted to identify fish vertebrae. From the transitional Middle to Late Woodland period, only the Carp River Mouth site (20MK261) (Smith 1993) analyses identified fish vertebrae. The Ekdahl-Goodreau site (Smith 1983), the Ten Mile Rapids site (20DE188) (Martin 1984), and the Whitefish Bay View site (47DR167) (Dirst 1987) are the only accounts from Late Woodland sites/occupations that explicitly reported identifications based on fish vertebrae. In cases where fish were decapitated at the point of capture or processing, only the postcranial elements would be deposited in habitation sites or at the point of consumption. Compounding the scenario of variable fish vertebrae deposition and identification with the taphonomic issue of variable element preservation underscores the importance of considering vertebrae in identification and may be critical to providing a comprehensive view of all species exploited at a site.

The application of flotation and fine-scale water screening varies widely among the sites in the region. Soil samples from the Fisher Lake (20LU21) (Brose 1975) and Summer Island (20DE4) sites (Brose 1970) were floated. From the transitional period, the East Bay site (20GT58) (Hambacher, Dunham, and Branstner 1994, 73), Pine River Channel site (20CX19) (Holman 1978), and Carp River Mouth site (Smith 1993) soil samples were floated. Fine-scale recovery techniques were employed at the Late Woodland sites of Point Arcadia (20MT120) (Hambacher 1988), Thunder Lake (20ST109) (Franzen 1987), Ten Mile Rapids (Roper, Weir, and Rutter 1984), Shanty Bay (Dirst 1995a), and Whitefish Bay View (Dirst 1987), and these samples produced evidence of fish.

An example of the importance of flotation and the identification of vertebrae is the Carp River Mouth site, located in the Straits of Mackinac. This is a transitional Middle to Late Woodland site where three whitefish vertebrae were identified. A comparison of the quarter-inch mesh-screened sample and floated sample revealed that 98.4 percent of the fish sample was recovered from flotation. The analysis also showed that without flotation the whitefish and sucker elements may well have been missed entirely, and these important species would not have been identified in the assemblage (Smith 1993, 138).

A further source of bias in the assemblages results from incomplete reporting of faunal findings. In most cases, only NISP (number of identified specimens) and occasionally only presence/absence are reported. Rarely is MNI (minimum number of individuals) calculated nor is the raw data presented so that MNI can be calculated from the report. Since most measures of taxonomic diversity, richness, and relative abundance rely on MNI data, statistical calculations of significance cannot be undertaken with any degree of confidence (Grayson 1984). For example, T. Martin reports that more than thirty thousand fragments of Lake Sturgeon bone were recovered from the Ten Mile Rapids site but that he could not estimate the number of individual sturgeon represented by the assemblage (Roper, Weir, and Rutter 1984). Together with sites where only presence is reported, such as the O'Neil site (20CX18) (Lovis 1973), the variability in reporting of faunal assemblages renders them difficult to compare statistically.

Sample size is yet another bias that affects the interpretation of the faunal assemblages. The amount of excavated area varies widely among the sites in the study region. The Ogontz Bay site (20DE296) faunal assemblage was recovered from only 2m² of excavation, whereas the Juntunen site assemblage comes from 450m² of excavation (Anderton and Weir 1991; Martin 1985). In reference to sample size and sampling error, Grayson states that

> interpretation of relative abundances may prove to be primarily the interpretation of the size of the samples from which the abundances have been derived. The presence of such a correlation does not necessarily mean that changing sample sizes have caused the changing relative abundances, but it does mean that the cause of the correlation must be explored before further analyses of those abundances are conducted. (1984, 130)

Sample size is, of course, also affected by recovery technique and by variability in taphonomic factors that affect fish bone preservation.

The seemingly insurmountable variables that contribute to bias in the fish faunal assemblages from the region include taphonomic factors, faunal analysis and reporting, archaeological recovery, and sample size. It is no wonder, therefore, that authors such as Cleland and Martin sidestep the details of the fish faunal assemblages from the region and apply more general or simulation methods of analysis respectively. However, the fish faunal assemblages can still provide hints about the trends inherent in Woodland strategies of fishing.

Middle Woodland Period Fish Fauna

Seven sites in the region have produced fish remains, and all of these sites indicate a mixed economy with spring spawners, which commonly include pike, suckers, catfish/bullhead, bass/sunfish, drum, and especially walleye and Lake Sturgeon (Table 5.1). The Fisher Lake site is located approximately four and a half miles inland from the Lake Michigan shoreline, and the Middle Woodland occupation has been interpreted as a small fishing site "probably utilized during the spring sturgeon spawning season" (Brose 1975, 80). The lower levels of the multicomponent Ekdahl-Goodreau site produced evidence of Northern Pike and Yellow Walleye (Smith 1983). The Middle Woodland occupation at the Summer Island site is considered to have been a fishing station that concentrated on Lake Sturgeon exploitation (Brose 1970). The Mero site on the Door Peninsula in Wisconsin is also dominated by Lake Sturgeon, although Yellow Walleye was an important species in both the lower and intermediate levels of the Middle Woodland occupation (Cleland 1966).

Three of the Middle Woodland sites in the region that have produced a range of fish species also have evidence for the exploitation of salmonids. The Gyftakis site (20MK51) in the Straits of Mackinac produced an assemblage dominated by Lake Sturgeon and Yellow Walleye and includes less amounts of White Sucker, Freshwater Drum, and one Lake Trout element from Middle Woodland features (Cardinal 1978). At the Winter site (20DE17), the fish assemblage is dominated by salmonid remains identified as Round Whitefish or Lake Herring; six additional species, including Lake Sturgeon and Yellow Walleye, are also identified at the site (Martin 1980). The Fayette Cliffs site is a mortuary locality where large individuals identified as Lake Trout, Lake Whitefish, Black Bass, and suckers are present (Martin 1995).

Transitional Middle to Late Woodland Period Fish Fauna

Four sites have produced fish assemblages that are considered to represent the transition between Middle and Late Woodland periods (see Table 5.1). The fish remains recovered from these sites are scant. The East Bay site produced only one unidentifiable vertebra fragment and sixty-two additional unidentifiable fragments recovered by flotation (Hambacher, Dunham, and Branstner 1994, 73). At the Pine River Channel site, sucker and Yellow Walleye are identified (Holman 1978). The Portage site (20EM22) produced Lake Sturgeon and Largemouth Bass (Smith 1983).

Table 5.1 Middle Woodland and Transitional Middle to Late Woodland Site Fish Fauna (NISP)

Taxon ID	Common Name	Middle Woodland								Transitional Middle to Late Woodland			
		Fisher Lake 20LU21	Gyftakis 20MK51	Ekdahl-Goodreau 20ST1	Summer Island 20DE4	Winter 20DE17	Fayette Cliffs Delta	Mero Wisconsin Lower	Mero Wisconsin Inter.	East Bay 20GT58	Pine River Channel 20CX19	Portage 20EM22	Carp River Mouth 20MK261
Acipenser fulvescens	Lake sturgeon	49	51		678	1		10	10			15	2
Lepisosteus osseus	Longnose gar				1								
Salvelinus namaycush	Lake trout		1				89						
Coregonus clupeaformis	Lake whitefish						3						
Coregonus sp.	Whitefish/Chub sp.												3
Prosopium/Coregonus sp.	Round whitefish/Lake herring				127	7							
Coregonidae sp.	Whitefish family												
Salmonidae/Coregonidae sp.	Trout/Whitefish family			5									
Esox lucius	Northern pike				2								
Esox sp.	Pike/Muskellunge sp.												2
Catostomus catostomus	Longnose sucker						1						
Catostomus commersonni	White sucker		11								1		
Catostomus sp.	Sucker sp.		8		2		5						4
Catostomidae sp.	Sucker/Redhorse family									24		22	
Ictalurus punctatus	Channel catfish							2	2				
Ictaluridae sp.	Bullhead/Catfish family				7								
Morone chrysops	White bass					2							
Micropterus dolomieui	Smallmouth bass						1						
Micropterus salmoides	Largemouth bass								2				
Micropterus sp.	Bass sp.	2			5		4						
Perca flavescens cf.	Yellow perch												
Stizostedion vitreum	Yellow walleye		45	2	18	2	180	3	15		1		
Stizostedion sp.	Walleye/Sauger sp.												
Percidae sp.	Walleye/Perch family												1
Aplodinotus grunniens	Freshwater drum		1		1	2	1		1				1
Subtotal		51	117	7	707	141	289	17	29	0	26	16	38
Osteichthyes sp.			1629	29	707	14	81	17	29	64	141	26	243
Total		51	1746	36	707	155	370	17	29	64	141	42	281

The most diverse fish assemblage from this cultural period is reported from the Carp River Mouth site, located near the Straits of Mackinac. A minimum of thirteen individuals, representing a minimum of seven fish species, are present in the assemblage. While the suckers are of a moderate and uniform size, the pike/muskellunge, walleye/sauger, Freshwater Drum, and Smallmouth Bass elements represent relatively large individuals. This site has also produced three Corigonidae (whitefish/chub/cisco) vertebrae, representing two individuals (Smith 1993, 132, 136).

Late Woodland Period Fish Fauna

Late Woodland sites in the northern Lake Michigan basin are more productive in terms of documenting the exploitation of a wider variety of fish species, including Lake Whitefish and Lake Trout. Seventeen Late Woodland sites and/or occupations and a cluster of sites in the Menominee River basin have produced fish remains, and nine of these assemblages include the remains of Lake Trout and Lake Whitefish (Table 5.2).

The major portion of the Late Woodland sites in the region show evidence of a rather eclectic assemblage of fish, which includes Lake Sturgeon and a range of species from the pike, sucker/redhorse, bullhead/catfish, sunfish/bass, perch/walleye, and drum families. The O'Neil site (Lovis 1973, 214–215), Thunder Lake site (Masulis and Martin 1987), Ogontz Bay site (T. Martin in Anderton and Weir 1991), and Summer Island site (Smith 2000a), and in Wisconsin the Shanty Bay (Dirst 1995a), Mero and Heins Creek (Cleland 1966), and Whitefish Bay View (Dirst 1987) sites, fit this general scenario. Also present in the diverse fish assemblages from some of these sites—including the O'Neil, Ekdahl-Goodreau, Ogontz Bay, and Summer Island sites—are proportionately small numbers of fall-spawning salmonids, Lake Trout, and/or Lake Whitefish. The small assemblage at the Beyer site (20MK45) in the Straits of Mackinac area also produced one Lake Whitefish element as well as Lake Sturgeon and Yellow Walleye (Cardinal 1974).

Some Late Woodland period sites seem to represent a fishing strategy that targets certain species with some degree of intensity. The Point Arcadia site is located on the margins of inland Lake Arcadia in proximity to the Lake Michigan shoreline (Hambacher 1988). The flotation sample from a Traverse phase (post-A.D. 1100) feature produced an assemblage of small fish, dominated by Yellow Perch, that were likely captured with a seine net during the warm weather season (Smith 1988). The other

Table 5.2 Late Woodland Site Fish Fauna (NISP)

Taxon ID	Common Name	Point Arcadia 20MT120	Fisher Lake 20LU21	O'Neill 20CX18	Juntunen 20MK1	Beyer 20MK45	Scott Point 20MK22	Ekdahl-Goodreau 20ST1	Thunder Lake 20ST109	Ten Mile Rapids 20DE188	Ogontz Bay 20DE296	Summer Island 20DE4	Sturgeon River 20DE75	Menominee River Sites MI	Shanty Bay WI	Mero WI	Heins Creek WI	Whitefish Bay View 47DR167
Acipenser fulvescens	Lake sturgeon			P	888	4	77	10		30000	18	75	1	70	215	13	12	24
Lepisosteus osseus	Longnose gar			P	29							2						
Salvelinus namaycush	Lake trout		37		36	1	25	1			2	3						12
Coregonus clupeaformis	Lake whitefish				262		10											8
Salmonidae/Coregonidae sp.	Trout/Whitefish fam.			P	2		345											
Esox lucius	Northern pike							1	2									6
Esox sp.	Pike/Muskellunge sp.	1			3		11				3				1		2	
Notropis cf. *cornutus*	Common Shiner																	
Cyprinidae sp.	Minnow/Shiner fam.				1													
Moxostoma anisurum	Silver redhorse				6													
Moxostoma macrolepidotum	Shorthead redhorse				4													
Moxostoma sp.	Redhorse sp.			P							2							
Catostomus catostomus	Longnose sucker				28						2							
Catostomus commersonii	White sucker			44	18		25					1		1			10	1
Catostomus sp.	Sucker sp.										20							
Catostomidae sp.	Sucker/Redhorse fam.	1			7		10			1								7
Ictalurus natalis	Yellow bullhead	1																
Ictalurus nebulosus	Brown bullhead				2													
Ictalurus punctatus	Channel catfish			P	3									1			7	
Ictalurus sp.	Bullhead/Catfish sp.			P					1									
Ictaluridae fam.	Bullhead/Catfish fam.																	
Lota lota	Burbot										2							
Lepomis macrochirus	Bluegill	6																
Pomoxis sp.	Crappie sp.	1																
Pomoxis/Lepomis sp.	Bluegill/Crappie sp.	1																
Micropterus dolomieui	Smallmouth bass	1	5		7											2		1
Micropterus salmoides	Largemouth bass				12		4				41	1			3		15	
Micropterus sp.	Bass sp.			P			4								3			
Centrarchidae sp.	Bluegill/Bass family											P			8		3	
Ambloplites rupestris	Rock bass				1													
Perca flavescens cf.	Yellow perch	201		19	16		2				5	2			1			5
Stizostedion vitreum	Yellow walleye			P	61	1	1		1		112	5			6	3	9	4
Stizostedion sp.	Walleye/Sauger sp.							1								3		
Percidae sp.	Walleye/Perch family	102					2								1			
Aplodinotus grunniens	Freshwater drum	2			7							1			8		5	5
Subtotal		317	42	63	1393	6	515	13	4	30001	207	90	1	75	248	21	55	76
Osteichthyes sp. (vertebrae)		1161		N/A	23371	31	1044	107	2	12	425	5			994			
Osteichthyes sp.					8332			5										
Total		1478	42	4172	33096	37	1559	125	6	30013	632	95	1	75	1242	21	55	76

sites suggest an intensive strategy of warm-weather fishing targeting the Lake Sturgeon. These sites, on the Upper Peninsula, include the Ekdahl-Goodreau (Smith 1983), Ten Mile Rapids (Martin 1984), Sturgeon River (Smith 2000b), and Menominee River sites (Buckmaster 1979).

Lake Whitefish is a dominant fish species in only four Late Woodland sites. The stratified sites of Juntunen (Cleland 1966) in the Straits of Mackinac and Scott Point (Martin 1982) on the Upper Peninsula of Michigan also have a strong representation of salmonids as well as a high proportion of Lake Sturgeon and a varied array of other fish species. The Fisher Lake site Late Woodland component is another example (Brose 1975). The Oneota component of the Whitefish Bay View site (Dirst 1987) on the Door Peninsula is similar to the aforementioned sites in terms of the relatively high proportion of salmonids; this site has produced the only evidence to date of fall-spawning fish, including Lake Whitefish, at sites around Green Bay.

Trends in Fish Faunal Assemblages in the Woodland Period

There is evidence of continuity both in site location (Martin 1985) and in the ubiquity of fish between the Middle Woodland and Late Woodland periods. One simple measure of diversity is the number of zoological families of fish represented in each site. Habitat preference and other behavioral characteristics of fish tend to be similar within zoological families, making this a useful category for comparison of sites (Figure 5.2).

Ten sites/occupations had only one to three different families of fish. A consideration of site location and archaeological factors may help to explain these assemblages. Five of the sites are located inland (more than two miles) from the Lake Michigan shore; they are small, at least in excavated area, and produced small and less varied fish assemblages. Both the Middle and Late Woodland occupations of the Fisher Lake, Sturgeon River, Ten Mile Rapids, Thunder Lake, and Menonimee River sites fit this description. The Ekdahl-Goodreau site also produced little variety, but only 9m² of this shoreline site were excavated, no flotation samples were taken, and the stratigraphic complexity of the site resulted in difficulty assigning a cultural occupation to certain levels (Martin 1985, 284). Although the Portage site excavations were more extensive (65m²), the stratigraphic complexity and lack of flotation are reminiscent of the Ekdahl-Goodreau site (275). The Pine River Channel site produced little variety in the fish assemblage, and as Holman (1978, 416) concludes, the

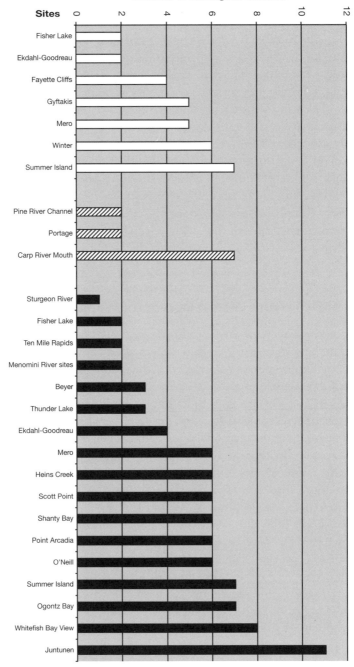

Figure 5.2 Diversity in Fish Taxa by Family

fish assemblage indicates a spring occupation at this warm season site. Finally, the Beyer site also produced little variety of fish fauna, and only six elements could be identified from a small fish assemblage of thirty-seven specimens (Fitting and Clarke 1974). This may reflect poor preservation of fauna, which is unusual for sites in the Straits of Mackinac.

Eleven of the twenty-seven Woodland period sites/occupations produced evidence of the use of four to six different families of fish. All of the remaining Middle Woodland period sites, except Summer Island, and almost half of Late Woodland period sites fit this category of diversity.

Six sites produced evidence of more than six different fish families. High diversity is not confined to the Late Woodland period, since the Middle Woodland and Late Woodland occupations of Summer Island, the transitional period Carp River Mouth site, and the Late Woodland Ogontz Bay, Whitefish Bay View, and Juntunen site assemblages produced a diverse assemblage of fish. High diversity does not in this case appear to be directly correlated with assemblage size. The total number of fish elements from the Scott Point site is approximately two and a half times greater than the number from the Ogontz Bay site, for example, yet the Ogontz Bay site assemblage is slightly more diverse.

A closer examination of the fish species identified at these regional sites provides additional evidence of trends in the use of fish through the Woodland period. While acknowledging the uniquely high preservation rate and ease of identification of Lake Sturgeon, the ubiquity and probably the importance of this species in Woodland subsistence is difficult to deny. A total of twenty-one of the twenty-five sites considered in the study area produced evidence of Lake Sturgeon, and especially in inland sites the anadromous Lake Sturgeon is an important species.

In regard to the number of sites/occupations in each cultural period where select species are represented, there is a tendency for Yellow Walleye to decrease in importance through time; it is present in 86 percent of Middle Woodland sites and declines to 61 percent of Late Woodland sites. Salmonids and suckers, on the other hand, increase in their presence from 43 percent of Middle Woodland sites to 61 percent of Late Woodland sites.

The overall picture of fish selection throughout the Woodland period conforms to Martin's (1985) observation based on site locational characteristics. While certain species are more commonly found in different periods and sites, there is strong consistency through time regarding fish exploitation. The dominant species of fish exploited throughout the Woodland period include Lake Sturgeon, suckers, and Yellow Walleye with a consistent presence of species of the pike, bass, catfish/bullhead, and drum families. There are also salmonids present in both Middle and Late Woodland sites, but can the presence of Lake Whitefish and/or Lake Trout necessarily indicate the use of the gill net during the Middle Woodland period?

The Middle Woodland Period and Evidence for the Use of the Gill Net

Martin has suggested that the consistency in site locations throughout the Woodland period implies a consistency in both subsistence strategy and extraction technology, that is, gill nets, due in large part to the presence of salmonids and net sinkers in Middle Woodland sites. It is important, therefore, to consider this argument and to look more closely at the Middle Woodland sites that have produced salmonid remains.

Firstly, the assumption that the presence of any salmonid is evidence for gill net fishing because all salmonid species spawn in the fall is problematical. The gill net is not the only method of capturing Lake Trout and Lake Whitefish. Cleland (1982), Martin (1985), and others have carefully examined the ethnohistoric records for data about traditional fishing technology. In the early historic period, large Lake Trout were commonly taken with spears and harpoons in the Straits of Mackinac. Hook-and-line fishing was also practiced, especially through the ice, throughout the Upper Great Lakes. Artifacts from archaeological sites in the region provide strong support for an argument extending the ethnohistoric accounts of these fishing technologies into the past. The dip net fishery of the St. Mary's rapids for Lake Whitefish is yet another technology that is well documented ethnohistorically. Therefore, the mere presence of these species is not unilateral evidence of gill net technology.

Secondly, the presence of net sinkers is not unequivocal evidence for gill nets, since all sites from both the Middle and Late Woodland periods have spring-spawning fish present and at least some of these species, especially suckers, are commonly and efficiently taken in seine nets. Seine nets also require stone net sinkers, and unless stones are notched it may be difficult to identify them as cultural artifacts. Martin (1999, 225) notes that whitefish elements and net sinkers do not co-occur in any northern Lake Michigan sites. However, it is possible that both nets and their sinkers would have been stored on beaches where, in the cold weather of November, people would avoid placing their dwellings. If so, net sinkers may have been deposited in the same localities as fish heads, away from domiciles.

Another line of evidence that has been suggested to indicate the use of gill nets is the presence of diving, fish-eating aquatic birds. To explain the high number of Common Loon (*Gavia immer*) elements at the Juntunen site, McPherron suggested that loon would have been caught in the gill nets while feeding on fish (1967, 196). Since it is freeze-up that forces the Common Loon to its winter grounds on the seacoasts (Godfrey 1986, 22), this species would likely be in the area when gill nets are set in November in the Upper Great Lakes. Common Loon is also identified from the Late Woodland Scott Point (Martin 1982), Ogontz Bay (Anderton and Weir 1991), Mero (Cleland 1966), and Whitefish Bay View (Dirst 1987) sites and from the Gyftakis site and Summer Island site Middle Woodland occupations.

The strongest line of evidence to support the use of gill net technology is a relatively uniform size distribution of an assemblage of Lake Whitefish individuals. This would be expected since gill nets are highly selective in terms of size of fish caught. Generally, small fish swim through the mesh and large fish bump off the net, but fish within a certain size range swim into the net until they can no longer continue, then, in attempting to back out, get their gills caught in the mesh. As McCombie and Fry (1960, 182–183) state, "a gill net will take very few whitefish as long as the perimeter of the mesh is greater than the girth of the fish." Contemporary studies of gill net selectivity indicate that there is a strong correlation between mesh size and size of fish selected (McCombie and Fry 1960; Regier and Robson 1966), although the size range of individuals captured in a 14-cm net can be as great as 25cm (Carlander 1970, 125). The vast majority of individuals, however, will conform to a more restricted size range.

Sites dating to the early historic period have provided a strong argument for gill net technology by considering the size range of Lake Whitefish in assemblages. The majority (56.9 percent) of Lake Whitefish at the P-Flat site measured 40–48cm in length (Colburn and Martin 1989, 118–119, 130). The assemblage of Lake Whitefish from the Marquette Mission site (20MK82) was dominated by individuals measuring between 42cm and 45cm in length (Smith 1985, 101). The Providence Bay site (BkHn-3) on Manitoulin Island also produced a Lake Whitefish assemblage dominated by individuals ranging from 40cm to 45cm in length (Smith and Prevec 2000).

The three Middle Woodland sites where salmonids have been identified require further discussion in light of the possible lines of evidence for gill

net technology discussed above. These are the Gyftakis site, the Fayette
Cliffs site, and the Winter site.

The Gyftakis site is complex. Because an intensive series of overlapping
occupations is found along much of the shoreline of downtown St. Ignace,
Michigan, it is necessary to isolate and date features rather than sites. In
a Middle Woodland feature, one Lake Trout element was identified. The
two Lake Whitefish elements, attributed to the Middle Woodland by Martin (1985, 98), come from a "modern" feature (Cardinal 1978). The single
Lake Trout element is not compelling evidence of the use of a gill net.

The Fayette Cliffs mortuary site produced human and animal remains
from a small niche in a limestone cave (Martin 1995). The fish bone represents the remains of fourteen large individuals. Five of the Lake Trout
at this site averaged 64cm long; the other Lake Trout measured 40–48cm
long; three suckers, three Lake Whitefish, and one Black Bass all measured
approximately 40cm or more in length. Worked beaver incisors, Passenger
Pigeon (*Ectopistes migratorius*), duck, shorebirds, and small perching birds
comprise the rest of this assemblage. If this is a single burial event, the
season is estimated to be late April through late August based on the presence of the Common tern (*Sterna hirundo*) (Martin 1980, 4). This seasonal
estimate is inconsistent with the spawn of salmonids, when a gill net
would be used.

At the Winter site on the south shore of Michigan's Upper Peninsula, a large salmonid assemblage (N=127) has been identified as Round
Whitefish or Lake Herring (Martin 1980). This assemblage comes from
the upper occupation of this site and therefore dates to the more recent
end of the A.D. 150–350 estimated date of occupation for the site (91).
The Winter site salmonid assemblage is unique to the region since no
other site has produced a similar assemblage of this/these species from
the Middle Woodland or any other cultural period. As such, this site is
the best candidate to support an argument of gill net technology in the
Middle Woodland.

In terms of the biology, Lake Herring and Round Whitefish are somewhat different from the Lake Whitefish. While all these species spawn in
the late fall, the Lake Herring and Round Whitefish require colder temperatures, 38–40% F, than the Lake Whitefish, which spawns when water temperatures reach 46% F. The spawning depth of the Lake Herring can be quite
shallow, from three to ten feet. The Lake Whitefish spawn in less shallow
water that is rarely deeper than twenty-five feet. Round Whitefish spawn
at depths of twelve to forty-eight feet (Scott and Crossman 1973, 239, 271,

288). The most significant difference between these species is their average size. Lake Herring and Round Whitefish are relatively small species, averaging eight to twelve inches (20–30cm); record-sized individuals rarely exceed thirteen inches and twenty inches, respectively, in Lake Michigan (Scott and Crossman 1973, 240, 289). Lake Whitefish, on the other hand, average fifteen inches (38cm) and commonly reach a total length of seventeen inches (43cm) as young as three years of age and may reach twenty-three inches (58cm) by nine years of age (Scott and Crossman 1973, 273).

Terrance Martin states that the Winter site represents "an example of experimentation with subsistence scheduling that was later successfully adopted by Late Woodland inhabitants of the area" (1980, 91). Given the known behavior and availability of these species, it does indeed seem that the Winter site represents the exploitation of salmonids in the late fall/early winter in the Middle Woodland period. Martin does not suggest any possible technological strategies of exploitation or report MNI's for the assemblage, nor does he comment on the range of sizes of individuals in the assemblage. The small average size of these species might indicate that seine nets could have been used to collect the salmonid species from the Winter site, since the whitefish collected in gill nets at historic sites tend to be much larger.

The evidence for the presence of the gill net in the Middle Woodland is equivocal at best. While fall-spawning salmonids, especially Lake Trout, are present in Middle Woodland assemblages, their minor presence and the evidence of alternate ways of collecting these species makes it difficult to conclude that the gill net was a feature of Middle Woodland technology.

The Juntunen Site and the Emergence of Gill Net Technology

Trends in the fish faunal assemblages through the Woodland period might suggest an increasing use of nets in general. Transitional Middle to Late Woodland site assemblages suggest that while Yellow Walleye may decline in importance, suckers seem to become more common in sites. Perhaps this indicates a trend toward a more intensive use of seine nets for the anadromous species of sucker at the expense of the more individual collection techniques, such as hook and line, for Yellow Walleye. Moreover, faunal assemblages from the Middle Woodland clearly indicate that people were exploiting Lake Whitefish, Lake Trout, and other salmonids and perhaps, if the Winter site is any indication, experimenting with netting species that congregate in the fall for spawning as well as those that spawn in the spring.

These trends in species selection and extraction technologies during the Middle and Transitional Middle to Late Woodland periods differ, however, on both a quantitative and qualitative level from the nature of the faunal assemblage from the Juntunen site. In its earliest level of occupation, the Mackinac phase (A.D. 800–1100), whitefish are the second most common animal in the assemblage behind Lake Sturgeon. The earliest occupation of the Mackinac phase (Level A) is the most productive in terms of faunal remains, and all Mackinac phase levels at the site produced 125 whitefish and 22 Lake Trout elements. The 31 whitefish elements from the Bois Blanc phase (A.D. 1100–1250), and 30 whitefish elements from the Juntunen phase (A.D. 1250–1450) raise this species to the most commonly represented animal at the site (Cleland 1966, 185).

It is important to recognize that the fish assemblage at the Juntunen site is derived from archaeological excavation techniques that predate fine-scale recovery. Regarding taphonomy, Cleland (1966) states that while "general conditions for the preservation of bone material were quite good, the actual number of identifiable specimens was quite small relative to the total amount of bone. . . . In areas of intense occupation, the bone was apparently subjected to much trampling under foot" (187). Moreover, Cleland did not identify fish vertebrae in his analysis, although he records 23,371 vertebral specimens (62 percent of all fish remains) and found that much of the fish bone was "fragmented beyond identification" (187). Although varying through the occupation strata, the proportion of fish relative to other classes of animals in the Juntunen site assemblage ranges from almost 80 percent to 99 percent (192). Furthermore, the Juntunen fish assemblage is highly varied; 18 different kinds of fish are identified, representing eleven zoological families (see Figure 5.2). It is difficult to contradict Cleland's assertion that "by Late Woodland times this economy was keyed on fish production" (1989, 606).

Interestingly, Cleland notes that the whitefish assemblage from Juntunen is characterized by an extensive size range and "must have been taken by a method that did not strongly select for size. Either a seine or small mesh gill net is thus indicated" (1982, 772). If the Juntunen site does indeed represent the emergence of the gill net, it would be expected that the earliest gill nets were modeled after the small mesh seine net and, only later, became more selective with an increase in mesh size.

The other sites in the northern Lake Michigan basin where Lake Whitefish are numerous postdate the Mackinac phase of the Juntunen site. The Fisher Lake site Middle Woodland fish fauna is dominated by Lake Sturgeon, whereas the Late Woodland occupation, dated to about A.D. 1100, is dominated by Lake Whitefish (Brose 1975). At the Scott Point site, whitefish is not present in the Mackinac Phase but is present in the Bois Blanc phase around A.D. 1000–1100, and by the Juntunen phase at A.D. 1200, Lake Whitefish and Lake Trout increase in importance (Martin 1982).

In the Green Bay region, the transition in the Late Woodland from Heins Creek to Oneota is heralded by the post-A.D. 1100 addition of tropical domesticates to an economy that also incorporated the harvesting of wild rice in the fall (Mason 1981). Given the evidence of Lake Whitefish and Lake Trout from the Whitefish Bay View site, possible evidence of the use of gill nets appears in Green Bay at this time (Dirst 1987).

Elsewhere in the Upper Great Lakes, fish faunal assemblages interpreted as possible evidence of gill net technology appear only in the late fifteenth century. This observation has been made for sites in Huronia (Needs-Howarth 1999, 59) and is consistent with findings from sites in the homeland of the historic Odawa in Georgian Bay, such as the Providence Bay, Hunter's Point (BfHg-3), and Shawana (BkHk-1) sites (Prevec 1988, 1991; Smith 1989).

For most archaeologists, the Late Woodland represents a major shift in settlement pattern. As Holman and Brashler state, "Seasonal aggregation of large groups was possible at 'central place' Late Woodland sites in most regions of the Lower Peninsula" (1999, 215). One of the earliest of these "central places" was the Juntunen site and, like several later Late Woodland sites in the northern Lake Michigan basin, the gill net to extract fall-spawning Lake Whitefish and Lake Trout was added to the existing fishing technology, resulting in the "Inland Shore Fishery." At the same time, Martin's analysis reveals that the transition from Middle to Late Woodland period settlement did not involve the abandonment of localities that had previously proven productive for the critical spring fishery. Martin sees "the persistent reuse of a few areas of high, multiple-season subsistence potential in spite of, not because of, the prominence of a single technology" (1989, 603).

Conclusion

This essay consolidates the currently available fish faunal data from Middle Woodland, transitional Middle to Late Woodland, and Late Woodland archaeological sites in reexamination of the disparate models regarding the emergence of gill net technology in the northern Lake Michigan basin.

A consideration of taphonomic, recovery, and analytic variables that impact the utility of fish faunal remains to accurately reflect subsistence strategies and extraction technology is presented and, while the biases are substantial, faunal remains are the only direct empirical evidence of the species exploited at archaeological sites.

A review of the archaeological fish fauna recovered from northern Lake Michigan sites reveals that certain clear trends can be observed in the data. Inland sites have less diversity in the kinds of fish exploited than do shoreline sites and, at most shoreline sites, four to six different zoological families of fish are present. High diversity of fish is observed not only in Late Woodland sites, but in Middle Woodland sites as well. Furthermore, there is evidence to suggest that Yellow Walleye, an important species throughout the Woodland period, declines in importance relative to suckers, which may signal an increased use of netting technology as the Late Woodland period approaches.

Fall-spawning salmonids, including whitefish, are not confined to the Late Woodland period. This analysis has reviewed the possible lines of evidence that may be employed to indicate that these species were captured using gill net technology. It is concluded that while experimentation using nets for salmonids occurred at certain localities in the Middle Woodland period, such as the Winter site, it was not until the Late Woodland period that fall fishing with gill nets became an entrenched part of the subsistence strategy.

There is a continuation of the use of sites during the Late Woodland where a well-established spring fishery is documented for the Middle Woodland and transitional Middle to Late Woodland periods from Traverse Bay, Michigan, to Green Bay, Wisconsin. However, the earliest site where convincing evidence of the gill net first appears is still the Juntunen site at A.D. 800. By A.D. 1100, several sites around the region display evidence of the use of the gill net to take whitefish in the fall, and the technology is seen outside the Lake Michigan basin by the late fifteenth century.

The Jesuits, in their rather exaggerated yet surprisingly insightful way, called the Straits of Mackinac the fishes "native country" (Thwaites 1959, 55:167). Until further empirical evidence is presented to the contrary, it seems that the Straits of Mackinac is also the native country of gill net technology in the Upper Great Lakes.

6

Heins Creek Pottery

Reexamining the Wells Collection

Carol I. Mason

The Heins Creek ceramic complex was defined from the site of the same name on the east shore of the Door Peninsula of Wisconsin. It is an early Late Woodland manifestation with signs of developing into Madison ware. Material from excavations at the site are reexamined from the point of view of physical separation in the ground of two separate Heins Creek occupations and what they might mean for understanding such development.

THE PLACE WHERE little Heins Creek enters Lake Michigan south of Baileys Harbor in Door County, Wisconsin, has a long history as a well-known archaeological site (Figure 6.1). Archaeological remains extend along the shore on both sides of the creek within an area of migrating sand dunes, in part stabilized and in part eroding completely away; the site itself may be coterminous with this sandy area. It was originally thought to extend at least fifteen hundred feet north of the creek and about five hundred feet inland, bordered on the east by Lake Michigan and on the north and west by swampy ground. Parts of the site have undoubtedly been washed away by Lake Michigan over the centuries. Exactly how large the site may have been is now unknown, owing to extensive cottage construction along and back from the shore.

The site officially entered the archaeological literature in 1918 when J. P. Schumacher recorded it in his *Wisconsin Archeologist* article of the same year as probably the largest site on the Door Peninsula. The above figures on site dimensions are his. Later, Charles E. Brown (1925) included it in his survey of Door County, using information derived from Schumacher. In the Wisconsin Archaeological Codification files, maintained by the

Figure 6.1 Map of the Door Peninsula with Site Locations

State Historical Society of Wisconsin, the Heins Creek vicinity is listed as Dr-1 and Dr-2 although both designations most likely refer to a single site, Dr-1 being the record of a burial or burials once found "along Heins Creek" and Dr-2 referring to the whole area. In 1961, Ronald J. Mason and Carol I. Mason with a crew from the Neville Public Museum in Green Bay excavated in one of the stabilized dunes in hopes of finding an intact land surface, and the resulting monograph (Mason 1966) has been the major source on this extensive and important site.

Others have excavated in the Heins Creek site in one capacity or another. Over the years, it served as a favorite picnic and recreation area for local people with its beautiful sandy beach and adjacent swimming area. Part of the attraction of this site was certainly the fun of discovery as generations of children and adults dug in the sand looking for "Indian relics." Door County residents have even described a large "motor launch" that cruised the shore buying "relics" from whoever found them. At times the surfaces at Heins Creek were sufficiently disturbed as to make it doubtful whether anything at all had survived intact. One comment on its appearance compared it to a bombed out battlefield. The accessibility of the site and its consequent poor condition gave it low priority in field excavation programs designed to understand Door Peninsula prehistory: undisturbed sites offered more information with fewer interpretative problems.

In addition to so much random destruction, a number of careful excavations were actually made at Heins Creek by Edward W. Wells, a well-known and respected avocational archaeologist from Forestville. He worked at the site on an irregular basis from April 1951 to May 1968, always carefully covering his tracks and concealing his work to avoid having his efforts wrecked by the thoughtless weekend looters. He had learned from experience that any evidence left on the surface was an open invitation for casual and not-so-casual digging; in fact, he learned to do his fieldwork in early spring or late fall when the weather was chancy to avoid the "visitors" who immediately went in where he left off. This meant sometimes working in sleet and/or snow, one of the many challenges of doing fieldwork in Door County.

For the most part, Ed Wells worked alone or with the help of his son, John, and his fieldwork was careful and meticulous. He sought permission to excavate from owners when he could find them, which was not always an easy job; he kept profiles, photographed what he found or saw, systematically mapped the site, and carried on years of excavation motivated by a desire to know what had happened at Heins Creek as well as to add to his extensive collections. When the Mason excavations took place, no evidence had been left on the surface to distinguish the Wells excavations from pot hunters' pitting, and no one in the Neville Public Museum crew was aware that other archaeological recovery had occurred there. Wells subsequently contacted the museum, conferred with Ronald J. Mason, and was urged to publish on what he had found. This he did in a 1969 article in *The Wisconsin Archeologist*. It did not have as great an impact on an understanding of Heins Creek as was expected, in part because the photographs reproduced poorly and surface features of the pottery were hard to distinguish. In 1999, some of Ed Wells's archaeological collections, principally pottery, were generously donated by his family to Lawrence University in Appleton, and his Heins Creek material was made available for further work. What has emerged from this restudy is the subject matter of this report.

The Wells excavations (Figure 6.2) consisted of one 10×5- and twenty 5×5-foot units put in between 1952 and 1968. Work began there in 1952 with four units taken out partly in April and partly in June before the rush of summer visitors. Another test pit was completed in 1953, and then there was a hiatus of seven years when he occupied himself with locating and collecting from other sites in northeastern Wisconsin and probably visited Heins Creek only to surface collect. In 1960 he began excavations at the site with five units opened between then and 1962, and during 1963 and 1964 he began to concentrate his work in one area with six more units excavated. For the next four years, he averaged one test pit per year, ending in the summer of 1968. No records exist of his having done any more work there after 1969, but considering his deep regard for the natural beauty of the area and his concern for the site, it is hard to imagine that he abandoned it completely. A few photographs of Heins Creek taken in 1970 are the only surviving evidence of his being there after completing his major excavations.

The significant portion of the Wells collection is from a cluster of eight 5×5-foot test pits on the top of Dune A, the major remnant of the original beach surface, where two sequential Heins Creek deposits were found.

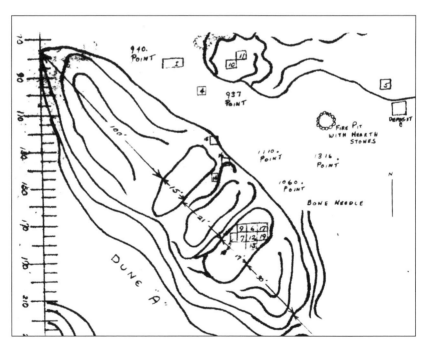

Figure 6.2 Edward Wells's Original Field Map

These eight test pits (numbered 6, 7, 9, 12, 13, 17, 18, and 19; see Figure 6.2) were contiguous and formed a single excavation unit, although the pits were not all excavated at the same time nor was a continuous profile kept open. In between Dune A and other smaller remnants, the deposits have been blown away, dropping the contents of formerly segregated horizontal layers in an unsorted surface deposit. Thus, the few places where intact stratigraphy has been preserved are of critical importance in determining two things: how Heins Creek can be characterized at different periods in its life history and how much discernible internal evolution has occurred. The length of time between the two Heins Creek levels has not yet been determined, but it was long enough for a respectable layer of windblown sand to have built up between them, in some places up to a foot thick, although varying, of course, with the topography and presumably with factors of possible sheltering and wind direction not now recoverable. Exactly how long it takes for sand to move along Lake Michigan's shore during a storm is unknown, but forces of wind and water are notoriously strong there, and the internal interval represented by the sterile layer between the occupation layers may not be very great.

The two horizontal layers in the dune top test pits were labeled II and III. In some areas there was also a discrete Level I, which, when identified, was described as windblown sand with occasional lens-shaped traces of old humus, running between five and eighteen inches thick. Level I contained scattered artifacts, but there was no continuous buried humus layer. In the field notes, this layer is occasionally identified as "Late Woodland," and whatever it was it did not represent a heavy occupation. Level II could be segregated in all of the eight test pits on the dune top. It ranged from a thin deposit of only four to six inches to an appreciably thicker deposit of more than fourteen inches. In all cases, Level II was a black compact layer with varying artifact content and no discernible features. In some places it contained concentrations of fish bones, occasional dolomitic beach cobbles, and considerable cultural material; in others, it yielded little. Level III, separated from Level II by windblown sand, was another black compact layer ranging from six to twelve inches thick. Artifact density was variable with some hot spots and some loci with little content. Levels II and III diminished in thickness as excavation proceeded southward, petering out completely to the west and south. Dates for the two lowermost levels may be forthcoming from carbon encrustations on some of the sherds.

One of the major stratigraphic problems in connecting the Wells excavations to the Mason excavations of 1961 is correlating either Level II or Level

III with the single homogeneous deposit referred to then as Level b of Locality 1 (see Mason 1966). The options for relating Locality 1 to these levels are several: Is the Locality 1 deposit to be equated with Level III with the overlying windblown sand and Level II eroded away? Or is it Level II in a portion of the dune where Level III—for whatever reason—did not occur? A final possibility, based on an *ex post facto* assessment of artifact content, is that the Locality 1 horizon had lost, or did not originally have, the intervening windblown sand layer and is both Levels II and III conjoined. Elevation data would be helpful in deciding, but none exist for the dune top test pits.

The Locality 1 assemblage has come to stand for Heins Creek, and its constituent pottery has become the important Heins Creek ceramic series (Mason 1966) widely used in comparative studies (e.g., Buckmaster 1979; Dirst 1993, 1995a; Halsey 1999; Kreisa 1992). R. Mason (1966) early on saw changes within Heins Creek and linked the complex both to North Bay, where a bridging ceramic complex is represented by pottery from the Rock island site (Mason 1991, 127–128), and to Late Woodland as cord-impressing replaced cord-wrapped stick impressing, sometimes combining both techniques on the same vessel (see the discussion for Level II vessels below). The test pits in the dune top offer a further opportunity to examine the changes and separate Heins Creek clearly into an earlier and later version if the sample is sufficient to tease out differences and the differences are marked enough to be useful.

The Dune Top Test Pits
Level I

The scattered material from Level I includes eight rim sherds and two cord-marked body sherds (Figure 6.3; see also Wells 1969, 18, Fig. 9, d-3, d-5, and d-6). Because there are so few body sherds, the suspicion is that all the artifacts retrieved from that level are no longer in the collections, but Ed Wells's field notes are particularly explicit on the scanty yield from Level I wherever he identified it. In some of the pits he found nothing he might call Level I, insisting instead that it had all "blown away." Level I can in no way be considered equivalent to the dense black middens that are Levels II and III. It is fugitive and simply not physically comparable.

The pottery from Level I is best described as various with five vessels identified from rim sherds and two more provisionally identified from body sherds (see Figure 6.3). Two of the vessels (Nos. 1 and 2) are smooth-surfaced and undecorated except for corded stamping across the rolled lip in Vessel 1; the paste

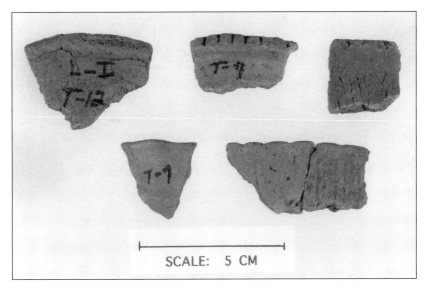

Figure 6.3 Level I, dune top test pits. Top row, left to right, Vessels 5, 1, 7. Bottom row, left to right, Vessels 2, 6.

of these two vessels is chalky and gritty, not like the usual Heins Creek ware. Two other vessels (Nos. 6 and 7, represented by three rim sherds) are straight-sided and cord-marked to the lip. In both cases, the potter fiddled with the lip, in one instance putting knotted cord punctations on the flattened lip (No. 6) and cord-roughening on the others. Vessel 6 has a Heins Creek paste and falls loosely within the Heins Creek Corded-stamped category, but the other has a more chalky paste. The last vessel (No. 5) is represented by two rim sherds from the dune top test pits and a third that came from Test Pit 1, level unknown. It has a Heins Creek paste, although sandier than most, and a smoothed exterior surface; if originally cord-marked, it was subsequently smoothed so effectively as to leave no traces of cord behind. Indication that cord-marking might have been present on this pot comes from the rolled lip, which is covered with crisscrossing cord-marking that may have come from a cord-wrapped paddle or a fabric-wrapped hand. The upper interior rim bears a horizontal row of knotted cord punctations immediately below the lip. Two cord-marked body sherds, each clearly from a different vessel and unrelated to any of the rim sherds, completes the inventory (Nos. 3 and 4).

What exactly does this material from Level I mean in the larger context of site history? The sample is very small, and it represents enough vari-ability to render any conclusions extremely tentative. One of the vessels

(No. 6) and one of the cord-marked body sherds (No. 4) would slip right into Heins Creek without a ripple. The remaining vessels are either not conformable with Heins Creek (Nos. 1, 2, and 5) or marginal enough to be unclassifiable (Nos. 7, 3). The former are smooth-bodied, sandy, or chalky-pasted and in two cases have rolled rims very unlike either Heins Creek or Madison ware. The rim/lip configuration almost looks like the beginning of a collared assemblage, but the absence of any single-cord impressing plus the presence of plain surfaces make comparisons with local collared wares untenable. Level I is only informative in a negative sense: it does not contribute to an understanding of changes in Heins Creek nor does it point to anything new.

Level II

Level II contained a total of 235 sherds, representing a minimum of 20 vessels (Table 6.1). The Heins Creek vessels from Level II, defined from both rim sherds and body sherds, conform to the ware and surface finish descriptions as originally published (Mason 1966, 14–16, 202–204): they continue to reflect the same tightly conceived recipe of what should go into the clay and on the body of the vessel. In all cases, the vessels are represented by only a few rim sherds and in some instances by only one or two very small sherds, compromising somewhat the characterization of each whole pot. The assemblage further reflects some of the same difficulties as in the original description: the ubiquitous cord-marked body sherds from all the types represented are so uniform as to make joining them to rims or discrete vessels almost impossible, and the sherd—and vessel—type Heins Creek Cord-marked undoubtedly includes many a sherd that would

Table 6.1 Ceramics from Level II, Dune Top Test Pits

Level II	All Sherds	Vessels
Heins Creek Corded-stamped	23	5
Heins Creek Cord-wrapped Stick	2	2
Heins Creek transitional	8	5
Madison/Heins Creek Cord-marked	49	1
Heins Creek Cord-marked	3	3
Fabric impressed	1	1
Oneota-like	7	1
Unclassified	10	2
Cord-marked body sherds	132	—
Totals	235	20

SCALE: 5 CM

Figure 6.4 Level II, dune top test pits, Heins Creek Corded-stamped Vessels. Top row, left to right, Vessels 2, 5, 3. Bottom row, left to right, Vessels 1, 4.

be classified otherwise could it be reconstructed into a whole pot. Thirty-six cord-marked body sherds out of a grand total of 132 probably belong specifically to Heins Creek vessels, based on ware characteristics, but more of those presently unassigned cord-marked body sherds surely would be included as Heins Creek were their rims still attached.

As in the Mason excavations at Locality 1, Heins Creek Corded-stamped (Figure 6.4; Vessel Nos. 1, 2, 3, 4, and 5) is a prominent constituent of the body of identifiable pottery from the Level II dune top test pits: five vessels represented by twelve rim sherds and eleven body sherds (including both body sherds belonging to rims and unattached corded-stamped sherds). They conform to the type description with cord-marked bodies, flattened lip treatment consisting of cord-wrapped stick stamping on the lip and rim and occasionally on the body proper (Mason 1966, 16–18). The type definition is here extended to include a slight variation not found in the Locality 1 excavations and not mentioned in the original type description. This variation can be illustrated by a typical Heins Creek Corded-stamped vessel (Vessel 5, represented by seven rim sherds and seven body sherds) with interior and exterior stamping at the rim and lip juncture, not impressed so heavily as to produce the common sinuous lip in this example but stamped nonetheless. In fact, the stamping is so faint it resembles

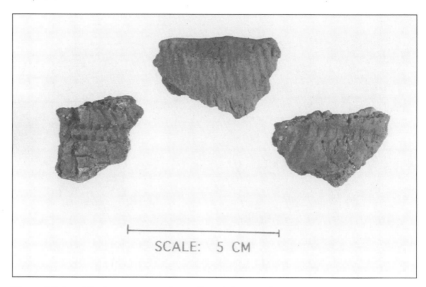

Figure 6.5 Level II, dune top test pits. Left to right, Vessels 15, 17, 18.

fingernail impressions even though it clearly is cord. Subsequent to this stamping, the lip itself was smoothed, flattened, and then punctated (probably with the tip of the same tool as was used in stamping). The punctations are 2–3mm in diameter and sometimes show coarse striations from what was evidently a bone or wooden tip. Another rim sherd from an entirely different vessel exhibits the same combination of flattened, punctated lip, but the sherds are too small to reveal whether or not stamping was also present on the lip exterior. What is going on here may simply be the substitution of poking the clay with the pointed end of the stamping tool rather than laying the same tool across the lip.

Clearly identifiable Heins Creek Cord-wrapped Stick rim sherds in the full sense of the term are entirely absent from Level II test pits. This characteristic Heins Creek complex pottery type may possibly be represented by a single cord-marked rim sherd, with cord-wrapped stick impressions placed diagonally across the lip (Vessel 6). In the absence of any other rim sherd even vaguely assignable to a Cord-wrapped Stick vessel this particular sherd looms large, but it may very well be part of a Corded-stamped vessel. There are only two body sherds (counted as representing two vessels, Nos. 15 and 18) with cord-wrapped stick impressing on them, a single line of coarse cord-wrapped stick impressions across an otherwise undistinguished body sherd and a sherd with a double line of fine cord-

Figure 6.6 Level II, dune top test pits, Transitional Vessels. Top row, left to right, Vessels 12, 13. Bottom row, left to right, Vessels 19, 16, 14.

wrapped stick (Figure 6.5). The whole message concerning Heins Creek in Level II is that corded stamping persists, but cord-wrapped stick has for all practical purposes disappeared.

What has replaced Heins Creek Cord-wrapped Stick ceramics is something more nearly allied to Madison ware in the use of single twisted cord decoration. The pottery uses twisted cord where cord-wrapped stick used to be, with typical Heins Creek lip treatment retaining the cord-wrapped stick stamping. There are five vessels (represented by five rims and three body sherds thought to belong to those vessels, Nos. 12, 13, 14, and two vessels based solely on three decorated body sherds, Nos. 16 and 19) of these transitional forms from the dune top test pits (Figure 6.6). They deviate from the standard Heins Creek ware only in that they may be a slightly finer pottery: denser, thinner, harder, and better made. Decoration consists of horizontally placed single-cord impressions encircling the vessel in rows of at least three (in two cases, four) either on the exterior or interior or both, always on a cord-marked body. Where the lowermost line of cord impressing is preserved, vertical, apparently doubled, cord impressions hang down like a fringe in banks of at least five in a group alternating with banks of five corded-stamped punctations, also appended to the lower line of cord impressions. Lips are flat with either interior or exterior corded stamping or both, sometimes faint and casually placed and sometimes boldly executed, resulting in the appearance of that precisely formed undulating or sinuous rim that is such a common trait of Heins Creek ware. Where corded-stamped rims are not of the dramatic undulating sort, single-cord impressions (one or several) have been laid horizontally across the flattened lip to achieve a decorated effect. A sixth vessel, Madison Cord-marked (?), is represented by one rim (see Figure 6.5) that probably belongs to forty-eight body sherds (Vessel 17), and it was classified solely on the basis of its distinctive ware characteristics; a reasonable argument can also be made that it is an excellent example of Heins Creek Cord-marked. It is a thin (5–7mm), hard pot with fine vertical cord-marking to the lip and no decoration except for vertical corded stamps on the lip interior. The lip itself was flattened and then smoothed after the body was cord-marked, leaving a few faint cord markings under the smoothing. Vessel shape seems to be a simple deep, wide-mouthed bowl with gently incurvate rim and rounded body.

Another vessel from Level II in the dune top test pits is an odd grit-tempered Oneota-like vessel represented by three rim sherds and four body sherds (Figure 6.7). This vessel was small (probably only about 120mm high with an estimated orifice diameter of 80mm). It stands out among the pots from the dune top test pits by reason of its thinness (4–6mm), type of surface finishing, and form of decoration. The temper is a medium to occasionally coarse grit, certainly not like either Heins Creek or Madison wares. The surface is entirely plain with careless wipe marks visible, and with horizontal smoothing around the rim; pairs of trailed vertical lines were placed at wide intervals around the rim, reaching at most 50mm from top to bottom. The vessel outline is of an elongate globular pot with a slightly outflaring rim; it does not fit comfortably within any of the Oneota material from the Mero site (Mason 1966) or Rock Island (Mason 1990) and looks more Mississippian if the trailed lines and grit temper are ignored.

A single fabric-impressed body sherd also occurred in Level II. It is only a tiny sherd, but it is distinct enough to warrant identification as a separate vessel (No. 20). The fabric was coarse and irregularly applied, possibly originally part of a string bag. Assessing the significance of fabric impressing here is of interest in view of the recovery of a fabric-impressed vessel from Test Pit 15 (Vessel 15-1) and Locality 1.

In summary, the Level II contents of the stratified test pits in the dune top indicate the presence of standard Heins Creek ware expressed almost

SCALE: 5 CM

Figure 6.7 Level II, dune top test pits, Oneota-like Vessel 11.

wholly by Heins Creek Corded-stamped vessels (at most 5 out of a total of 20 identified vessels) and Heins Creek Cord-marked vessels (3, Nos. 6, 7 and 17). Cord-wrapped stick impressing is present on two body sherds from 2 different vessels but is not identifiable on any rims. A kind of transitional pottery, one combining the decorative patterning and ware characteristics of Heins Creek with twisted cord in place of cord-wrapped stick is as common as Heins Creek Corded-stamped. Two vessels (Nos. 8 and 9) could not be classified. The grand total of 132 cord-marked body sherds should represent mainly Heins Creek, given the larger number of Heins Creek vessels; in ware characteristics they are uniform and conform to the type description (Mason 1966). However, some of them could come from the twisted cord-impressed vessels cited above; in ware characteristics, at this site at least, the body sherds from these transitional forms cannot always be easily distinguished from Heins Creek since the former is only different by degrees rather than absolutely so. The presence of a single, odd Oneota-like vessel and a fabric-impressed pot completes the inventory. What the contents of these pits suggest is that Heins Creek is fading into or giving way to something more like Madison ware, that cord-wrapped stick impressing has given way to single-cord impressing, and that an anomalous Oneota-like vessel is not a harbinger of things to come.

Level III

Level III, because it is the lowermost of the two strata, ought to be different from Level II in significant ways if it is to be of any chronological or typological use. The ceramic inventory is indeed different from that of Level II although not in ware characteristics, which conform to the Heins Creek standard. The grand total of all sherds in Level III is 342, represented by a total of 35 rim sherds, 212 cord-marked body sherds, 48 decorated body sherds, and 47 sloughed sherds (Table 6.2). Unlike Level II and Locality 1, Cord-wrapped Stick is not such a minority ware; it comprises 14 vessels represented by 13 rim sherds and 28 body sherds, nearly half the total of 34 vessels. Corded Stamp is still close with 9 vessels represented by 5 rim sherds and 9 body sherds, but it clearly does not dominate the collection as it did in either Level II or in Locality 1. A number of other kinds of pottery occur here, some of which are surprising—for example, an incised-over–cord-marked vessel.

The Cord-wrapped Stick vessels include one (Vessel 1) with a cord-marked body heavily wiped so regularly, first in one direction and then in another, as to seem deliberately patterned (Figure 6.8; see also Wells 1969, 16, Fig. 8, B-2). This vessel (five rims, sixteen body sherds) has three closely spaced encircling rows of cord-wrapped stick impressing beginning 20mm below the lip with the lip itself decorated with interior and exterior corded stamps at the lip and rim juncture and with an additional row of small corded stamps on the rim interior. The flattened lip has been further impressed with a continuous line of cord-wrapped stick all the way around the vessel, an attribute that characterizes most of the Cord-wrapped Stick rim

Table 6.2 Ceramics from Level III, Dune Top Test Pits

Level III	All Sherds	Vessels
Heins Creek Corded-stamped	14	9
Heins Creek Cord-wrapped Stick	40	14
Madison Cord-marked	5	1
Heins Creek Cord-marked	47	3
Unclassified	5	3
Cord-marked body sherds	212	—
Unclassified incised over cord	3	1
Dane incised?	13	1
Miniature cord-wrapped stick	3	2
Totals	342	34

Figure 6.8 Level III, dune top test pits, Cord-wrapped Stick Vessels . Top row, left to right, Vessels 1, 2. Bottom row, left to right, Vessels 3, 16.

sherds recorded from Level III on the dune top and that does not occur in Level II at all. The heavy body wiping, which so resembles deliberate pattern-ing but is not, is paralleled on the interior with heavy wiping in much the same way. This heavy crisscross body wiping was noted in the Mason exca-vations at Locality 1 where it was singled out as possibly "incised" (Mason 1966, 24–25). The presence of similar deep, but not crisscross, wiping on the interior of the dune top pot supports the contention made here that the potter was a more-than-ordinarily heavy-handed wiper, not a deliberate but a careless inciser. A second vessel (Vessel 2, with two rims, three body sherds) is very similar except in having at least four lines of cord-wrapped stick and no over-the-body wiping at all (see Figure 6.8; see also Wells 1969, 16, Fig. 8, B-1). It has additionally short lengths of cord-wrapped stick impressions fringed on the bottommost line, although how extensive or discontinuous they are is unknown.

The continuous line of cord-wrapped stick impressing on the lip oc-curs on seven of the thirteen Heins Creek Cord-wrapped Stick rim sherds. Half of these are large enough to additionally show accompanying groups of cord-wrapped stick lines around the bodies, but some are not deep enough to indicate whether such lines occur. Since cord-wrapped stick impressing may begin as far as 36–38mm beneath the lip, only exception-ally deep rim sherds would reveal its presence. The expectation is that the line of cord-wrapped stick impressing on the flattened lip is always accompanied by parallel lines of cord-wrapped stick impressing on the body proper, but the data are not sufficient to confirm it. A further expectation, based on the presence of this attribute in Level III but not in Level II, is that the line of continuous horizontal cord-wrapped stick impressing on the flattened lip is a signature for a somewhat earlier Heins Creek, just as the presence of many cord-wrapped stick vessels seems to be.

The other Heins Creek Cord-wrapped Stick vessels include a typical example (see Figure 6.8, Vessel 16) with interior lip corded stamp, horizontal cord-wrapped stick impressing on the flattened lip, and at least three rows of cord-wrapped stick impressing beginning at 19mm below the lip. Another (see Figure 6.8, Vessel 3) combines cord-wrapped stick impressing with the typical interior/exterior corded stamped lip, creating the neat sinuous effect so typical of Heins Creek Corded-stamped pottery (for body profiles, see Mason 1966, 128, Fig. 7, a–h.) In all cases where enough of the body has been preserved to observe the lines of cord-wrapped stick impressing, the number of rows is at least one and up to at least five (Nos. 7, 8, and 9). Where final rows of cord-wrapped stick impressing survive, four of the five examples have corded stamped punctations or sections of cord-wrapped stick fringing the lowest row.

There are nine vessels (Figure 6.9) included as Heins Creek Corded-stamped, represented by five rims and nine body sherds. Two of them (Nos. 19 and 23) have the typical interior/exterior corded stamped lips producing a sinuous lip flattened on top. Neither of these rims is large enough to tell whether or not cord-wrapped stick impressing or single-cord impressing might have been below the breaks, thus requiring a different identification. The other rims are small and remarkable only for the lip treatment: interior and/or exterior corded stamps and in two cases annular punctations on the lip and in a row 12mm below (Nos. 22 and 32). Corded stamping on the bodies includes banked stamping from below 20mm on the rim to an unknown extent on the body and simple isolated rows of corded stamping (Vessel 25).

Two miniature vessels occur in Level III (Vessels 5 and 12). Each of these is decorated with cord-wrapped stick impressing, but both have entirely smooth surfaces, removing them from being included as Heins Creek ware. That they belong to the Heins Creek complex is undoubted, but they are different. One of them (Figure 6.10, Vessel 12; see also Wells 1969, 16, Fig. 8, B-6) has a single row of crudely overlapping cord-wrapped stick impressing bordered on top and below with corded stamps and a row of similar stamps

Figure 6.9 Level III, dune top test pits, Heins Creek Corded-stamped Vessels. Top row, left to right, Vessels 19, 23, 22. Bottom row, left to right, Vessels 25, 32.

on the lip. The decoration on this vessel uses so much corded stamping that it is almost within a corded stamped category; it is one of those in-between examples that bedevil taxonomy. In other respects it is unusual: it has an estimated orifice diameter of approximately 50mm and was apparently a little globular pot with a gently outflaring rim; it has an almost chalky paste with what may be fine limestone tempering. The other miniature vessel (Vessel 5) is represented by two body sherds (see Figure 6.10, Vessel 5; see also Wells 1969, 16, Fig. 8, B-3 and B-5). It has a plain exterior with the surface smoothed to reveal tiny particles of dark grit. Decoration consists of at least three rows of cord-wrapped stick impressing, 2–4mm apart, the last row having a fringing line of corded stamps. The lip is missing, and the interior is smoothed and crudely modeled. It was a tiny jar with a globular body and constricted neck, and it could not have been more than 55mm in diameter and perhaps 50mm high. Miniature vessels such as these are often described as children's pots, as indeed they may have been, but other interpretations may be offered: mortuary vessels, perhaps? What is evident is that these little pots are too small for culinary use of any kind, although they could have been used as cups.

A single incised-over–cord-marked vessel (Figure 6.11, Vessel 18, represented by five rim sherds and eight body sherds) was recovered in Level III. It is a different kind of a thing than the Heins Creek material: it is heavy and crudely made. The paste is sandy, coarsely tempered with crushed grit and unsmoothed on the interior; it ranges from 10 to 12mm thick on the body, 10 to 11mm at the rim. The body was first cord-marked and then incised in lines parallel to the lip. On the preserved section (see Figure 6.11; see also Wells 1969, 19, Fig. 10 B), the potter seems to have done the incising in sections, and the lines of the first group do not match the second although clearly intended to do so. Fourteen lines of incising survive in the largest sherds, but there were probably more; they begin 18mm below the lip and continue down the body at least as far as 80mm. The vessel seems to have been fairly straight-sided with only the slightest outflare at the neck. The lip is slightly rounded and decorated just below on the exterior with vertical fingernail impressions all the way around. The interior has a similar but somewhat fainter row placed closer to the lip itself. Two deep circular punctations occur on the lower rim below the fingernail impressions, but not enough of the rim survives to indicate whether these encircle the vessel or not. In places the lip bears traces of the original cord-marking up and on the exterior of, but not over, the lip.

SCALE: 5 CM

Figure 6.10 Level III, dune top test pits, Cord-wrapped Stick Decorated Vessels. Top row, left to right, Vessels 7, 8, 12. Bottom row, left to right, Vessels 5, 9.

Figure 6.11 Level III, dune top test pits, Incised Over Cord-marked Vessels. Top row, Vessel 18. Bottom row, left to right, Vessels 33, 17.

Almost any incised-over–cord-marked vessel is still often labeled Dane Incised in spite of growing evidence that the type name is being used to cover a lot of temporal territory and typological variability. (See Farnsworth and Emerson 1986 for discussions of some of the issues.) At the Mero site, similar pottery was associated with the earliest part of North Bay II, thus giving it an Early Middle Woodland association (Mason 1966, 94–99). Another incised-over–cord-marked vessel from Shanty Bay (Dirst 1995a, 37) has a 195 B.C. ± 50 date, which would put it even earlier. Some sherds originally interpreted as incised-over–cord-marked came from the

Locality 1 excavations at Heins Creek, but these were the heavily wiped Heins Creek vessels referred to earlier, not true incised-over–cord-marked. The presence of this incised-over–cord-marked vessel in Level III of the dune top test pits is a gratifying indication of the earlier status of that level, but in this instance it is too early. What such a goose of a crudely made pot is doing among the swans of Heins Creek is unknown: it would be more appropriately associated with Middle Woodland material. (See Mason 1991 for a discussion of this point.)

Two other vessels (Nos. 17 and 33) may also represent incised-over–cord-marked but of a distinctly peculiar kind (see Figure 6.11; see also Wells 1969, 19, Fig. 10, c–1, and 21–22). The surfaces of these two, represented by four rim sherds and one body sherd, look like a checkerboard marked out into 2- to 3-mm squares by lines going vertically and then horizontally over cord-marked surfaces. The vessels themselves were small to medium globular pots with excurvate rims and smoothed, rounded or flattened, and totally undecorated lips. Temper is the ordinary Heins Creek crushed grit. Although provisionally identified as incised-over–cord-marked, these two vessels are sufficiently different from anything that might be classified as Dane Incised that they should not be grouped with it.

At the other end of any proposed temporal spectrum is the presence of pottery decorated with single-cord impressing. Five body sherds with lengths of single-cord impressing occur in Level III. In only one case is enough of the body present to even guess at placement or patterning. This is a sherd with cord impressions approximately 30mm long, much like the fringing often appended to final rows of cord impressing on Madison ware (Figure 6.12, Vessel 35). All the other examples are simply small lengths of cord-impressing over cord-marked bodies, and a vessel count was considered unwarranted.

The 212 plain cord-marked body sherds from Level III range all the way from thin (4mm) to thicker (10mm), but none approaches the heavy thickness of North Bay. They are sometimes covered with very fine cord-marking and sometimes with medium to thick cord-marking. Most are black or buff with buff bloom common on black sherds. Efforts to tie any of these sherds to rims or decorated body sherds were unsuccessful.

A final ceramic object is what appears to be a small beak-shaped lug with two deeply incised lines running parallel to its long axis. It is 31mm long, 14mm wide at its widest, and 12mm thick. It has a slightly concave lower edge that is smooth and rounded, as if it were made to slide on to some other surface. The butt end is well-rounded, and the opposite end is pointed. If it were a lug, it is too small to have been a useful one.

Figure 6.12 Level III, dune top test pits, Madison Ware Vessel 35.

Level II and Level III in the Dune Top Test Pits: Discussion

In balance, what distinguishes Level III from Level II is a series of small shifts in the ceramic inventory. One trend is from cord-wrapped stick impressing in the former to single-cord impressing in the latter. This shift mirrors a change from Heins Creek as a complex to the emergent Madison ware tradition. In this site, in these test pits, the emergence of Madison ware is indeed an evolutionary one, with not only replacement but also step-by-step replacement as certain attributes shift by increments, sometimes visible on a single pot (Mason 1966 for other examples). It is tempting to think that single-cord impressing was somehow easier or more efficient than cord-wrapped stick impressing and that the change was a perception of time and effort saved. Efficiency, however, is not the mother of style, and the emic reasons behind the shift remain unknown and, for that matter, unknowable.

Level III also includes a respectable sample of lips with horizontally impressed cord-wrapped stick. Where Heins Creek Cord-wrapped Stick vessels survive as rim sherds in Level III, all but one of them has a continuous line of cord-wrapped stick impressing placed horizontally into the flattened lip. This distinctive feature is nonexistent in the (admittedly small) sample from Level II and did not occur in the sample from Locality 1 at all. The material from Shanty Bay includes a few small rims with lines of horizontal cord-wrapped stick impressing, but it is not a prominent trait in the collection (Dirst 1995a). If the prominent presence of this decorative motif is in fact an indicator of early status, then it argues for both Locality 1 and Shanty Bay including a slightly later Heins Creek occupation.

Additionally, the substitution of punctuations for corded-stamps on the lips may represent a shift within Heins Creek. The sample is very small, but it may represent something real going on in the choices made by potters. The presence of punctuations instead of corded stamps is most striking on the lip, but it also occurs elsewhere on the site (e.g., Test Pit 1-14; see also Mason 1966, 255) on the body as fringing to lines of twisted cord and as banked decoration where banked corded stamps might be expected to occur.

Another observation from the dune top test pits is the near absence of Oneota pottery. Only a single unusual vessel from Level II that might be Oneota attests to a brief overnight stay or trade or intermarriage or war captives or whatever. There are additionally very few stray shell- or grit-tempered Oneota sherds in the collections, almost none from the surface and mixed deflated areas. Anyone who has worked on the Door Peninsula can testify to the ubiquity of Oneota materials and their universal presence, even in the most unlikely places. Why was there no Oneota occupation at Heins Creek? The site itself attracted human settlement as early as North Bay, if not before. Whatever attraction it possessed for aboriginal people cannot have suddenly ceased once Oneota settlement on the Door Peninsula began. Heins Creek is surrounded by major Oneota sites—Mero (Mason 1966), Whitefish Bay View (Dirst 1987, 1993), and Porte des Morts (Mason 1970)—and a reasonable expectation is that the long sandy stretches at Heins Creek would prove as attractive to Oneota people as to their predecessors. In terms of actual evidence to support such an expectation, there is nothing worth considering.

Materials from Other Test Pits at Heins Creek

The Wells excavations identified separate levels in several other test excavations both in the dune and elsewhere. In his report, however, Wells (1969) lumped all his Level II material together and all of his Level III material together, regardless of where they came from or whether they were all from comparable horizons. Since these other test pits are not contiguous and the depositional history of the site is very complex, there are some clear problems in deciding whether or not any of these other materials can be equated with the dune top test pits or even with each other. Three of these pits—Test Pits 14, 15, and 16—are particularly important since they are also in the dune, and if their stratigraphy can be shown to be trustworthy, they are an additional potential source of information. However, their recorded stratigraphy is in some measure questionable.

For example, there is no profile drawing or profile photograph for Test Pit 15. And while Levels II and III are separated in the collection, there is no mention in the field notes of a sterile layer of sand separating them in the ground. Test Pit 14 has two somewhat blurred profile photographs with three levels labeled in the ground: there seems to be a layer between Levels II and III that might be a narrow band of sand, but the clear separation seen in the dune top pits is not present. Test Pit 16 has both a profile drawing and a photograph with a preserved sterile sand layer between Levels II and III. What these pits can add to the dune top test pits has to be carefully considered.

Level II in Test Pits 14, 15, and 16

Test Pit 14 was located by itself in the top of Dune A but to the eastern end, nearer the northern rim. The material recovered from Level II in the pit is scanty (Table 6.3)—four rims and eight body sherds—but there are three identifiable vessels, two with twisted cord impressions and a third with cord-wrapped stick (Figure 6.13). One of these pots, with four rim sherds (No. 14-1), is a miniature constricted necked, presumably globular-bodied vessel (see also Wells 1969, 18, Fig. 9, A-2). It is grit- tempered with some large black particles (2–4mm) in the pale, sandy paste, but for all the grit in the paste, it is a fine, almost dainty pot, roughly estimated at only 60mm in orifice diameter and measuring 4mm thick at the rim. The lip is slightly out-

Table 6.3 Ceramics from Level II, Test Pits 14, 15, and 16

Level II, Test Pits 14, 15, 16	All Sherds	Vessels
Test pit 14		
Heins Creek Transitional	4	1
Heins Creek Cord-wrapped Stick	1	1
Unclassified single-cord impressed	4	1
Test pit 15		
Heins Creek Corded-stamped	5	2
Fabric impressed	7	1
Cord-marked body sherds	33	—
Unclassified single cord impressed	2	2
Test pit 16		
Heins Creek Corded-stamped	6	6
Heins Creek Cord-wrapped Stick	2	2
Cord-marked body sherds	52	—

Figure 6.13 Level II, Test Pit 14. Top row, left to right, Vessels 14-1, 14-3. Bottom row, Vessel 14-2.

flaring and carefully rounded. The surface was impressed with slightly diagonally placed cord-marking, and the interior surface was neatly smoothed. Decoration consists of three rows of single-cord impressing encircling the rim some 8mm below the lip, each row separated from the other by 2–3mm. Appended to the lowermost cord is a row of impressions similar to a line of corded stamps encircling the vessel 4mm apart. The lip is nicked on the exterior all the way around at 3–4mm intervals, perhaps with a fingernail. The interior has a single faint line of cord approximately 7mm below the lip with what appears to be a row of corded stamping appended to it at 4mm intervals. Except for cord-impressing in place of cord-wrapped stick and the fact that the body is cord-marked, it is very like the two miniature vessels from Level III in the dune top. A second vessel (No. 14-2) with the same ware characteristics, and probably with the same arrangement of decoration down to the diagonally placed vertical cord-marking and the fringing row of corded stamps, is represented by a single body sherd, broken just below the final row of what would have been cord impressing on the first example but instead is cord-wrapped stick-impressed. This second vessel was 5mm thick and, judging from its almost flat profile, was very large compared to the first. A third vessel (No. 14-3) is represented by four small (plain?) body sherds with single cord-impressions in a pattern not recoverable from the remaining sherds, although it might be parallel horizontal rows with corded fringing appended to the bottom row. As far as Level II is concerned, the pottery from this test pit parallels the conclusions drawn from the dune top test pits except in the presence of one cord-wrapped stick-impressed vessel. The sample is limited, though, probably not representing the total, and the frequencies of any variety are simply unknown.

Test Pit 15 poses problems both in its stratigraphy and in its contents. It was located about five feet north and ten feet west of Test Pit 14; there is no profile drawing, but Level II was described as a midden four to six inches thick with dolomitic beach cobbles as well as a lot of fish remains. The fish refuse, judging from Test Pit 16 (which may not be a safe bet), was on top of Level II, meaning it may not have been associated with the pottery. The origins of the dolomitic beach cobbles, and the possible relationship to the much lower dune cobble layer, is unclear. Field notes describe a trench "adjacent to" Test Pit 15, but the field map (see Figure 6.2) shows no adjacent excavations at all, only the nearby Test Pits 14 and 16. The pottery from Test Pit 15 (see Table 6.3) includes a single fabric-impressed vessel (No. 15-1) represented by a rim sherd and six body sherds (Figure 6.14, Vessel 15-1; see also Wells 1969, 19, Fig. 10-A). The provenience of this vessel is mostly Level II, but one body sherd came from Level III and another occurred halfway across the dune in Test Pit 1. Five additional sherds from the same vessel came from the Locality 1 excavations (Mason 1966, 25) and are presently housed in the Neville Public Museum in Green Bay (catalog no. 6831/1982.53). In ware characteristics this is a Heins Creek pot, but fabric marking, an unusual surface treatment on this site, sets it apart (Mason 1966, 25). The fabric used in impressing the surface was coarse, possibly part of a string bag. The rounded lip is slightly thickened with vertical corded stamp alternately on the lip interior and exterior. The scattered provenience of this vessel does not inspire much confidence in Test Pit 15, Level II, as a tightly controlled stratigraphic entity.

Other pottery in Level II includes a corded-stamped vessel represented by one rim and three body sherds with both interior stamping and across-the-lip stamping (see Figure 6.14, Vessel 15-5) and a single thin, hard rim sherd also with across-the-lip corded-stamping (No. 15-2). All rims are from vessels with cord-marked bodies. Two other vessels, both represented by single body sherds, provide additional examples of horizontal single-cord impressing fringed with doubled cord or corded stamping. The thirty-three unattached body sherds from Level II in Test Pit 15 are all cord-marked and represent a broad ceramic palette in terms of body thickness. Among them are six body sherds (up to 10mm in size) that are thick enough to be

North Bay ware except for the relatively modest size of the tempering particles; even the interiors of some of them exhibit "kneading," a signature North Bay trait. Cord-marked body sherds are notoriously difficult to sort, and the presence of these North Bay-like sherds pushes the collection in an earlier direction than is warranted. The overly thick, crude, cord-marked sherds could be basal portions of Heins Creek pots rather than representing an unusually long-lived North Bay.

Level II in Test Pit 15 supports the conclusions from Level II in the dune top test pits in that cord-wrapped stick is absent, single twisted cord impressing has replaced it, and corded stamping persists. Only the fabric-marked vessel and the too-thick Heins Creek body sherds sound discordant notes.

Figure 6.14 Level II, Test Pit 15. Top row, left to right, Vessels 15-1, 15-2 (interior). Bottom row, Vessel 15-5.

Level II in Test Pit 16 is Heins Creek without anything else; there is no single twisted cord impressed pottery at all (see Table 6.3). Eight small rim sherds (Figure 6.15) from as many different vessels were recovered. One of these (No. 16-1) has a single row of uneven cord-wrapped stick below a rounded, out-flaring lip decorated at the lip/rim juncture with diagonally placed corded stamps, a row of which also appears on the rim interior. Appended to the single row of cord-wrapped stick is a row of large, crude punctations probably made by the tip of the same instrument used to make the decoration (Figure 6.15; see also Wells 1969, 16, Fig. 8, A-2). The presence of only a single row of cord-wrapped stick impressing rather than multiple lines is unusual, not having been observed at either the Mero site or in the Locality 1 excavations. Two additional body sherds bear cord-wrapped stick decoration, one of them (No. 16-9) in combination with banked punctations (see Figure 6.15; see also Wells 1969, 16, Fig. 8, A-5). The remaining vessels include four corded-stamped; a single possibly plain pot with annular punctations in the lip (No. 16-4); a rim with continuous, horizontal cord-wrapped stick impressing on the lip (No. 16-6); and a vessel with tiny interior and exterior punctations, more like pinpricks than corded stamps or their substitutes. A total of fifty-two cord-marked body sherds complete the inventory.

Two questions arise with this small collection: What can be made of the banked punctated patterns, and where does this group of vessels fit into the Heins Creek picture? None of the banked, punctated body sherds occurs in the stratified pits on the dune top or in Test Pits 14 or 15; they are similar, however, to those recovered from the Mason excavations at Heins Creek and also at Mero and Shanty Bay (Dirst 1995a, 38, Fig. 24). Their temporal or stratigraphic position is unclear, but in view of the wide range of punctation shapes and forms, perhaps punctations are corded-stamps evolving into something else—single-cord impressed sherds from this site

Figure 6.15 Level II, Test Pit 16. Left to right, Vessels 16-1, 16-9.

occasionally feature punctations appended to a line of cord impressing rather than corded stamp. The presence of cord-wrapped stick impressing argues against the idea of that design technique's waning as single cord-impressing waxes, but that particular cord-wrapped stick vessel is anything but ordinary. The additional presence of one rim sherd with horizontal cord-wrapped stick in the lip poses still additional questions. There is also the possibility that Level II in Test Pit 16, like those in Level II of Test Pits 14 and 15, may not necessarily relate to Level II elsewhere on the site. Level II looks backward with the presence of cord-wrapped stick impressing and the absence of single-cord impressing, and it looks forward with its banked punctations. The sample is so very small that not much can be made of it.

At least as far as Level II is concerned, Test Pits 14, 15, and 16 offer as much confusion as clarification. Test Pit 14 reflects a Late Woodland, single-cord–impressed assemblage while Test Pit 16 is all Heins Creek; Test Pit 15 contains an unusual fabric-impressed vessel in an ambiguous context. Both Test Pits 14 and 16 could be used to support what Level II says elsewhere—that single-cord impressing is replacing Heins Creek (Test Pit 14) and that Heins Creek is undergoing an attribute shift as banked punctations are added to the repertoire, presumably as a time change (Test Pit 16). The vessel with the single line of cord-wrapped stick plus appended punctations could be taken as an adumbration of this association. Test Pit 15 requires a different context to make adequate use of what information it contains, and, at this point, that context is not obvious.

Level III in Test Pits 14, 15, and 16

The material labeled Level III is scarce (Table 6.4) and does not lend itself to clearing up any questions about these three pits or what they can contribute to the overall interpretation of the dune top test pits.

Test Pit 14 contained three sherds of a single plain, cord-marked vessel (Figure 6.16, Vessel 14-1). It is either a globular or elongate globular pot with a constricted neck and outflaring rim, vertically cord-marked to the lip and then crudely wiped in the neck area inside and out by the same kind of heavy-handed wiper as went over the cord-wrapped stick impressed vessel in Level III of the dune top test pits. There is no discernible decoration. It cannot be confidently assigned to Test Pit 14 since the provenience on the sherds is conflicting, and some of it has been changed, presumably by Ed Wells. Provenience is, at this point, uncertain. Level III seems to be the only sure assignment, wherever that was. The small num-

Table 6.4 Ceramics from Level III, Test Pits 14, 15, and 16

Level III, Test Pits 14, 15, 16	All Sherds	Vessels
Test pit 14		
Cord-marked body sherds	3	1
Test pit 15		
Heins Creek Corded-stamped	2	1
Heins Creek Cord-wrapped Stick	1	1
Cord-marked body sherds	30	—
Test pit 16		
Heins Creek Corded-stamped	1	1
Heins Creek Cord-wrapped Stick	3	3
Cord-marked body sherds	20	—
Unclassified	4	—

ber of sherds from Test Pit 14 and the total absence of cord-marked body sherds is unusual on so rich a site. It may well be that most of Test Pit 14 is simply missing from the collection.

Level III in Test Pit 15 produced three rim sherds, representing two vessels, and thirty plain cord-marked body sherds (Figure 6.17; see also Table 6.4). One of them (No. 15-1) is Heins Creek Cord-wrapped Stick Impressed with at least two rows of cord-wrapped stick impressions beginning about 25mm below the lip, which was diagonally decorated with tiny corded-stamps; the interior rim has a line of more robust corded stamps impinging on the lip/rim juncture (Figure 6.17; see also Wells 1969, 16, Fig. 8, B-4). The other (No. 15-2) is represented by two small rim sherds whose only discernible decoration is corded stamping placed diagonally across the lip.

Test Pit 16 includes four vessels (Figure 6.18; see also Table 6.4) represented by a single rim and seven very small decorated body sherds; there are additionally twenty plain cord-marked body sherds in the collection. The single rim (No. 16-1) is from a flat-lipped, interior-exterior corded stamped vessel with a single, continuous horizontal line of cord-wrapped stick impressions in the lip; a reasonable expectation is that if more of the vessel were present, it would include body decoration of cord-wrapped stick. All the other vessels are decorated with cord-wrapped stick impressions, most often of lines (up to three) fringed with corded stamping, but with one example of a double row forming a chevron design (Vessels 16-2, 16-3, and 16-4).

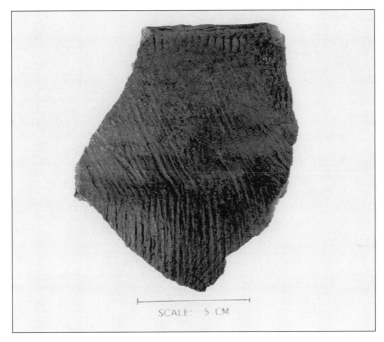

Figure 6.16 Level III, Test Pit 14, Vessel 14-1.

Figure 6.17 Level III, Test Pit 15. Left to right, Vessels 15-1, 15-2.

Figure 6.18 Level III, Test Pit 16. Top row, left to right, Vessels 16-1, 16-2, 16-4. Bottom row, Vessel 16-3.

What Level III in Test Pits 14, 15, and 16 provides is the possibility of using the test pits to buttress what has come from the dune top test pits and the probability that all of the data from these pits must be questioned. Test Pit 14, Level III, has almost nothing in it, an unlikely circumstance since the surviving material comes from only two distinctive pots with no extraneous body sherds at all; this, coupled with uncertainty about provenience, makes Test Pit 14 a poor candidate for contributing to the analysis. Test Pit 15 has the requisite Heins Creek Cord-wrapped Stick Impressed vessel in Level III, but the presence of possible North Bay material in the overlying Level II renders this a less than convincing sequence. Test Pit 16 has only cord-wrapped stick decoration with corded stamping as an addendum to rim-lip junctures or to the interiors of rims.

Test Excavations from Other Dune Deposits at Heins Creek

Test Pit 1

Test Pit 1, or Trench No. 1 in Wells's catalog, was the first formally excavated at Heins Creek by Ed Wells (1969, 3), and it was set into the edge of the dune near where the later Mason excavations would take place (see Figure 6.2). No profile drawing was made of this 10×5-foot test pit, nor is there any recorded stratigraphy except for a comment describing a single

Table 6.5 Ceramics from Test Pit 1

Test pit 1	All Sherds	Vessels
Point Sauble Collared	3	3
Heins Creek Corded-stamped	2	2
Heins Creek Cord-wrapped Stick	14	14
Heins Creek transitional	5	#3
Unclassified rimsherds	8	8
Smoothed cord-marked	1	1
Unclassified body sherds	15	—
Cord-marked body sherds	175	—
Totals	223	31

midden deposit and an ambiguous "refuse pit." Some differentiation must have occurred within Test Pit 1 since a small number of sherds are described as from the "upper portion" and others are more formally labeled "Level II" and "Level III."

The position of sherds from the "upper portion" or "top" assumes some importance since it is only here that Point Sauble Collared has been found in any kind of specific context at the Heins Creek site (Table 6.5). Four Point Sauble Collared vessels represented by eleven rim sherds and eight body sherds came from the single stratum at Locality 1, but their exact position within that layer was not determined at the time. Wells (1969) lists nine rim sherds of Point Sauble Collared pots from Test Pit 1, and these are the only sherds of that type recovered during his entire excavations. Only three of these rim sherds (Figure 6.19) survive in the collections, and it may be that these are in fact the only ones; six other "Late Woodland" rims representing four vessels are pictured on the same page as the Point Sauble specimens, and the total of nine may have mistakenly been made up of these in addition to the original three (Wells 1969, 18, Fig. 9, c and d). Be that as it may, all of these sherds came from the "top" or the "upper level" or even "Level I," although what this might mean in Test Pit 1 is a good question given the indication that a single midden layer was all that was recorded there.

All three of the surviving Point Sauble Collared rim sherds represent vessels typical of the original description (Baerreis and Freeman 1958): thickened or folded lip and conspicuous twisted-cord decoration rooted in the same stylistic changes that eventually led to the spread of the northeastern Wisconsin version of Madison ware across the Door Peninsula. The physical characteristics of the paste are very similar to those of Heins Creek; on this site, at least, the two are virtually indistinguishable. Exactly what the presence of Point

Figure 6.19 Test Pit 1, "upper" portion, Pt. Sauble Collared Vessels . Top row, left to right, Vessels 1-1, 1-3. Bottom row, Vessel 1-2.

Sauble Collared here means is hardly clear: it is a minority ware, as it seems to be throughout the area (but see Dirst 1995b on the Stockbridge Harbor site). On the northern half of the Door Peninsula, its distribution is spotty. It is more common at Mero than at Heins Creek (21 percent of all decorated Late Woodland vessels as opposed to 8 percent at Heins Creek); about as frequent at Heins Creek as at Shanty Bay (5 percent compared to 6 percent); present at Rock Island (17 percent of the decorated Late Woodland vessels) and at Whitefish Bay View (32 percent from the 1992 excavations). It also occurred in low frequencies on several sites across Green Bay in the Menominee water-shed: Riverside II, Reindel, Little Cedar River, Backlund, Pemene Falls, and Grand Rapids (Buckmaster 1979). The Stockbridge Harbor site, with Point

Sauble Collared comprising more than 50 percent of the total vessel count (Dirst 1995b), points to a more southerly increase in numbers; perhaps it is unfortunate that the type was named for a site so far north.

At Heins Creek, Point Sauble Collared is late in the sequence when it can be stratigraphically pinpointed at all, but how much later is unknown. The only ^{14}C date directly on the pottery itself is from the Mero site, where charred food residue produced a date of A.D. 689–897 (Mason 1992, 112). Considering its ware characteristics, its areal distribution, and the common Late Woodland urge to add collars to pottery (as, for example, Aztalan Collared and all the collared ceramics from the Northeastern Woodlands), it would not be surprising to discover that Point Sauble Collared in this area is another immediate descendant of Heins Creek, much like the Heins Creek/Madison ware transitional ceramics associated with Level II in the dune top test pits.

The remaining pottery from Test Pit 1 includes material that is not stratigraphically useful but adds more information on the dynamics of ceramic design change (Figures 6.20 and 6.21). Transitional forms include one vessel (No. 4 with three rims) with the usual cord-marked exterior and the typical flat Heins Creek lip vertically stamped on both exterior and interior rim/lip juncture to form a neat, crisp, sinuous outline when viewed from above, thus giving an appearance rather like rickrack. Below this the exterior rim has a fancy crisscross single-corded pattern bounded by a braided cord line. A second of these transitional vessels repeats the crisp sinuous lip, produced here by tiny vertical corded stamps in the lip/rim juncture and parallel lines of interior as well as exterior single-cord impressing beneath (No. 5), all on pottery with typical Heins Creek physical traits. Standard Heins Creek Cord-wrapped Stick Impressed accounts for four vessels, one of which belongs to a vessel from Test Pit 16, Level II; and ten other cord-wrapped–stick-impressed vessels are represented only by single small body sherds. In addition, two Heins Creek Corded-stamped vessels occur here also. One of these includes banked punctations (No. 11) up to and in the lip, and a single rim sherd (No. 13) much like the plain cord-marked vessel from Level III of Test Pit 14 (No. 1). These two pots, the one from Test Pit 14 and this one from Test Pit 1, are sufficiently unusual as to invite comparisons with materials from the Chautauqua Grounds site (Pleger and Lowrey 1994) and even with Point Peninsula (Wickham Plain?). Cord-marked body sherds (N=175) make up the remainder of material from Test pit 1.

Except for the suggestion of a stratigraphic position for Point Sauble Collared, Test Pit 1 is uninformative on the issues of internal change within the Heins Creek occupation. It has enough of the Heins Creek ceramic se-

Figure 6.20 Test Pit 1 vessels. Top row, left to right, Vessels 1-4, 1-5, 1-6. Bottom row, left to right, Vessels 1-13, 1-11.

Figure 6.21 Test Pit 1 vessel interiors, reverse of Figure 6-20. Top row, left to right, Vessels 1-4, 1-5, 1-6. Bottom row, left to right, Vessels 1-13, 1-11.

Figure 6.22 Test Pit 4 vessels. Top row, left to right, Vessels 4-1, 4-2, 4-3. Bottom row, left to right, Vessels 4-4, 4-5, 4-6.

ries to put its single occupation layer squarely within the territory originally marked out in the Mason excavations at Locality 1, but it adds little more.

Test Pit 4

Test Pit 4, the remaining Wells test pit in the dune (see Figure 6.2), was excavated a month later than the nearby Test Pit 1 and according to the field notes reflects the same stratigraphy. There is no profile drawing for Test Pit 1, but the drawing for Test Pit 4 has but one 8–12-inch thick artifact- bearing stratum, identical to Locality 1 in the Mason excavations and putting the three excavation units into the same frame of reference. Pottery from this pit consists of five vessels identified from rims (Figure 6.22, Vessels 4-1, 4-2, 4-3, 4-4, 4-5), two identified from body sherds (Vessels 4-6 and 4-7), and nine cord-marked body sherds. One of the rim sherds (4-4) is part of a vessel (No. 10) from Test Pit 1, which was nearby. Two of the vessels (Nos. 4-1 and 4-2) are both single-cord impressed and corded stamped, making them good candidates for Heins Creek transitional status. Vessel 4-3 is Heins Creek Cord-wrapped Stick Impressed even though only part of the rim survives; the cord-wrapped stick impressing consists of a single horizontal line in the flattened lip, which in the dune top test pits is an identifier of cord-wrapped stick impressing elsewhere on the body.

Table 6.6 Ceramics from Test Pit 4

Test pit 4	All Sherds	Vessels
Heins Creek Corded-stamped	1	1
Heins Creek Cord-wrapped Stick	1	1
Heins Creek transitional	2	2
Unclassified single-cord impressed	1	1
Cup/toy pot?	2	2
Cord-marked body sherds	9	—
Totals	16	7

A single sherd from a very small pot also came from Test Pit 4 (Vessel 4-5). It is tempered with crushed rock and has a plain, well-smoothed exterior surface. Decoration consists of tiny knotted-cord stamps in two parallel rows, about 3–4mm apart, beginning ca. 3mm below the lip. The lip is rounded and nicked all around, possibly with a cord. This sherd is nearly half of a little vessel with a diameter of ca. 32mm and a height of 35mm. It is well-made and may be a toy pot, a cup, or something else entirely. Another sherd from a different small pot has a smooth chalky surface and a partial line of tiny punctations (Vessel 4-6). The final identified vessel from this pit (Vessel 4-7) is a thick (9mm) grit-tempered pot with a cord-marked surface; it is of interest solely because it bears single-cord impressions, as of fringing on a horizontal line of single-cord impressions.

Test Pit 4, like Test Pit 1, does not allow any separation of the occupation zone into discrete levels. The most that can be said about it is that it reflects a Heins Creek occupation.

Nonceramic Artifacts in the Wells Collection

Besides pottery, the Heins Creek material from the Wells collection includes some stone, bone, and antler tools; two clay pipes; and a large amount of debitage, animal bone, and fish scales. The stone tools, both from excavated pits and surface, consist of more than fifty-nine whole and broken projectile points (fifty whole specimens originally cataloged plus others from more general collections) and an assortment of other tools.

Material specifically from the dune top test pits consists of a relatively small sample from each level and exhibits remarkable uniformity in material, workmanship, and tool types. The tool raw material is mainly from chert-bearing veins in the local cliffs, a grayish to whitish occasionally banded chert ubiquitous on the Door Peninsula. It is not usually fine-grained or even distinctive as a raw material for tools, but very occasionally a piece of better quality can be found, even in the limestone cliffs. The infrequent samples of really good chert, black or gray waxy material, probably come from pebbles retrieved from glacial gravels, but these are ordinarily very small and no finished tools from the dune top pits are made from them, although some occur in surface collections. Three flakes of Hixton Silicified Sandstone (two flakes from Level II, one from Level III), or perhaps its Upper Peninsula cognate, were found, but no finished tools of any kind, in either the dune top pits or elsewhere, were made of this material.

A single piece of a roughed-out granitic ground stone tool, probably intended as a celt, was present in Level II of Test Pit 12. What is interesting is that the crude flakes knocked off this, or other, ground stone tools in the first stages of manufacture are also present in the Level II collection, a reminder that even ground stone tools began as chipped ones.

Chipped stone tools consist primarily of triangular projectile points in three sizes (Figure 6.23). Almost all are simple isosceles triangles, remarkable for their uniformity and for the closeness with which they adhere to the original description (Mason 1966, 10). The small ones consist of seven specimens (ranging from 14mm to 28mm in length, averaging 23mm, and from 13mm to 18mm in basal breadth, averaging 17mm). The medium-sized points (30–40mm in length, 26–40mm in basal breadth) are only three in number, a tiny sample even for the dune top test pits, with an even tinier sample of the large ones, two in number (53–63mm in length, ca. 30mm in basal breadth) and one of those badly broken, probably in a fire.

The reason for intently examining the contents of Levels II and III is to see if any temporally relevant differences occur, and not much to meet this end has resulted from looking at the stone tools. There are few complete specimens, and what they have to say is ambiguous, reflecting sampling rather than any real shifts in tool types between the levels. This, of course, supports a conclusion that the time gap between the two levels is not a great one.

A number of observations can be made, however, reflecting perceived differences between the levels, although it must be strongly emphasized that these observations are being made on very small samples:

1. Level II contains six small projectile points, two medium, and one large. However, there are additionally five tips of broken large points. Level III has only one small point and one medium one with two possible tips of large points. Level II, therefore, has altogether a larger number of points from a site where points are relatively rare.

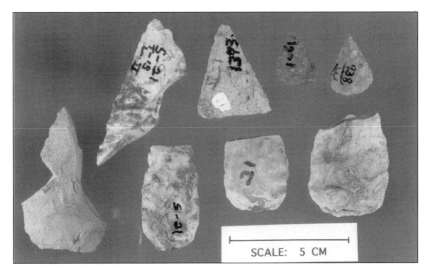

Figure 6.23 Bifacial Stone Tools

2. Level II additionally contains four small broken bifaces while Level III contains ten. With one exception, they are broken but apparently began as ovals with one pointed end and a straight or slightly convex base. They average ca. 28mm in breadth for both the Level II and Level III specimens. Workmanship is certainly no guide for separating these tools from projectile points, as both are relatively casually finished. How these bifaces or blanks functioned in the stone tool complex is unclear; the edges of some are so finished as to indicate complete tools, while others are clearly blanks designed to become other tools. Yet all are about the same size: those identified as blanks are too large to have served that function for the tiny projectile points and (mainly) too small to serve as blanks for the largest ones. The medium-sized projectile points are hardly frequent enough to justify so many blanks representing so few points. Additionally, some of the bifaces seem to have been used as scrapers or knives.

3. Both Level II and Level III contained minimally reduced blocks of chert on their way to becoming bifacial tools. These are more frequent in Level III (5:1), which is expected since most of the bifacial tools occur there, too.

4. Fragments of three different brachiopods came from Level III (two from Test Pit 17, one from Test Pit 13). Fossils—principally corals of many kinds as well as an occasional brachiopod—are common in the dolomitic limestone that forms the Door Peninsula. They are, however, not com-

mon sitting many feet up in a sand dune, and there is every likelihood that their presence indicates human transportation. Whether these three were selected as possible sources for raw material or for an entirely different purpose is unknown. They are all fragmentary (ca. 40 (26mm, 23 (23mm, and 38 (25mm) and were broken roughly in half, exposing a quartz interior. Breaking open a brachiopod requires deliberate effort and some force; perhaps the reason for doing so was to check the interior as a possible source for raw material. It would be useful in the future to watch for brachiopods in archaeological contexts in case they have a cultural meaning over and above their paleontological one. The nearby Mero site produced a large brachiopod with holes broken on each side as if for suspension; however, it was from a context where sure attribution as an artifact could not be determined, and the holes were not clearly of human origin.

5. Nine flakes of a distinctive dark chert with a tan rind came from Level III (Test Pit 17). A tenth piece was recovered from Level II of the same pit. A heavy-stemmed point (No. 1197 in the Wells catalog; Wells 1969, 7, top, No. 3) made from this unusual material has no within-site provenience and is probably from the surface. The presence of *any* stemmed points in the stratified dune top test pits would be surprising, but considering this raw material and its absolute absence anywhere else on the site, the point might indeed originally have come from Level III; certainly the debitage recovered from Level III in Test Pit 17 argues for it.

The three other stratified test pits in the dune, Test Pits 14, 15, and 16, yielded small numbers of the same kinds of artifacts as were present in the dune top test pits: triangular points, blanks or preforms, and fragments of bifacially flaked tools. The most curious distributional information to emerge from these pits is that most of the fragmentary bifacial tools come from Level II; these tools in Level II total ten in number—the same number as from Level III of the dune top pits. Level III in Test Pits 14, 15, and 16 produced only two fragmentary bifaces and one minimally shaped block of chert. Additionally, these three test pits had a recorded "Level I" containing five whole or fragmentary points plus one rectangular-based biface; stone tools from all the dune top test pits recorded for Level I number only three fragmentary, minimally worked bifaces. The disparity between what has come from Levels I, II, and III in the eight dune top test pits and the three others in the dune may mean nothing at all, but it may also mean that the levels are not really comparable across the entire dune and confirm that what comes from Test Pits 14, 15, and 16 should not be casually lumped with what comes from the dune top.

A number of bone and antler artifacts came from the dune test pits (Wells 1969, 10, Fig. 5, excluding the toggle-headed harpoon [Wells 1964]), but only a few of them are still with the collection. Judging from the specific locations of those illustrated by Wells, there are no differences between Levels II and III in either the dune top test pits or in Test Pits 14, 15, and 16 in the kinds of tools represented or in the materials used. The presence of harpoons certainly reflects a concern with fishing, amply seconded by net sinkers and fish remains. A tiny broken, grooved antler point from Level III in Test Pit 16 (Wells 1969, 10, Fig. 5, 3–4) was identified as a possible toggle-head, but the point has such a shattered base what it might have been is unclear.

Two tiny trumpet-shaped pipes came from the dune top test pits, both of them from Level II (Wells 1969, 13, Fig. 7-c); a third pipe fragment is missing. Both pipes are crudely made of finely tempered clay, and the complete specimen shows interior striations in the bowl that may have been caused by finger-hollowing. Bowl diameters are 19mm in one case, an estimated 20mm in the other; the complete pipe measures only 36mm in height and 37mm across. Neither is decorated, and both are so similar that they might have been made by the same person. No other pipes were recovered anywhere else on the site, including during the Mason excavations. Other Heins Creek-affiliated sites such as Shanty Bay, Mero, and Rock Island also produced no pipes. What this may mean is that smoking was an uncommon practice, materials for smoking were scarce, or smoking was introduced during the transition between Levels II and III, or perhaps nothing at all can be made of them. For whatever reason, the distribution of pipes across the archaeological landscape in northeastern Wisconsin is peculiar, given their abundant presence elsewhere in earlier and later contexts.

The Heins Creek Site: Comments Based on Analysis of the Wells Collection

Stratigraphy is the mother lode of archaeology, and the Door Peninsula with its elongate shoreline and many streams emptying into Lake Michigan was blessed with wind and water layering of strata for millennia. The interruption of these processes and this sequential layering by cultural deposition provides an almost textbook opportunity for watching culture change in action, especially where more than one segment of a particular prehistoric or historic occupation is represented. (See, for example, Mason 1966 for changes over time in North Bay, and Mason 1976 for historic changes on Rock Island). The extensive site at Heins Creek was evidently one of these textbook cases until erosion carried away much of the dune topography, leaving only a relatively small area intact. The Wells excavations took place in a part of this intact area where stratification was present on a finer scale than elsewhere on the site, enabling the recovery of small collections of materials from two separate Heins Creek occupations. In essence, these stratified contexts allow a subdivision of the single layer found during the Mason excavations of 1961 and provide for more powerful confirmation of trends observed in the analysis of those excavations. Ceramic development between Heins Creek and Madison ware over a very short time can be observed and suggestions for the course of ceramic development proposed. However, in all cases, the samples are small and the suggestions tentative. They are offered here with caveats and the deliberate intention of stimulating other fine-scale analyses of materials from other tightly controlled stratified contexts. There is yet more to be learned about the Heins Creek ceramic complex.

Acknowledgments

Thanks are owing to Mrs. Edward Wells and John Wells for the donation of the Wells collection to Lawrence University, to Ronald J. Mason for his logistical support and many insights, and to Charles E. Cleland for his commentary on this retrospective.

7

Backyards, Scrap Yards, and the Taphonomy of Riverine Urban Environments

Bay City, Michigan, as a Case Study

William A. Lovis

Urban areas present complex cultural formation processes that alter landscapes dramatically. These dramatic alterations give the perception that much of the early precontact Native American archaeology is largely disturbed or more likely destroyed. As such, urban contexts are not routinely incorporated into regional research designs but are more likely to be explored as idiosyncratic projects under either opportunistic or compliance-associated circumstances. Using Bay City, Michigan, as a case study, presented is a counter-perspective with the premise that late-nineteenth- and early-twentieth-century taphonomic processes of urban areas are systematic, can be identified, and should be employed to predict potential locations for the preservation of intact precontact surfaces. Such a perspective not only acts to place even isolated projects in broader problem domains, but additionally asserts that archaeologists addressing precontact problems must take a long-term view of the research potential of urban areas and systematically incorporate them into regional research strategies.

IT IS DOUBTFUL that when Chuck Cleland sent me to work at the Fletcher site (20BY28; Figure 7.1) in Bay City in 1967, while I was still an undergraduate at New York University, he had any inkling that his decision would result in an essay based on the archaeology of Bay City some thirty-five years later. Chuck never let me forget, or perhaps never forgave

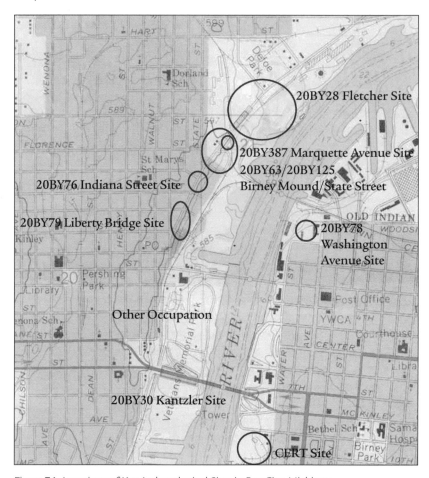

Figure 7.1 Locations of Key Archaeological Sites in Bay City, Michigan

me, that I was an urbanite. As the old saw goes, you can take the boy out of the city, but you can't take the city out of the boy. It is, therefore, only just that his deep-rooted suspicions be vindicated by my topic in this volume.

My early field trips with Chuck Cleland had a profound impact on the way in which I viewed both natural and cultural landscapes and their interaction. While Chuck devoted a small part of his attention to driving, he engaged the other and substantially larger part to an almost continuous monologue on geology, land forms, vegetation, fauna, history, architecture, and sundry other topics, imparting to his students a vast array of information that they could variably adopt and build on. This essay reflects part of that which I adopted.

Chuck Cleland at the time was also something of a barefoot prophet for historical archaeology, proselytizing both those who would listen and those who had little choice. I must confess that while I eventually agreed with Chuck at a philosophical level, and ultimately became a card-carrying Society for Historical Archaeology member, I was not sufficiently captivated to make this a primary research interest. My presentation here, while an oblique affirmation of the importance of historical archaeology, reflects this duality and asks, How does nineteenth-century urban development act to preserve intact precontact archaeological deposits?

This essay has as its goal the understanding of some of the primary processes of urban landscape evolution and development in Michigan, and the recognition of the relationship between those processes and the preservation of the precontact archaeological record. To achieve these ends, it will be necessary to first examine the framework of archaeology in urban areas, then explore issues of urban landscape development at a general level, and finally to empirically ground these issues. In many respects this study is a continuation of my ongoing interest in the relationship between research design and the formation of the archaeological record and the site populations that we observe in our research (Lovis and O'Shea 1994).

The majority of the case studies explored here will derive from a substantial body of archaeological data from an intensively researched urban area in Michigan's Lower Peninsula: Bay City, on the lower reaches of the Saginaw River in Bay County, Michigan. Research spanning thirty-five years by multiple institutions has developed an impressive record of precontact archaeological site (see Figure 7.1) and urban taphonomic data from this restricted area that will assist in the current task. While the focus of this discussion is on those processes associated with human residential and industrial development, it must also be recognized that such processes are interactive with natural processes of floodplain and shoreline taphonomy, both at the level of the case study, where, for example, reworked Middle Holocene materials have been found in shoreline contexts within Bay City (Larsen and Demeter 1979) as well as at a more generic or regional level (Monaghan and Lovis 2002).

Urban Archaeology, the Archaeology of Urbanism, and the Issue of Taphonomy

There is a sharp distinction between urban archaeology and the archaeology of urbanism. Urban archaeology is the implementation of research in the context of contemporary urban environments, while the archaeology of urbanism seeks to understand the social, taphonomic, and other processes responsible for the development of urban landscapes (Dickens 1982). The two are clearly not mutually exclusive, and it is often the case that urban archaeology is in fact directed toward issues of the archaeology of urbanism or some of its potential subsets, such as industrial archaeology. When such convergences are not evident, however, other questions arise. Those whose interests lead them to employ urban archaeology to understand the precontact past are confronted with substantial taphonomic questions related to the differential preservation of the natural and cultural landscapes that existed prior to urban development. This requires an understanding of both depositional and postdepositional processes. That is, at its most overt level, is the archaeological record of precontact native peoples preserved, if so to what degree is it preserved, and is it still systematically recoverable?

Locales such as urban contexts, large towns, and industrial developments experiencing intensive land use and population density in the present often reflect relatively similar patterns of locational choice to those made during precontact times. That is, there is a concordance of locationally significant places in the precontact, postcontact, and recent past, despite alterations of the cultural landscape. Examples of this phenomenon in Michigan are evident among several scales of nineteenth- and twentieth-century settlements across the state, including larger cities such as Detroit, Grand Rapids, Lansing, Saginaw, and Bay City; medium-sized towns such as Sault Ste. Marie, Lyons-Muir, and St. Ignace; and smaller locations such as Charlevoix or Norwood. In large part, this convergence of significant locations is a product of both natural and cultural factors.

While certainly not the only factor responsible for this spatial synchrony, river and lake transportation was significant for indigenous pre- and postcontact populations as well as Euro-American immigrants to the region, so a premium was placed on locations important to waterborne movement by both mobility systems. Under such circumstances, locations of importance in both domains might include prominent narrows such as the Straits of Mackinac and Detroit areas, or the outlets of major streams into lakes such as Bay City or Saginaw where the Saginaw River enters or at one time entered Lake Huron, or at locales near the confluences of significant streams such as Lansing, to name a few. As such, there is an expectation that there should be evidence for indigenous, precontact use of areas currently occupied by both light and heavy urban development, and that particular attention should be paid to areas undergoing redevelopment in postindustrial context.

Lack of systematic attention to such heavily developed natural contexts has also led to the erroneous impression that urban development was largely destructive of precontact cultural landscapes and, even if not totally destructive, that such contexts and landscapes were either heavily altered or not readily recoverable by standard archaeological procedures. Thus, the degree of visible land modification resulted in a perception of substantial land-form alteration or destruction. In fact, prior to the implementation of environmental and culturally focused legislation, the ability of archaeology to systematically understand urban areas in terms of either their changing archaeological roles or landscape development processes was limited, not so much because of difficulty or lack of interest, but rather due to a lack of significant access. Consequently, archaeological entrée to these contexts was most often idiosyncratic and opportunistic, rather than an integral aspect of continuing regional research design. Focused or intensive research was typically conducted either when specific landowners were favorably disposed toward archaeological research and/or researchers, or when enticing finds captivating the public interest were inadvertently recovered and reported.

Within the Bay City case study, both factors came into play with the inadvertent "discovery" of the Fletcher site (20BY28) during dredge spoil disposal in 1967, which subsequently resulted in a multiyear archaeological field effort by Michigan State University (Lovis 1985; Mainfort 1979). Such exciting discoveries tended to shift the weight of public opinion toward archaeological research in a salvage framework. The outcome of these more opportunistic investigations has been, and at times continues to be, the sporadic archaeological investigation of important locales in restricted time frames and budgets, with limited potential for the compilation of systematic comparative data sets.

Fortunately, the current legislative and political milieu of archaeology has in many respects changed the research environments within which the archaeology of urban areas is approached and has made it imperative that the relative preservation of prehistoric sites within urban landscapes, and their potential for addressing regional research questions, be systematically addressed as one facet of review and compliance. Regularized advance project review and the incorporation of archaeology at early project stages has largely but not completely ameliorated the issues of short time frames and funding allocation for proper research. The accumulation of more than thirty years' worth of information from compliance- and noncompliance-based research projects has increased substantially our knowledge of the urban archaeological record, provides the basis within which to cast future research in a larger problem framework, and equips researchers with a sound foundation for comparative and synthetic studies. It has also brought archaeology to the point where we can no longer accept as given that precontact landscapes are either absent or even potentially heavily altered in urban contexts, that they cannot be incorporated into larger regional research agendas, and that they are not regularly and systematically recoverable.

Urban Taphonomy: The Michigan Case

A discussion of some key taphonomic contexts and processes can provide an understanding of many major components of urban development and will provide a basis for the development of focused research designs specifically directed to precontact archaeological sites in specific urban contexts. The contexts to be addressed here include the broader perception and role of floodplains and riverbanks, processes of industrial development, processes of residential development at the household lot level, and the development of various types of transportation corridors. Each of these contexts has its own peculiar set of associated processes allowing systematic assessment of preservation potential.

Of significance to this discussion is a recognition of the temporal framework within which these processes are addressed. Certainly, current urban locations were often occupied by Euro-Americans early in the postcontact history of Michigan, as early as the late seventeenth century in some cases. Thus, there is a record of contact and fur trade era archaeology from many of these areas that substantially predates the period of primary interest here. Rather, it is the time period from approximately the Civil War era (1861–1865) through World War I (1914–1918) that is of particular concern. It is during this period that Michigan experienced the development of locations with large and relatively permanent Euro-American population aggregates, extractive and manufacturing industrialization, and the expansion of transportation networks designed to make efficient the movement of people and goods between these locations (Dunbar 1980; Farmer 1969; Fuller 1939; Parkins 1918). Land-use histories from Bay City demonstrate that local-level development of this river town is consistent with the broader, state-level trends articulated (Branstner and Branstner 1993; Coir-Hambacher 1993). It is the residue of land development from this period that conditions the potential of the current landscape to preserve precontact surfaces.

In Michigan, as well as other parts of the Midwest, Midsouth, and Eastern United States, urban areas are often associated with rivers, either interior segments of rivers or locations where rivers enter larger water bodies, such as wetlands or lakes. In large part this is a consequence of the use of waterpower for industrial purposes, and the advantages and early dominance of rivers for transportation prior to the advent and growth of the railroad and intensive use of horse-drawn and motorized vehicles for long-distance commerce. In general, and recognizing that substantial variability in land form exists both regionally and subregionally, such situations often have one or more of several topographic features in common. These features include a riverbank, a floodplain, one or more terraces, and a bluff top or upland. Depending on the specifics of location, these features might also include a Great Lake or interior lakeshore (Monaghan and Lovis 2001). Each of these topographic features normally underwent differential sets of natural formation processes as well as human-induced landscape development.

Construction and engineering procedures between the mid-nineteenth century or post–Civil War era and World War I, while certainly capable of massive land alteration when such was demanded, nonetheless placed a premium on minimizing costly endeavors such as substantial cutting and filling, opting instead for more labor- and cost-effective approaches utilizing natural features of the landscape wherever feasible. Furthermore, disposal processes at both the household and industrial levels were less formalized than during subsequent periods, providing abundant opportunity for accretional processes to operate on a regular basis. It is toward these twin phenomena of land-form development and accretional disposal that much of the following discussion is directed.

Urban Floodplain/Riverbank Contexts

In many respects, currently visible riverbanks in urban areas are false phenomena, being the result of early decisions about navigability, and sometimes arbitrary decisions about where the "river" ended and "land" did or should begin. It is in Michigan, therefore, an issue of nineteenth-century perception. To generalize, prior to intensive Euro-American development even the most developed urban riverine contexts were initially complex suites of multiple natural habitats of varying water depth and associated animal and plant communities, including deeper channels, shallower slack water situations, and true wetlands less than a meter in depth and harboring substantial shallow-water plant communities. Figure 7.2 (Macomb 1856) clearly demonstrates this phenomenon along the banks of the Saginaw River within the limits of Bay City during the pre–Civil War era. The "riverbank," therefore, could be in multiple locations, depending on how or why one wanted to perceive it. Where industry and riverine access for transportation were of paramount importance, the riverbank was often perceived as the area where the river had navigable depth, with the latter issue typically decided by federal agencies with either an interest in or responsibility for navigation, such as the various bureaucratic compartments of the Departments of War or Defense, the Corps of Engineers, or the U.S. Coast Guard. The riverbank was, therefore, an engineered decision on the part of these agencies, dictating the type of land alteration that was allowable. Anything landward of the defined riverbank, which might be in several feet of water, could be subject to fill and other alteration, whereas the river or navigable channel side of the defined riverbank could not be so altered. Riverbanks, and adjacent exposed land that might also be subject to periodic or seasonal flooding, that is, the floodplain, were open to accretion and development.

Depending on the specifics of local fluvial-system evolution, the filling of such areas for future, primarily industrial, development (Branstner and Branstner 1993, 10, 23) could result in the preservation of intact soil surfaces. Observed archaeological examples presented in greater detail later in this chapter include the use of pilings for structure footings, the use of log cribbing to stabilize riverbank mucks, the dumping of industrial waste as fill to create usable land surfaces, and the disposal of dredge material from the enhancement and maintenance of navigable ship channels. At times, multiple sets of these processes were employed to enhance such areas for future use. It may therefore be impossible to reconstruct from current land surfaces either the position of the original floodplain, the juncture of original floodplain and the riverine wetland, or the endpoint of the original riverine wetland, all important considerations for precontact archaeology.

Nineteenth-century historical maps of Bay City amply illustrate the fashion in which this phenomenon of river edge expansion and development alters the configuration of a developing waterfront. Several historic maps in particular will be employed here, spanning a period of three decades overlapping the Civil War–era expansion of Michigan's urban

Figure 7.2 1856 Macomb map of Saginaw River in Bay City. Note extensive riverfront wetland, sloughs, and limited industrial development.

Figure 7.3 Detail of 1867 Ruger bird's-eye map of Bay City waterfront. Note modification of wetland by cribbing, fill, and causeways. Also note mill raised on cribbed fill in lower left.

Figure 7.4 Detail of 1879 Ruger bird's-eye map of Bay City waterfront. Note extensive riverbank fill on far bank of Saginaw River and definition of navigable river channel boundaries by fill, causeways, and buoy markers on near shore. Also note use of level river terrace for railroad right-of-way.

settlements: the 1856 Macomb map (Figure 7.2; Macomb 1856) titled *Lower Saginaw River and Bar in Front* and the 1867 and 1879 panoramic and bird's-eye maps of Bay City (Figures 7.3 and 7.4; Ruger 1867, 1879). Portions of the Macomb map, which was produced by the Department of War prior to the Civil War, are centered on the Saginaw River in Bay City. Among the most noticeable features of the map are the relative lack of structures, industrial or otherwise, adjacent to the original riverbank and the substantial shallow wetlands that fringe that feature. In this relatively pristine configuration the navigable channel is at a great distance from the riverbank.

By the late 1860s through late 1870s, however, this same area is depicted with expansive tracts of claimed land extending out to the navigable channel, often inset with slips for shipping, or wharves parallel to the river, and industrial structures dominate the landscape (see Figures 7.3 and 7.4; Ruger 1867, 1879). Such changes would suggest that little in the way of intact precontact surfaces would remain. However, the archaeology of these same locations would suggest otherwise, as the following section reveals.

Industrial Complex Contexts

Nineteenth-century riverfronts were bustling hubs of industrial activity, with wharves, warehouses, and manufacturing and storage facilities lining the riverbank. At face value, when confronted by such scenes, one would be dubious about the potential of such contexts to preserve original ground surfaces and attendant archaeology. In many respects, however, industrial development acted as a handmaiden to riverbank evolution and contributed significantly to the accretional activities necessary for preservation of original surfaces and incorporated archaeological deposits.

In large part, the industrial phenomena of the nineteenth century engaged in waste disposal practices that acted beneficially to seal original ground surfaces under, in many cases, several meters of industrial fill. Therefore, an understanding of the technological organization of both industrial development and disposal practices during this period creates the ability to isolate several urban contexts amenable to modern investigative techniques and practices.

In general, original industrial riverbank development took place on the more durable and level natural floodplains, which required little preparation in the form of grading and filling to provide appropriate construction surfaces. Floodplain locations provided access to water transportation as well as roadways and rail networks, as several of the map illustrations reveal. By building on the floodplain, an industry also gained recoverable "land" that extended to the official definition of the riverbank, which was often tens of meters offshore from the existing shoreline. This allowed industry to "claim" land by filling and to easily manufacture wharf facilities through the use of pilings, dredging, and filling. The need for stable and durable riverbanks often promoted the use of logs as cribbed fill to support the weight of industrial activity associated with the loading and unloading of water vessels by land-based transportation systems. Where less durability was necessary or desirable, dredged bottom sediments, derived from enhancement of defined river or navigable channel areas, could be dumped onto existing wetland to create additional usable land. Likewise, waste products from industrial activity, such as cinders and clinkers, foundry sand, scrap metals, wood chips and sawdust, dredged sediments, etc., could also be used as on-site fill, negating the necessity of hauling the refuse to a remote or alternate disposal site. Over the course of several decades, such accretional activity has resulted in multiple fill layers spread stratigraphically, but often discontinuously, over large areas of former riverbank, effectively sealing original ground surfaces.

While multistory brick and balloon-framed wooden industrial structures likewise give the impression of substantial impact to original surfaces, the end products of such activity might well be preservation of intact surfaces within the confines of the structures, as well as adjacent to them. Although one cannot deny that such construction does indeed alter existing land surfaces, the potential impact of such construction is largely a mistaken impression, and more an issue of degree than of kind. Even larger industrial structures were typically built on trenched foundation footings, albeit of greater depth and width than found in residential construction, rather than on large subsurface cellar excavations. These footing trenches were subsequently filled with concrete, or a mix of stone and mortar, sometimes poured into vertical forms in consecutive courses. Few large industrial structures have subsurface excavations that intrude on original ground surfaces. As with other types of lighter construction, the material from foundation trenches was ejected and spread adjacent to the structures, further preserving original ground surface in these locations beyond the perimeter walls. When durable flooring was desirable in such structures—for example, to house larger mechanical equipment—concrete of sufficient thickness would be poured within the confines of the foundation, either on the original ground surface or with minor leveling. Alternatively, wooden floor beams would be laid within the foundation and plank surfaces then laid on the joist network, or prepared stone flooring laid on the existing ground surface.

A number of reported archaeological contexts from Bay City well illustrate several of the preceding points regarding processes of riverbank development and/or the preservation of intact precontact surfaces as a consequence of such development. Site 20BY78, at the west approach to the Liberty Bridge over the Saginaw River (see Figure 7.1), displayed evidence of intentionally placed massive log cribbing over intact river-bottom deposits, an approach clearly designed to stabilize the expanding industrial riverbank in this area, as well as over substantial deposits of wood chips employed for the same purpose (Figure 7.5; Lovis 1993a). Associated site 20BY77, at the west approach to the same bridge (see Figure 7.1), displayed a more complex fill stratigraphy resulting from waste disposal as well as intentional deposition. At this location, a complex fill sequence consisting of a layer of wood chips and bark, the detritus of a woodworking mill complex, lay beneath a heavy deposit of cinders associated with a local railroad yard complex evident on Sanborn insurance maps (Sanborn Map Company 1912). With the subsequent abandonment of the railroad

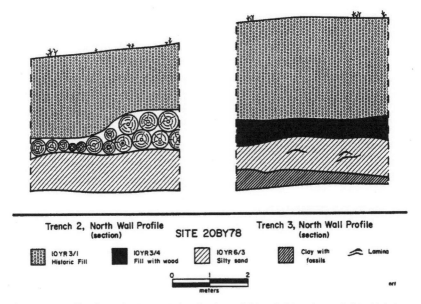

Figure 7.5 Profiles from site 20BY78 showing log cribbing (left) and wood chip (right) fill sequences.

yard and alteration of land use to scrap metal recycling, a thick layer of mixed scrap metal fill further capped the deposit. Of importance to the current discussion is the fact that the basal nineteenth-century deposit of wood chips and bark capped and sealed an intact albeit compressed A soil horizon beneath which were intact Late Woodland storage and hearth features (Lovis 1993a).

Both the Fletcher site and Marquette Viaduct locales of the Fletcher site, 20BY28 (see Figure 7.1; see also Lovis 1985; Lovis et al. 1996; Mainfort 1979; Prahl 1987), on the west bank of the Saginaw River to the north of the Liberty Bridge in Bay City exhibit similar processes. At these locations, nineteenth- and twentieth-century fill and stabilization activities effectively sealed an intact Late Archaic through eighteenth-century archaeological sequence beneath a bed of cinders associated with railroad activities and several layers of dredge spoil derived from channel maintenance of the Saginaw River. In some areas these accretional deposits exceeded a meter in thickness.

Perhaps the most striking example of riverbank stabilization and the preservation of intact precontact soil surfaces in Bay City, however, derives from the extensive work on the Center for Environmental Resource Training (CERT) project, on the east bank of the Saginaw River (see Figure 7.1). At this location, intact soil surfaces with Late Woodland occupation with identifiable and datable organic materials were recovered from beneath up to 5m of riverbank fill (Demeter, Robertson, and Egan 1994), revealing that at times substantial effort in unlikely places is likely to yield significant research results.

The Residential or Household Context

Household or residential lots form one of the most basic and abundant land divisions in urban situations. While lot sizes may vary both in width and depth, the basic architectural units found within such lots are generally quite similar, consisting of a main residential structure, possibly with an attached or detached garage, possibly with some small backyard outbuildings, and formally or informally paved areas for a walkway and driveway. Residences that date to periods prior to the introduction of centralized utilities, such as water and sewage disposal, may have had privies in the backyard, and these probably migrated locationally over time for sanitary and pragmatic reasons. Moreover, by the 1880s it is likely that many residences had been transformed to above-ground tank privies, and even indoor plumbing (Branstner and Branstner 1993; Weir and Demeter 1991). Most often, the city-owned easement along the road frontage contains a public sidewalk. Given such lot-level or scale development, what are the construction and development processes that might result in differential preservation of intact soil surfaces, potentially containing precontact occupation materials, within the lot? Specifically, lot-level accretional processes associated with the capping of original surfaces, either with construction materials, waste disposal, or ejectum from excavation, become of paramount concern, as does the degree of subsurface disturbance as it relates to differential development of the residential lot.

Perhaps the most common construction situation that results in preserved surfaces occurs when material is ejected from construction or cellar excavations and subsequently deposited above intact original soil surfaces adjacent to the construction. Three types of construction excavation can be identified: footing trenches, so-called crawl spaces or shallow interior subfloor excavations, and full cellars bounded by foundation walls. Some construction may have combinations of these three types of excavation. In each case the ejected fill is thrown outward from the construction area and graded outward from the foundation or footing wall. It is rarely transported from the site and may even be beneficial in that it assists drainage away from the foundation and cellar. Consequently, while the excavation areas themselves might be disturbed, those areas directly or closely adjacent to a residence may have high potential for finding intact and preserved soil surfaces sealed below a cap of fill. This is true as well for any footings that might be associated with garage, privy, or outbuilding construction. In fact, outbuildings other than garages and privies may sit directly on top of the soil surface.

While initial construction efforts may effectively preserve archaeological surfaces, the cumulative addition of centralized subsurface utilities has, over time, a marked impact on the preservation of certain lot segments, particularly front yards. As sewage disposal, water, gas, electric, and phone lines are placed underground, several substantial impacts to the original surfaces are notable. First, the main trunks of such utilities are often placed in linear excavations along the front-lot lines within the city or municipal easement, along curbs, and adjacent to or under public sidewalks. Thus, preservation potential in such areas may be quite limited although not categorically so. Second, each residence has entry points from the main trunk of a utility to the household itself. Thus, gas, water, electric, sewage, and perhaps telephone (and now high-speed cable) will have independent subsurface excavations that crosscut the front lot of the house and will often reduce the area of intact surfaces substantially.

Back lots or backyards, on the other hand, often have the greatest potential to preserve intact soil horizons, due largely to a lack of major architectural features, the relatively temporary nature of outbuilding construction, and a general lack of utility disturbances. The primary impacts to such locations on residential lots are the intrusions of privy excavations, which may result in several subsurface disturbances over time prior to the development of centralized waste disposal. However, the actual so-called footprints of the latter are very small relative to yard expanse or area.

Pavements of varying type are often associated with residential lots, including walkways, driveways, and public sidewalks on municipal easements. Walkways may be constructed of either concrete, paving stones, or brick. For such types of construction, it is often the case that a shallow 8–10cm excavation will precede either the laying of paving stones or the pouring of concrete slabs. Concrete slabs rarely exceed 7–9cm in thickness in residential contexts. At times, clean fill sand is employed prior to construction, thereby sealing underlying deposits. Similar types of construction are employed for public walkways. Entry drives to garages and parking areas often pose a somewhat different type of construction situation, particularly on lots that predate the transition from coal to either oil or gas heating. There is, in addition, a socioeconomic aspect to entry drives. Higher status households may have paved driveways constructed in a fashion similar to that previously described for walkways, but oftentimes of greater thickness or depth. Lower status households may have unpaved drives. It is this latter class of drive that often results in accretional activities that act to preserve intact surface deposits.

Prior to the burning of "clean" fuels such as oil and gas in household furnaces, the burning of coal was common as a household heating fuel. The burning of such material resulted in waste material commonly known as "clinkers" or ash, which needed to be periodically cleaned and removed from furnaces and subsequently disposed of. While some municipalities engaged in formalized disposal of such waste (I recall as a child seeing long lines of metal trash cans filled with such detritus lining the curbs), it was also a common practice to dispose of clinkers at the household level, often by spreading it on the surface of driveways. The cumulative result of such disposal patterns is the creation of a highly compact, often cemented and compressed, mass of durable aggregate in the driveway, acting to seal and preserve original ground surfaces. Regardless of the specific type of impact from these processes, however, both driveways and sidewalks result in only low-level impacts overall.

The outcome of this cumulative set of anthropogenic processes on urban residential lots is the identification of a series of accretional or buffering contexts that may act to preserve the original ground surfaces and any incorporated precontact occupation materials. Specifically, back lots hold the highest potential for undisturbed deposits. Secondarily, areas sealed beneath ejected fill from footing or cellar construction also hold high potential for preserved deposits. In addition, driveways, particularly those filled with disposed waste materials, and possibly private and public walkways, hold lower but still significant potential. Finally, front lots should hold low potential for preserved deposits due to intrusion by subsurface utility easements. This latter context is extendable to public easements near curbsides and between public walkways and streets or other thoroughfares.

Fortunately, these processes and their archaeological signatures are well represented in research from reported sites in Bay City. Research at the Trombley House, on the east bank of the Saginaw River, gives a clear indication of how ejected fill from builders' rather substantial foundation trenches and full basements can preserve intact precontact deposits adjacent to historic structures. Fill removed from the trench was spread on the outer edge of the structure, effectively sealing the original A horizon with its Woodland and earlier occupation assemblage and allowing the systematic recovery of intact prehistoric occupation deposits (Prahl 1990). That this is not idiosyncratic is demonstrated by the redundancy with which such observations are made. Recent work on the Columbus Avenue Neighborhood Park in Bay City has also recorded the presence of intact precontact deposits under 50–70cm of expelled basement fill (Branstner 2001).

This situation was replicated on a larger scale during excavation at site 20BY79, on the western approach to the Liberty Bridge (see Figure 7.1; Lovis 1993a). Research at this locale took place in a former residential area with the remnants of several nineteenth-century structures. Site 20BY79 revealed intact precontact deposits under sidewalks, under cinder driveways, and under ejected fill from basement and foundation excavation. Research on the Broadway/Washington Corridor Project on the east bank of the Saginaw River in Bay City revealed intact A soil horizons containing systematically recoverable Late Woodland occupation materials under sidewalks on the east side of Franklin Street (Hambacher, Dunham, and Branstner 1995).

Overall, backyards were less prone to disturbance than front yards, the former displaying clear evidence of intact soil horizons. These observations led to some preliminary statements about the preservation potential of residential neighborhoods, in this case one that was occupied for as much as a century (Lovis 1993b). An important outcome of this work is the demonstration that there is in fact predictive potential for the systematic incorporation of such contexts into continuing regional archaeological research designs.

Land Transportation Corridor Contexts

Horse-drawn and motorized vehicle roadways and railroad rights-of-way are the two primary transportation corridor contexts that must be addressed in the archaeology and taphonomy of urban areas. Of paramount importance in understanding the early development of such transportation systems is that existing land forms were employed to reduce initial per-mile construction capital expenditures. Level, linear surfaces were sought by engineers because they minimized the amount of cutting, filling, and leveling needed to provide a surface with acceptable grades for the motive power, traffic, and conveyances it was to serve. Consequently, existing land forms such as floodplains, river or lake terraces, or bluff tops were often the primary choice for major early transportation rights-of-way. (See Ruger maps, Figures 7.3 and 7.4, for examples of railroad right-of-way placement in Bay City.)

Railway right-of-way construction is a fundamentally accretional activity in such locational contexts, if one eliminates locations where the cutting of grade into existing surfaces is necessary. Initial railway construction techniques were minimalist. Often, wooden crossties were initially set on an existing surface that was subject to little if any preparation. As the need for enhanced drainage became apparent or desirable, the entire roadbed could and would be physically lifted and gravel ballast added under and around the ties, or the original roadbed would be capped by subsequent rebuilding processes. A graphic example of this latter process was revealed during earthmoving activities on an abandoned New York Central Railroad (originally the Southern Railroad) right-of-way in southeastern Michigan near the town of Adrian. Original 1840-era roadbed with timber ties and wooden rails with iron strapping was found under clay and ballast that had been applied to raise the right-of-way and increase drainage (M. Branstner and K. Lewis, personal communication, 2001). Regular applications of ballast, coupled with tie and rail replacement, eventually resulted in a roadbed that effectively sealed the original ground surface under many centimeters of fill, although such preserved surfaces would, admittedly, be subject to compression forces (a consequence noted at sites 20BY77 and 20BY387 in Bay City; see Figure 7.1). Importantly, however, the locations of such rights-of-way are often in areas of highest precontact site potentials: terrace edges, floodplains proximal to the river, and the level areas of nearby bluff tops and uplands.

Early urban roadways for horse-drawn and motorized vehicles also placed a priority on those locations sought by railroads, that is, level surfaces, often paralleling a river, such as terraces and floodplains. The earliest roads were constructed with a mind toward minimal alteration, and while they may initially have been unpaved, they were subject to subsequent improvements. Common initial improvement often included the laying of half-timbers for the creation of so-called corduroy roadways. Later, gravel, brick, concrete, and asphalt became more common, and at times form a cumulative record of road resurfacing and improvement. Depending upon when such timbers or other surfacing materials were laid, it is possible that sealed ground surfaces could be preserved under many centimeters of cumulative reconstruction materials. It should be noted, though, that many such early roads are currently being completely reconstructed and that much of the earlier protective construction material is being removed, with new subroad bed often intruding into intact subsurface deposits. These development situations provide abundant potential for the recovery of precontact occupations.

Bay City provides several examples of transportation corridors preserving precontact surfaces, although for our present purposes we will limit these examples to the west bank of the Saginaw River between the Liberty Bridge and the Fletcher site (20BY28), an area several blocks long encompassing both a lake terrace and floodplain and possessing both vehicle roadway and railroad corridors (see Figure 7.1). Paved roadway is present on the level lake terrace above the floodplain, and a railroad right-of-way is present on the level floodplain at lower elevations. Recent research on the major north-south road, Marquette Avenue, revealed that only marginal grading activities had taken place during early episodes of road construction, although even this activity had the effect of either removing the original A soil horizon or greatly modifying it (Lovis 2002). Basal aeolian and lacustrine sands were left intact and protected beneath the road surface, which displayed several reconstruction episodes, sequentially including corduroy road, gravel aggregate, coursed brick, poured concrete, and rolled asphalt layers. Of significance, however, was the fact that the road capped a series of well-preserved Late Archaic Red Ochre as well as

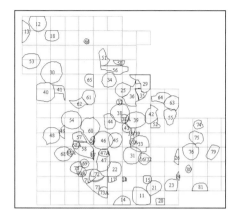

Figure 7.6 Plan View of Pit Feature Field under Bridge Approach at Site 20BY387

Woodland period burial features excavated more than a meter into the basal sands. Where this roadway was extended onto an elevated bridge approach, substantial volumes of sand fill capped an extensive Late Archaic pit field and occupation (Figure 7.6), although as previously noted the A soil horizon exhibited both compression and vertical displacement. Nonetheless, site 20BY387 revealed intact and recoverable precontact deposits.

Data recovery at sites 20BY77 and 20BY79 at the west approach to the Liberty Bridge (see Figure 7.1) were arbitrarily considered separate sites due to the presence of an intervening right-of-way of the Detroit and Mackinac Railroad (currently the Central Michigan Railroad right-of-way). Subsequent to archaeological mitigation of this pair of sites, the trackage in the area between them was being moved to accommodate the new bridge construction, providing an opportunity to observe but not systematically recover associated geological and archaeological information. On December 23, 1984, upon removal of rails, ties, and several accretional layers of limestone ballast, excavation by construction crews revealed an intact 30–50-cm thick A soil horizon underlying the ballast. Late Woodland pottery and lithics were observed in this horizon by the author and Earl J. Prahl (Lovis, field notes).

Conclusion

Urban areas have tremendous archaeological potential for understanding prehistoric use of highly desirable spaces. Idiosyncratic, intensive, and costly responses to specific endangered locales are insufficient if our goal is to understand the broader range of temporal and functional uses, and associated behaviors, currently encompassed by urban development. The only way to properly tackle such problems is with the development of systematic research designs directed at long-term exploration strategies.

The foregoing discussion of the processes associated with the development of complex urban environments, the potential contexts for accretional deposits, and illustrations of archaeological contexts in which intact precontact land forms and surfaces have been searched for, discovered, explored, and recovered leads to the clear conclusion that systematic research designs can be developed and implemented in such contexts. No longer can archaeologists work from a perspective that negates the potential of these areas to provide information on the prehistoric use of current urban areas, nor can we pretend that urban developments within larger study areas are fundamentally unexplorable. Rather, it is critically apparent that we have the predictive ability to isolate contexts in which such deposits will be preserved.

It has taken archaeologists almost thirty years since the advent of compliance legislation to recognize the potential of cumulative data sets to provide insights into the development of research problems and strategies. Existing historical site file data, coupled with opportunistic, regionally based, and compliance-based research data, when properly integrated, can provide substantially new perspectives on long-standing research problems. This is a point well made by Brashler and Mead (1996) in their compendium of Woodland research in the Grand River basin and by Monaghan and Lovis (2002) in their recent synthesis of geoarchaeological data from southern lower Michigan. These types of research models, designed to understand the systematics of the archaeological record, if replicated in urban contexts have the potential to dramatically alter the contributions archaeology can make to our understanding of the prehistoric past.

For those interested in urban research, either at the regularized compliance level or from other vantage points, such undertakings can be initially effected by the development of intensive land-use histories of urban areas, employing map, insurance, and other documentary data to understand patterns of development and land-form alteration. Land-use information must then be set against the backdrop of data available on the early or precontact configuration of these areas. Such initial work must, perforce, be properly coupled with ground truthing in advance of more intensive and expensive archaeological fieldwork. At a practical level, this implies the directed use of heavy equipment in a systematic exploratory framework designed to understand local-level land formation and depositional processes and to correlate stratigraphic information across broad areas that may have experienced heterogeneous developmental processes. With these data in hand, it is often possible to target areas of highest preservation potential for intact deposits and design both discovery and excavation strategies that focus on such preservation potential.

In many ways, what is being said here is neither new nor novel. Those working in archaeological compliance confront such problems on a regular basis, and with the exception that compliance-based projects are essentially idiosyncratic, meaning that they are not often part of a larger ongoing urban research strategy, such compliance efforts implement essentially the same type of program outlined here. However, it is to the exception that the current argument is directed. Archaeologists must take the long view on the archaeology of urban environments. Compliance and other forms of research effort directed at precontact problems in urban contexts require placement in systematic research designs that appropriately accommodate known taphonomic processes. There are many such urban contexts in Michigan and the Great Lakes region that could benefit from such attention.

Acknowledgments

My early field trips with Chuck Cleland had a profound impact on the way in which I viewed both natural and cultural landscapes and their interaction. I thank Chuck for acting as the catalyst for the observations presented here. Honing the presentation to its final form was assisted by several readers, including Dr. Kenneth Lewis, Mr. Mark Branstner, and Dr. Margaret Holman. Ken Lewis, in particular, assisted tremendously with the structure of the essay and kept the arguments both honest and, I hope, logical. Mr. Mark Branstner of Great Lakes Archaeological Research, Inc., and Drs. James Robertson and Michael Hambacher of Commonwealth Cultural Resources Group, Inc., provided citations, unpublished reports, and copies of maps, which strengthened the substantive components of the essay. Finally, I owe a debt of gratitude to the City of Bay City and the various federal, state, municipal, and private funding agencies that have supported the many decades of Bay City archaeology and made this essay possible.

8

Michilimackinac Archaeology and the Organization of Trade at a Distance

James A. Brown

The North American fur trade is often held up as another typical example of the exploitative history of Europeans in the early world economy. Lost sight of is the long period during the eighteenth century in which this highly atomized trade was subject to negotiation between trappers and traders, a condition that Richard White calls the "middle ground." The slow transformation of the middle ground to the fully integrated world economy of the nineteenth century calls for a theoretical perspective that focuses on process. The distance parity theory of Gil Stein provides that focus by relating distance to the effective implementation of power. This theory views fur trade history as neither the triumph of European might nor the unfolding of native acculturation, nor of native economizing.

The history of a nodal place in the fur trade network is used to show the power of Gil Stein's concept of effective distance to integrate disparate types of documentary and archaeological evidence. As a trading post at the Straits of Mackinac from 1715 to 1781, Michilimackinac bridges an important shift in the effective distance with which European power could reach into the continental interior. Starting around 1733, the site was transformed from an endpoint depot to a distribution and resupply center. Both the actions taken there and the material record signature demonstrate the impact that effective distance had on the slowness with which the entrepôt grew. The pattern that is emphasized is the growth in capacity to invest in an extractive economy that had a fundamental impact on the degree to which European power became consolidated in the vastness of the continental interior.

— • —

History is not the study of origins; rather it is the analysis of all the mediations by which the past was turned into our present.

— Sir Herbert Butterfield,
The Whig Interpretation of History

THE FUR TRADE in Canada and the Great Lakes region seems, from the vantage point of the twenty-first century, to have had the history of a typical colonial enterprise. Once Europeans discovered that profit could be made from trade in furs, they embarked on a program of exploitation. After depleting fur-bearing animals in one area, traders moved on to fresh trapping grounds. As native trappers became increasingly dependent on European technology, their economic relations with Whites turned from native autonomy to subordination to a metropolitan core. Colonization soon followed claims of European sovereignty, thereby creating ever-increasing stress on Indian-White relations. The competition among European colonial powers—the British, Dutch, French, and later Americans—over control of access to furs led to a fateful reduction of Indian cultural alternatives. The increased pressure on resources subjected locally self-sufficient Native Americans residing in the prime fur-bearing forests to the role of specialist pieceworkers in a global political economy. All told, the impression one gathers from one account (Hickerson 1973) was that throughout the northern forests European domination was inevitable once Indians engaged in the first opportunistic trade with overseas visitors on Atlantic shores. In a sense, this conception of the pathway toward contemporary conditions looks upon each battle, each settlement founding, each colonial policy move, and each technological innovation as steps in a direction toward the condition of dependency we know today.

A verdict that ascribes so much to the first fatal footfalls is tantamount to taking the outcome as a ratification of a particular historical pathway. But recent scholarship has shown that the dependency identified with contemporary fur trade conditions was not foreordained as Hickerson (1973) implied in his account. The path was anything but straightforward (Eccles 1988; Ray 1996; White 1991).

Although European leverage in the trading relationship increased over time, factors external to the trade itself—to say nothing of events on the continent of Europe—were of utmost influence in bringing the fur trade economy to its present condition. It is pertinent, therefore, to ask, were it not for the fiscal strength and economic growth of the metropolitan centers, the pressure of population growth in the American colonies, and the fall of Montreal (to name some central factors), might the weakness of European powers up until the early seventeenth century have led easily to a long-term equilibrium of relations in the forest with trade being continually negotiated in what Richard White has termed the "middle ground"? After all, it took three centuries for Indians of the nineteenth century to become subordinated within the fur trade political economy (Eccles 1988; Ray 1996; White 1991).

The transformation of the Great Lakes fur trade over time represents an opportunity to return to certain issues regarding the expansion of colonial European powers into areas lacking the local resources necessary to support a large European population. How was expansion accomplished without a substantial resident population base to serve as a springboard? More specifically, what role did distance play when Europe served as the sole effective logistical and financial base for imperial expansion? The various ways in which distance has been a factor has been usefully explored by Gil Stein (1999). He has identified effective distance as a critical dimension along which to measure any center's relationship with its periphery.

When applied to the fur trade, the distance decay principle carries us a long way toward explaining various aspects of the trade in the northern forest. As a consequence, the distance decay principle helps dismiss the claims to causation that commonly assumed European powers had the inherent potential to overpower all native resistance from their first toehold on the continent. This posture, when transferred to an interpretation of the postcontact archaeological record, whether Indian or White, tends to resolve itself into a matter of the strengths and weaknesses of specific colonial powers. The different European players deemed to have the greater inherent potential to triumph become those who have most successfully incorporated the tenets of liberal economics. What has been overlooked is the processes by which imperial power relationships have been constrained economically and logistically by effective distance.

Testimony to the distance parity theory is often elusive in the documentary record. But when the material record is enlisted, such testimony emerges forcefully in the details. It is just such detail that this essay turns to in explicating the model in the archaeology of Fort Michilimackinac in the Straits of Mackinac area.

History of the Fur Trade Political Economy
Historical Processes

At this point it is useful to identify the critical steps in the transformation of imperial and colonial organization of the northern forests in the Americas. Economic, fortunes of war, and logistical and population growth factors can be identified in the history of the fur trade in the Great Lakes area.

As early as the first decade of the sixteenth century, western European fishermen began to trade in furs with peoples on the Atlantic Coast as opportunity presented itself (Trigger 1985, 118–125). After one hundred years of this kind of trade, fur became a staple of its own (Eccles 1988, 324). The French, the Dutch, and later the English undertook this trade from newly established permanent posts. The early establishments of the seventeenth century were low-cost affairs that minimized the settled presence of Europeans. As the fur trade developed, it differentiated into a concentration on beaver pelts in the northern forests and deer skins in the southern. Both the beaver and deer populations responded comparatively well to intense trapping and hunting, respectively. Hence, the long-term productivity of the beaver and deer skin trade was supported by the resiliency of these animals to continued harvesting.

Sporadic fighting among the representatives of France, Holland, and England stimulated investment in both additional resources and human capital. France took the novel approach of using the proceeds from the trade to support Jesuit missionizing (Eccles 1988, 326). This led to an energetic outreach of Jesuits and traders into the lower and upper Great Lakes. Expansion in this period brought France into deadly conflict with the Iroquois (Abler 1992). Alarmed by the terror that the Iroquois brought to the fledgling settlement of Montreal on the St. Lawrence, the French Crown took the step of bolstering the colony with a few thousand settlers.

In 1663 the French Crown also reorganized the trade as a Crown monopoly. The intent of this act was to stabilize the market with guarantees to purchase all furs at fixed prices. Many of the men who were brought from France took advantage of the opportunity of such price supports to move into the bush, thereby laying the foundation for a class of coureurs de bois (Eccles 1988, 327). The French Crown attempted to discourage these men from pursuing their unregulated trade by instituting an unsuccessful licensing scheme (Eccles 1974, 1988). The result, however, was a barely regulated trade frontier that tended to expand willy-nilly and brought traders into increasing conflict among themselves and with native peoples. The intensity of the trade accelerated during France's war with the English (1689–1697). By 1701, the uncontrolled accumulation of furs resulted in a glut of pelts that caused the French king to shut down the trade to all but a small number of trading posts (Eccles 1988, 327). Michilimackinac and two other central posts were allowed to remain in business in order to sustain peace-maintaining gift-giving.

Up to this time the French depended on established low-cost practices to minimize investment in personnel and infrastructure. The cooperation of Native American middlemen such as the Iroquois, Huron, Ottawa, and Fox was momentarily convenient, but the maturation of the fur trade necessitated a more costly undertaking if it was to avoid irreversible decline. The urgency to do so came, however, from a national policy level that regarded the English colonies on the Atlantic seaboard as a threat to French claims to the interior. Detroit, New Orleans, and other small towns were established to reinforce French claims. As self-sustaining settlements, these towns were also viewed as potential staging places for effective trade into the interior. Although this move was successful, French success was largely offset by the failure of these settlements to induce a peaceful settlement among nearby tribes.

Trade was reopened in 1714 after the long war over the Spanish Succession had depleted the French treasury. Posts were created to tap territories beyond the Great Lakes. By the 1730s the trade had penetrated to the Saskatchewan River. However, this necessitated trade with the Sioux, the mortal enemies of the Fox. The latter's reaction led to two wars against that tribe (Edmunds and Peyser 1993).

The Seven Years' War (1756–1760) brought the Anglo-French rivalry to a head with the fall of Montreal to the British. The consequent transfer of New France into British hands became a blow to the Indian's bargaining position because they could no longer play France against Britain (Eccles 1988, 331). Although the volume of gift-giving initially was reduced by the British, they discovered upon Pontiac's Uprising in 1761 that previous levels had to be sustained in order to maintain harmony in the forest. The Seven Years' War had brought disruption to the trade and its system of gift-giving (Eccles 1988, 331). As the trade rebounded, competition between the different Montreal groups and Hudson's Bay Company set the trade in a direction of increasingly sharp practices, sometimes to native benefit but destructive in the long run due to the widespread use of alcohol (Eccles 1988, 332).

The American Revolution (1775–1883) raised a direct challenge to the customary state of affairs in the interior. The threat of dispossession that population expansion west of the Appalachians presented was well understood by natives. British authorities attempted to shield Indians from settler intrusions with various acts that proved ineffective. The British even tried to maintain control of the strategic Straits of Mackinac after their defeat. But the Indian negotiating position was considerably weakened within the new American territory because they had sided with the British in the conflict.

Between 1790 and 1821, the economic and political position of natives underwent significant and lasting erosion (Ray 1996, 299–300; White 1991). In British America (Canada), the competition among trading companies (there were no longer any independents) led to a depletion of game and to what Ray (1996, 300) has called "the central role which alcohol had assumed in the business." The transfer of trading company rivalry to Indian factionalism shows the depths to which the collective bargaining position of bands had deteriorated. With the ascension of George Simpson to the head of the Hudson's Bay Company in 1821, the fate of the Indian trapper was sealed by the cessation of gifts and the conversion of gifts into lines of credit (Ray 1988, 1996). In addition, the assertion of the color bar created a class line between traders and trappers in the bush. In the United States, the declining bargaining position of Indians culminated with the War of 1812 and the defeat of Tecumseh (White 1991).

Triumphal Themes

The foregoing account touches on several oft-repeated themes that obscure the action of such factors as different financial capacities of various European powers and the contingent effect of such events as the fall of Montreal on native bargaining power (Anderson 2000). Prominent among these factors and events is the dramatization of fur trade history as the contest for exclusive domination by one or another imperial power. French competed with the Dutch, then with the British, and after the American Revolution the British competed with the Yankees. Traders of each block vied with each other for the allegiance of native trappers. They, in turn, were not averse to switching their trade in the event that they felt slighted. Out of this competitive history the British emerged triumphant in what is now Canada. Over time this triumph has taken on the aura of inevitability with an implication of inherent superiority.

This triumph has fostered its own list of "just-so stories." To explain the outcome the issue usually reduces to one over trade and, if that, then in material and economic terms. One of these is the notion that British goods were cheaper or better in quality. In point of fact, contemporary records only give qualified support for this thesis (Eccles 1988, 328). In many instances the French had the upper hand in both quality and price (Eccles 1983, 349).[1] The one good that emerges consistently to give the British the advantage in quality is their stroud cloths (Eccles 1979; White 1991, 120–121, 138).

What is missing is an acknowledgment that the British possessed a powerful edge in their innovative method for financing national debt (Ferguson 2001). In the King George's War of 1744–1748, the British waged a spoiler fight over market share in the Levant and Latin America in order to counter and perhaps overturn an increasing French success in overseas trade. A successful blockade allowed the British to achieve their goal (Eccles 1988). Later, in the Seven Years' War, Britain emerged victorious with its finances in better shape than the finances of its adversaries. This favorable fiscal condition has been traced in part by more than one historian to its management of finances (Kennedy 1987, 113). In consequence, Britain was able to invest in British America to a degree that eluded France.

Economic Determinism

A second theme is contained in the economic determinism of Harold Innis (1962) and his followers (e.g., Hickerson 1973; Hunt 1940). The publication of Innis's The Fur Trade in Canada in 1930 cast the history of the Great Lakes fur trade into economic terms, with Indians jostling for middlemen roles and Europeans adjusting their imperial policies and administrative practices to allow greater profit to be made trading in beaver pelts and other furs (Eccles 1979). In this view European revenue motives drove colonial policy. The profit motives of the French (and later the British) traders were readily transferred to Indians by conferring on strategically advantaged tribes the role of middlemen.

Of the many issues involved, only two need to be dealt with here. The first of these is the so-called profitability of the fur trade. The demand for achieving profit dictated the steady expansion of the area under colonial control. The pressure for profit not only dictated extension into the

---

1. The myth has arisen that traders foisted onto the trappers inferior and poorly performing firearms (Hamilton 1976). There is no contemporary support for this belief, and what little testimony we have speaks strongly against it. For instance, Hamilton (1976, 6) cites a document in which the cost of the "fine" arms to the firms was twenty-two shillings, whereas the "ordinary" ones were twenty shillings, a 10 percent spread in cost hardly indicative of cheapness. We do not find archaeologically the burst breeches that are the mark of bad arms-making (Hamilton 1976). The myth probably has its genesis in the policy of the Hudson's Bay Company to cheapen the quality of its goods in the 1820s (Ray 1996). Subsequent reaction to this step shows what a radical departure this decision was.

interior in quest of untapped territories, but also created an evolution in the role of the trapper as primary producer, first as middlemen and subsequently as workers whose independence was steadily compromised by indebtedness to company traders in return for European manufactures. Indians became trapped into dependency as goods produced in European shops became increasingly regarded as necessities. Eric Wolf (1982, 194) cast this transformation in terms of the replacement of a kinship mode of production with one resembling debt peonage.

Wolf's account neglects the weakness in fur trade yields. Precisely how much profit was truly realized has been difficult to measure (White 1991, 484). The windfalls from exploiting untapped territories (or those ironically left unharvested because hunters and trappers were diverted by warfare) undoubtedly represented a great incentive for traders. But the complete balance-sheet in the beaver pelt trade was commonly assessed by contemporaries as being scarcely worth the effort of French and British logistic support.

Neither side saw the fur trade as completely profit-driven. The French Crown subvented it to a large degree. Revenues from the fur trade were designated for Crown projects overseas—initially, during the 1640s, to underwrite missionary efforts (Eccles 1988, 326). Later, after the War of the Spanish Succession, the French Crown earmarked the profits toward the advancement of scientific knowledge, specifically the discovery of the route to the Pacific (Eccles 1984, 3–5). On the other side, Indians manipulated the fur trade to support individual tribal agendas, and in any case they were imperfect consumers (Eccles 1988; White 1991, 122). As White phrased it, "Indians might lose on direct trade but balance their losses by gaining on the gifts they received, on the debts they refused to pay, and on thefts that went unpunished" (White 1991, 484).

For Europeans, international politics assumed primacy. Fundamentally, these politics were driven by religious enmity and the use of overseas economic interests as pawns in domestic contests, including land wars and the rights of succession to foreign thrones (Eccles 1988, 327–328).

Innis's economic thesis has distorted the history of Indian-White relations. It presents the evolution of subordinate relations in classic economic terms, whereby economic development is portrayed as progressive, while the record from the 1500s to the twentieth century reveals a more complicated picture. No single feature of the economic perspective has undergone revision more than the so-called middleman role of the Huron, Fox, and other tribes (e.g., Hunt 1940). As Charles Cleland expressed it in Rites of Conquest,

It is assumed that they were motivated to enhance their economic position by interdicting or manipulating the supply of furs in order to effect demand. This would put potential competitors at an economic disadvantage by controlling the flow of goods. In short, they behaved like rational capitalists. This conclusion stretches credulity, because it requires us to believe that trade goods were critical to survival and that, to acquire these goods, traditional values of economic exchange were rapidly discarded.... Remembering that exchange to Indians was not just an economic venture but a political and social relationship ratified by a transfer of property, trade was like a marriage between two families sealed with a dowry. Once the French began to exchange with a tribe's neighbors, the social and political value to the group, in Indian eyes the main basis of continued trade and friendship, had slipped away. (1992, 110)

The "middle ground" was conceptualized by Richard White (1991) as the forum in which Indian-White relations were conducted in the Great Lakes area during the fur trade. In this arena all manner of relations were negotiated, whether they involved economic transactions, permission to use a parcel of land, or recruitment for war. The concept rests upon the fact that neither Indians nor Whites could project their customary usages on the other. Thus, while French and British claimed dominion over the Great Lakes (at various times as a projection of European royal prerogative and property rights), Indians uniformly regarded themselves as masters of their homeland and the Europeans as their as guests. French and British policy was to use the middle ground to play out relations with indigenous populations. This arrangement, however, could not withstand pressure from Anglo-American settlers that proved to be greater than either Indians or colonial administrators could deal with. In the end, a major factor in transforming the role of Indians into workers took place when British colonial administration dropped its protective policies, inherited from the French, and allowed the large fur trade companies to convert what had formerly been presents into dependency-creating credit.

Over time, the middle ground took on a new political format as the relative economic, demographic, and military advantages of its participants underwent change (White 1991, 104). Because European leverage was relatively weak in the centuries before the 1800s, power was exercised with corresponding condition. After the early 1800s the native side weakened as traders, now organized into vertically integrated companies, created debt relations out of what had been gift-giving (Eccles 1988).

The upshot of this reinterpretation has been to show that economics did not play its classical role; indeed, economic relationships were somewhat marginal until the end of the eighteenth century. Richard White (1991) found that all aspects of Indian-White relations were continually undergoing negotiation and that trade and war underwent historical changes in which relative advantages of the parties involved shifted over time. For most of the period Indians held the advantage, at least up to the French surrender of North American to the British in 1760. Thereafter, the balance moved gradually but definitively in the direction of European (mainly British) and American domination.

Native Dependency

Another issue is the alleged weakness of Indian resistance and the consequent fate for Indians of dependence on European goods. This verdict might seem to apply in retrospect, but any such assessment has to be placed in historical context. Richard White (1991, 482–484) distinguishes dependency in its far-reaching economic and cultural aspects from simple reliance on European goods, a condition with which dependency is often conflated (Hickerson 1973).

Trade for European goods did not alter Native American technologies to the point of dependency until the end of the eighteenth century. From the perspective of the straits history, Fitting (1976) concluded that up to and through the seventeenth century trade goods did little to dislocate local native technologies. A broader study by Ehrhardt (2002) underscored this conclusion from much more detailed information. White (1991, 129–141) reiterates this point by arguing that dependency was slow to appear—this despite repeated declarations by Frenchmen on a number of occasions that native provisioning systems would break down were it not for a constant inflow of trade goods. But Indians remained incomplete consumers for some time (Gilman 1982; Ray 1980). The main threat to their independence was the flow of alcohol into the political economy (Eccles 1983, 350).

Hickerson (1973) contrasted a self-sufficient precontact Indian economy with postcontact dependency. Characteristically independent tribes possessed economic autonomy. A stepwise directional change away from this autonomy was spelled out by Hickerson (36). Indians were first drawn into reliance on European trade goods, then intimidated into stepped-up trapping through "the ever constant threat of the withdrawal of the trading post," and then drawn into dependency through the "debt system." To account for the ever-expanding reach of the fur trade, a corresponding Indian demand has to be posited for trade goods (39).

All too frequently to us moderns, European interests from the outset had a capacity to overwhelm Indian trade customs and to prevail in their quest for profit. Europeans had only to apply the requisite force to exercise their will over natives. But we judge such force from our understanding of later military capacities, not by sixteenth- and seventeenth-century ones when the fur-bearing forests did not readily provide the basis for a population upon which cheap logistic support could depend. Contemporaneous conditions were much more fluid. For instance, the simplified view of the encounter between Indians and Whites has been reevaluated (Axtell 1992; Cleland 1992; Eccles 1979; Jennings 1984; White 1991). As a result, the contact history of Indians with Whites has now become less predetermined.

Since the 1980s, historical scholarship has disclosed the contingencies that led the fur trade from being an opportunistic one for many generations to a contractual one. Some of those events were the result of actions and processes outside of the fur-bearing forests. Only with the strengthening of transportation and military infrastructures and the buildup of European populations on the continent did the conditions governing the trade begin to alter significantly. Even more importantly, our contemporary preconceptions overlook the stepwise changes that took place in essential features of the trade since its simple opportunistic beginnings in the 1500s.

Distance Parity Theory—An Alternative Perspective

The foregoing review of fur trade history raises important questions about some conventional academic positions. These questions impel us to shift focus from terms coming from retrospective justifications to other factors, some to which even contemporaries were alert. Prominent among these is the dilution of power that comes with increasing distance from any source. Gil Stein (1999) formalized this factor as the distance-parity theory. In Stein's hands, distance becomes a factor (varying by circumstance) that mitigates the effect of dependency: "Under conditions of technological and demographic parity between two regions at different levels of sociocultural complexity, the power of the more developed ('core') region to control its 'periphery' will decay with distance" (62).

Like most intervening variables, the distance-decay of power does not attract much attention today, although it is as relevant to the colonial fur trade as it has been for the Near East of the fourth millennium B.C.

Stein identified as primary determinants the costs of transport for both military forces and trade goods. These costs and the relative access of each trading partner to population size (and health), natural resource base, and "military, productive, and transport technology . . . also structure the balance of power in interregional interaction" (Stein 1999, 62).

> The distance-parity model, then, sees interregional interaction as a continuum where the balance of power is subject to the constraints of transport costs and technological parity. In this model, we would expect variation in power and exchange relationships, not just between different interaction networks, but also between different parts of the same network. When the primary form of interaction is exchange, we can use the trade-diaspora concept to describe the different configurations of economic and political relations among homelands, trader, and host communities in different parts of the network. Under conditions of technological parity, relations among polities at different levels of complexity and the diasporas that link them would show a trend from power asymmetries between close neighbors toward progressively more symmetric interaction with increasing distance from the more developed core states. (Stein 1999, 64)

Applications to modern history are not new. Dan Rogers (1990) provides a concrete example from his examination of the impact of Europeans on various aspects of Arikara material culture. He was able to distinguish between two periods: 1681–1775, when Arikara sites lay outside and beyond the fur trade proper, and 1776–1805, during which direct engagement occurred. Because Europeans were infrequently sighted prior to 1775, European goods were treated with special respect. Relative remoteness to the sources of supply ensured an independence from the fur trade system, although European objects had trickled into Arikara hands through down-the-line trade. A parallel sequence was advanced by Trigger (1985, 219–224) for the history of Iroquois and Eastern Algonquian Indian responses to the European fur trade.

In the Great Lakes area, trading posts were established with minimal intrusion into the local social fabric. This has to be a classic instance of Stein's distance effect:

> Only at Detroit, Kaskaskia, and Cahokia in the Illinois country, and on the lower Mississippi, were they able to establish small agricultural settlements. Elsewhere they merely maintained fur-trade posts consisting of three or four log buildings surrounded by a palisade.

> Always these posts were placed in an area that no Indian nation claimed as its own—Detroit, for example—or were established with the express permission of the dominant nation of the region. . . .
>
> The land on which the trading posts stood they considered still to be theirs, the French occupants being mere tenants during the Indians' pleasure. (Eccles 1983, 348, 349)

The French maintained forts at considerable expense and risk to intertribal rivalry.

> With the exception of the Sioux nation, who always kept the French at arm's length, most of the nations were glad to have these posts on their territory. Although the French maintained that the posts gave them title to the land, their claims were made to exclude the English, not to deny the Indians' title, something they did not dare do. The French were certainly not sovereign in the West, for sovereignty implies the right to impose and collect taxes, and to enforce laws—and they were never able to do either. The Indians never considered themselves to be French subjects, and the French were never able to treat them as such. Moreover, the Canadian voyageurs who transported trade goods and supplies to the western posts and took the furs back to Montreal always had to travel in convoy for protection against the Indians through whose lands they passed. (Eccles 1983, 349)

From these statements it is evident that Stein's distance effect is relevant to far more of the fur trade operations than customarily acknowledged.

Charting the Shrinkage of the Distance Factor

Gil Stein held that the distance effect impacted several key aspects of intergroup relations—military power, transport technology, population size, and natural productive base. Of these, changes in transport technology had the most obvious impact on changes in the Great Lakes fur trade. Others that stood in the background were improvements in naval technology (transport again, but off-site so to speak), the beginnings of the industrial revolution, and a fiscal management policy that was capable of financing imperial economic expansion.

These technological changes, coupled with the logistical ones necessitated by enlargement of the reach of the fur trade with greater shipping efficiency, explains a great deal of the material changes registered in Great Lakes archaeological sites from the 1730s onward. These changes had little to do with royal revenue needs, or rising prosperity, in the view espoused by Heldman (1991, 201).

A number of critical junctures can be identified in this historical review that make sense in terms of Stein's effective distance model. First is the establishment of permanent, self-sustaining European populations in fortified settlements with maritime connections to the mother country. Montreal is obviously one of these; New Amsterdam, Boston, and Philadelphia are others. These communities and their hinterland settlements provided the manpower and productive energies that made possible the military, logistical, and economic initiatives on the American continent. With each advance of European populations and their livestock came ecological change that had the immediate effect of creating centers for disseminating European disease vectors. The second step was the placement of fortified self-sustaining settlements in the interior. Detroit represents this development for the northern forest. Third was the triumph of the British over the French in 1760, with the subsequent loss of bargaining power to the indigenous inhabitants. Fourth, beginning in the 1770s, was the population surge west of the Alleghenies by Euro-American populations.

To examine these critical points in detail, we need to bring into discussion the material record. It is the small things of this record that bring the broader trends into the sharpest relief. Among the different ways distance decay can be examined, here we examine the material history at a single location in the northern forest, at the Straits of Mackinac, to show how changes at that settlement were a response to specific reconfigurations in the military, fiscal, and logistic organization of imperial economics, irrespective of the specific governments involved.

Fort Michilimackinac

Changes at the Straits Area

The Straits of Mackinac area remained strategic throughout the duration of the fur trade. Although reasons for its importance shifted in response to changes in the complexity of the trade, transportation remained fundamental. The straits lay at a key juncture into Lakes Michigan and Superior from Lake Huron. These lakes brought access not only to the fur-bearing territory west of Lake Superior, but to the fertile lands of Green Bay and the Illinois Country as well. The straits area itself had poor agricultural potential. Hence, the area had to be provisioned externally to support the enlarged local population when the locale became a key link in a restructured logistic system. After 1730, Fort Michilimackinac became an entrepôt as the transportation linkage to Montreal doubled when the fur trade expanded into the Northwest (White 1991, 161).

Initially, posts were located in the straits area to cater to the immediate needs of the traders and missionaries. As early as 1671, the strategic value of the Straits of Mackinac was recognized when the French chose a bay facing the straits on the upper peninsula of Michigan to establish the Fort de Baude trading post. At this location resided a substantial native population. There the Jesuit Marquette mission (1671–1705) was placed in the bay of St. Ignace (Figure 8.1).

Later a military purpose became of overriding concern, and thus Fort Michilimackinac was established across the straits on the northern tip of the southern peninsula. The date for the first post on the south side of the straits is usually set at around 1715, although it might have been a few years later (Stone 1974, 8). The context was clearly that of French preparation at the straits for mounting a large military expedition against the Fox Indians over Lake Michigan, although the written sources are silent about the connection (Edmunds and Peyser 1993). In 1716, the French launched the first Fox War in an attempt to circumvent the tribe's objection to French trade with its enemy, the Sioux. Afterwards, a small garrison remained at the fort. In keeping with its military purpose, it is logical that Fort Michilimackinac

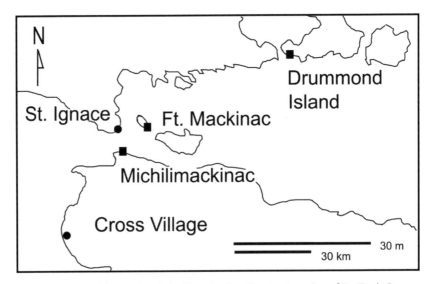

Figure 8.1 Map of the Straits of Mackinac Region Showing Location of Fur Trade Posts

should be repositioned against surprise attack from the west.[2] It is evident that the new south shore location was motivated by practical defensive considerations, not where native populations were located.

This fort "consisted of a small, square stockade with bastions, a mission, two guard houses, and a forty-foot-long structure which housed military personnel" (Stone 1974, 8). The number of permanent inhabitants was small. The legend on a circa 1717 map states that this newly established post had "a commandant, some habitants, even some French women." In contrast to this small permanent population were the number of transient voyageurs. As the map legend states, "In 1716 about 600 coureurs-de-bois were gathered there during trading time" (Stone 1974, 8, Fig. 3; see also Maxwell and Binford 1961, 11–12; Miller and Stone 1970, 12, 14).

There the fort remained until 1781, when another defensive alert during the American Revolution prompted the British to abandon the now-vulnerable position for a more defendable one across the Straits of Mackinac on the heights of Mackinac Island. The British, forced by the provisions of the Jay Treaty of 1794 to relinquish this island post to the Americans, replaced their strategic interests with a post at Drummond Island north of the international line at that time (see Figure 8.1). Each of these moves was dictated by strategic interests with scant regard for the interests of natives.

Emergence of the Fortified Supply Station

Early in the 1730s the fortified settlement on the south side of the straits took on new functions as the effective distance to Montreal suddenly changed. This large fortified post and rendezvous place of temporary construction was required to provide logistical support to a newly established field of front-line posts. In 1732, the Crown approved a petition "to rebuild Michilimackinac completely as 'a more solid fort' to accommodate the growing fur trade." (Heldman 1991, 205). By 1734, La Verendrye stated publicly that Michilimackinac would be his probable supply station for Fort St. Charles in place of the much more distant Montreal (Innis 1962, 93). At this time Michilimackinac was transformed from a square stockade to a larger, rectangular fortified village on the Vauban model with a broad side facing the waterfront (Heldman 1991).

---

2. The need to guard the western approaches to the straits is a plausible reason for the French to have relocated the post to a windswept location strategically placed at the tip of the southern peninsula. In 1749, Lotbinière remarked that both the eastern and western approaches could be monitored from this single location (Gerin-Lajoie 1976).

Enlargement was dictated by the needs of a much expanded trade network reaching to the Rockies. It took place at a time when the French had embarked on extending their trade network by reorganizing their string of posts with entrepôts at break-points in travel from Montreal. The growth in the size of the trading territory necessitated increased differentiation of the parts of the system. This change came in response to the fort's promotion to an intermediate collecting station and service settlement for distant connections between Montreal and the primary fur trade posts deep in the interior. Detroit and Michilimackinac were two of these entrepôts (Innis 1962, 92, 112). Each differed in important respects. Detroit was sufficiently south to act as a center for provisioning the system from local production, but Michilimackinac was too far north to be locally self-sufficient. Its strategic location combined with its far-forward position for trade in the fur-bearing forests of the far Northwest offset its lack of self-sufficiency (Russell 1939). The effect on site planning at Michilimackinac was immediate, although implementation would take decades to fully realize.

Entrepôt as Distributional Center

An account of the materiality of the fur trade as part of a world system economy has been sketched by Tordoff (1983). In her account, the fur trade was a network of size-sorted posts arranged in a well-ordered economic hierarchy. She sought to demonstrate this application of settlement hierarchy by comparing archaeological assemblages from the Great Lakes and Midwest in terms of their place within the pre-1761 French fur trade. Tordoff's model obviously pertained to the period following the rearrangement of the 1730s. In major ways, her hierarchical expectations were sustained. At in her terms "regional distribution centers" she found a greater variety both between different categories of European artifacts and among items within these categories. As an example of such a center, Fort Michilimackinac yielded greater variety of items of military issue and European artifacts associated with clothing in general. Tordoff's study measures up to expectations particularly with respect to variety. However, Anderson (1991) showed that canoe consignment documents clearly indicate Green Bay, a local point of trade, as the recipient of a larger amount of clothing and other artifacts (see also White 1991). This shows that the "hierarchy" was imperfect and asymmetrical. It also indicates that Michilimackinac had become an entrepôt or staging place for a diverse set of endpoints in the trade network (Keene 1991). A greater variety of goods actually passed through Michilimackinac (to Green Bay, for instance) than stayed there. Many of the material patterns reported by Anderson (1991) can be attributed to distance-related effects.

Any suggestion that this was an administrative hierarchy or anything but a distributional one flies in the face of the data. Using South's (1977) characterization formula, Fort Michilimackinac remained in the fur trade site type throughout its history (Heldman and Grange 1981). Detroit remained far different from Michilimackinac (Russell 1939).

Reduction of Effective Distance

In Stein's terms, the effective distance of Great Lakes Indians to both the metropolitan center and the colonies of the St. Lawrence basin posed constraints on the effects of exchange until around 1775. Preeminent among these were transport costs, since military technology and the production of hardware and dry goods had remained remarkably stable during the eighteenth century.

Transport of goods into the interior and the removal of furs for sale in the European market was a key feature of the trade. The network of lakes and rivers that provided the only feasible access to trappers presented a technical and logistical hurdle. By the very nature of their mode of acquisition of furs, trappers had to be scattered throughout the forest.

The canoe, for instance, was a highly fitted technology for travel that united commonly available raw materials with the swift and broken waterways of the glaciated interior. Early canoes were three-man affairs that were limited in their carrying capacity. In the 1720s the largest canoe (later known as a medium-sized eight-place bastard, or batard, of 9 to 9.5m in length) carried about 1,800kg.

By 1730, boat travel out of Montreal had reached the practical limits of a single round trip of canoes within a single warm season. As more distant fur fields came to realize a return on investment, staging settlements became of increasing importance to make the extension of trade into the Northwest practical. Into this context a new, larger version of the eight-place trade canoe was introduced around 1729 (Kent 1997, 95). This Montreal canoe, or canot du Maitre, measured 9.5 to 11m and carried 2,270kg, thereby adding 470kg to the payload (Kent 1997, 96). The invention of the Montreal canoe signaled the seriousness with which the French pursued their trade up to the Rockies. This type of eight-man canoe could carry an additional cargo of 25 percent over that of the largest existing inland watercraft. LaVerendrye used a mixture of the two sizes in his expedition beyond Lake Winnipeg. Data on the crew size of outfits authorized to depart from Montreal show a steady increase in the average size of canoe throughout the eighteenth century (Kent 1997, 89). These technological changes coupled with the logistic ones necessitated by enlarging the reach of the fur trade explain a great deal about the material changes registered in Great Lakes archaeological sites from the 1730s onward.

The French drew on a supply of highly skilled voyageurs to man the canoes fanning out from Montreal each year and were recognized as having a more reliable transport system than the British. Water transport underwent continued innovation under the French. The British only managed to outstrip the Montrealers' advantage with the invention of the York, a boat of wood plank construction that was both more durable than vessels made of birch bark and required fewer oarsmen to move equivalent cargo (Morse 1979, 24). But this triumph of the Hudson's Bay Company over the Montreal traders came only in the 1820s when Canada already was securely in the hands of the British.

Population Changes

The number of Frenchmen in the interior was always low (Eccles 1983). A great deal of the difference between French and British policies toward Indians of the Upper Great Lakes was dictated by distance to areas of continuous European settlement. Whereas the small, slow-growing population in the St. Lawrence valley, and scattered settlements elsewhere, constituted no threat to Indian land use in the Great Lakes, it was an entirely different matter with Anglo-American colonists whose populations were doubling every generation (Eccles 1988, 328). Indeed, population expansion within the American colonies probably forced the rift with the British Crown and in turn led to a deteriorated political, ecological, and economic landscape for Indians.

The population history of the Straits of Mackinac area charts a slow change in effective distance. Up to 1760, the French held a small garrison at Fort Michilimackinac. Lyle Stone reported that

> In 1729 there were no more than thirty-five soldiers, including officers, at the fort. In 1747 the troops numbered only twenty-eight. In addition to military personnel and their families, the fort housed licensed traders, craftsmen, missionaries, and itinerant coureurs-de-bois. Local groups of Ojibwa and Ottawa frequented the fort to trade. (Stone 1974, 8)

A significantly larger garrison was put in place by the British after 1761 in recognition of the increased investment required to hold the interior within the British economic network. The post had thirty-two men under arms when the post was retaken after Pontiac's Uprising in 1761. Their forces often doubled the size of the French. During British occupation, the fort intensified its military character (Stone 1974, 9). During the American Revolution, the men under arms nearly tripled. By 1781, one hundred men were stationed there under Sinclair's command (Michigan Historical Collections 1877–1929, 10:471).

Residential population growth accompanied this jump in military presence. As discussed earlier, the resident population of the initial fort was very small. Evidence from parish records indicates that after 1743 a much larger population, which included slaves as well as traders, merchants, and habitants, existed. In 1749, the engineer Lotbinière counted ten families (Gerin-Lajoie 1976, 9). In the 1760s, Alexander Henry re-

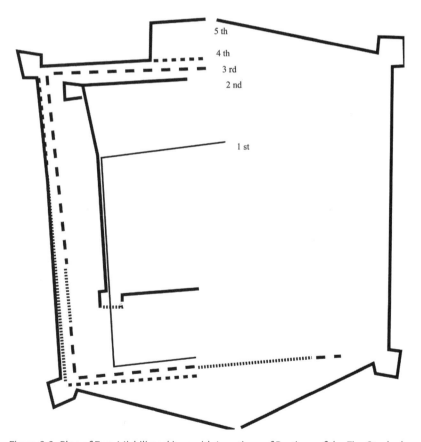

Figure 8.2 Plan of Fort Michilimackinac with Locations of Portions of the Five Stockades

ported thirty houses located entirely within the fort. Afterwards, the non-military population grew outside the stockade to the point that, in 1778, a resident trader counted nearly a hundred houses "in the Subarbs" of Fort Michilimackinac (Quaife 1928, 69).

The Material Traces of Changing Imperial Logistics
The Archaeology of Expansion

The sequence of stockade changes in size and configuration, shown in Figure 8.2, provides telling clues about economic and organizational changes that the Straits of Mackinac was undergoing during a period of increasing complexity in the fur trade network (1715–1781). As Table 8.1 shows, at least five stockades can be identified and dated.[3] Heldman's (1991, 201–209; Heldman and Grange 1981, 7–8) sequence of stockades is followed in Table 8.1 with some changes in interpretation. The first two (and perhaps others) were constructed prior to about 1733 with little regard for investment in permanent structures. Available archaeological evidence points to these structures as having been square stockades of relatively uniform size.

Archaeological evidence shows that the second of these posts was built on the sandy beach on a position downslope from the first post in a manner implying a need to adjust to a progressive drop in lake elevation. The level of Lake Michigan had dropped at least a meter as a result of the waning of the Little Ice Age (Larsen 1985a, 1985b). It seems that lake levels had a bearing on the preferred position of the water gate at the fort, which evidently was positioned as close to the lakeshore as practical. Alexander Henry (1969, 41) reported that the stockade line of the 1760s stood practically on the storm beach of eighteenth-century Lake Michigan. Since the establishment of the fort, lake levels had been oscillating steadily downward according to observations recorded in 1749 (Gerin-La-

---

3. The general sequence of successive fortifications was established by Maxwell and Binford (1961) through comparison of the first year's archaeological findings with various written accounts and with three maps made after the British undertook the modifications that created the fifth post. Subsequent fieldwork reinforced that picture, but not without uncomfortable gaps at certain places (Brown 1973; Miller and Stone 1970, 14; Stone 1974). Additional written records assist in providing greater precision. One in particular was a scaled map and accompanying description made by Lotbinière in 1749 (Gerin-Lajoie 1976). The text tells us that the fort was enlarged in 1744 by adding an outer palisade encircling the preexisting stockade line about one toise wide (equal to 6.4 English feet). These, and other details, settled an outstanding issue about the size and timing of fort expansion during the French occupation and allow for ready dating of all of the archaeological features except those associated with the second post.

Table 8.1 Sequence of Stockades with Estimated Sizes

Phase	Layout	Date	Area (m²)*
Stockade 1	square	1715–17	3190†
Stockade 2	square		3190
Stockade 3	rectangular	c.1733	7150
Stockade 4	rectangular	1744	7980‡
Stockade 5	pentagonal	a.1766	9070

* Excluding bastions.

† The first two stockades enclosed only about 3190m² if we use the distance between the north and south walls as a measure of both north-south and east-west dimensions. The distance between the north wall (F5) and the likely south wall (F273) for the initial fort is about the same as the distance between the north wall (F81) and the likely south wall (F241) of the second post. This correspondence, which differs from that made by Stone (1974), takes advantage of information acquired in the 1967–69 excavation. Enclosures of about 56.5m on a side are indicated for each. These distances are close enough to a multiple of the toise, a unit of measurement in common use by French engineers, to constitute the basis for credible dimensions. Stockade sides of 29 toises provide a close match: this length is equivalent to 174 French feet (185.3 English feet = 56.5m). A square of such a dimension would enclose an area of 841 sq. toises.

‡ Lotbinière included the bastions in his statement of side dimensions: "The sides measure from forty-seven *toises* [282 French ft. = 91.5m] up to fifty-three [318 French ft. = 103m], outside dimensions. The bastions have faces of eighteen and twenty feet and flanks of eight [5.8, 9.1, and 2.6m, respectively]" (Gerin-Lajoie 1974).

joie 1976, 9–10) and 1769 (Peckham 1938, 10–11). The preponderance of evidence points to this replacement installation as being of the same size and general square shape as the initial post.

In contrast, the third stockade, constructed around 1733, marked a change from fortified posts with temporary quarters for traders, habitants, and voyagers to a trade village with permanent quarters. A twofold increase in area marked the single greatest increase in the area enclosed by the fort since subsequent replacements added only relatively small estimated increases in space (see Table 8.1). This areal increment was coincident with a major change in settlement function. Heldman (1991) has shown that the site conformed to a standard town model organized according to a traditional rectangular format in which the long side faced the water.

The fourth post is represented by the construction of an outer stockade reinforced with corner bastions. Preparations against the British at the beginning of King George's War in 1744 led the French Crown to invest again in the fort by upgrading its military preparedness with corner bastions and the creation of an interior sentry beat between the palisade and the various private plots (see Figure 8.2).

By 1766, the British implemented a long overdue rebuilding embodied in the fifth post (see Figure 8.2). The aging structure they inherited was already more than two decades old. The major change in plan was the creation of the final hexagonal outline that modified the lakeside and opposite landward walls by bending outward the straight curtain alignments of previous walls (Heldman 1991). The space thereby created provided room for improved storage and military facilities (Maxwell and Binford 1961). Starting from the aftermath of Pontiac's Uprising, the British Crown attempted to consolidate existing military infrastructure and to invest in more permanent new facilities. Only upon their realization in 1780 that the post was vulnerable to attack by land from Americans did they abandon the south-side location for a more defensible position on Mackinac Island.

In sum, the first fifteen years or so of Michilimackinac's history on the southern straits was that of a post scarcely differentiated from others. The archaeological evidence points to a static, perhaps standard, plan. With new demands that the extended trade network placed on Michilimackinac, a protected town site was established in place of the earlier installation. The fort area was greatly expanded with a larger permanent population within. The impermanence of the early forts that such relocation implies stands in marked contrast with later stability, affirmed by civilian property rights within the stockade. Following fort plans represented consolidations of the existing location with minimal expansions.

Occupational Specialization

What archaeological evidence pertains to the period of doubling of the fort's area? First, new specialized structures are incorporated for the first time. The powder magazine presumably falls in the same relative position (Heldman 1991, 201; Heldman and Grange 1981, 7–8). The church of Ste. Anne was constructed within the stockade.[4]

Second, the land within the palisade became subdivided into private lots laid out on a uniform grid (Maxwell and Binford 1961, 34). Plots

---

4. Circumstantial evidence indicates that the parish church of Ste. Anne was incorporated into this enlarged post. The parish register states that a new church had been built by 1743, a year before the military strengthening of 1744 (Maxwell and Binford 1961, 33). Evidently, this was a replacement for another structure. The maps made in 1749 and in the 1760s show the church as being located in a space between the west-wall positions of the second and third stockades. Tellingly, in the three maps made after 1765, the walls of the church and priests' house are drawn further away from the stockade than the row houses in the southwest quadrant of the fort, thereby suggesting that the rebuilding of the post as a town site accommodated the placement of the walls to the church rather than the opposite.

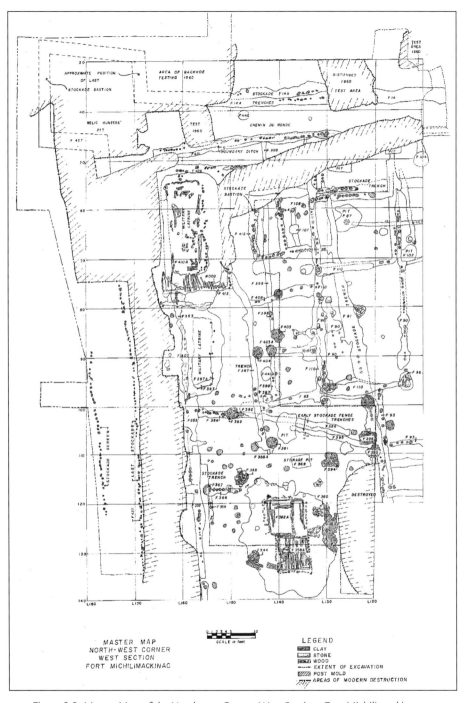

Figure 8.3 Master Map of the Northwest Corner, West Section, Fort Michilimackinac

within the fort were sold clearly to underwrite the cost of expansion in infrastructure (Wisconsin Historical Collections 1855–1911, 18:83). That the French would have selected such a method of internal improvement is entirely consistent with the self-supporting nature of their fur trade infrastructure (Innis 1962; Binford 1961). However, before this was fully implemented, the newly available space was occupied by buildings positioned on the former property alignments. An example of such construction in the northwest quadrant is the Early Northwest Rowhouse excavated in 1967 (Brown 1973) (Figure 8.3).

Archaeological evidence shows that the enclosed land created by the third stockade was not completely built upon before the stockade reinforcement of 1744. The row houses in the far southwest corner were erected after the fourth stockade was established. All of the row houses are recorded in place by 1749 on the map of Lotbinière (Gerin-Lajoie 1976).

It can be assumed that there would be considerable resistance to major changes in lot boundaries once these lots had been sold. Minor adjustments—subdivisions—are confirmed from what little archaeological evidence is available. One example of extension to property is illustrated by the increase in the depth of the garden plots in the southwest at the expense of the breadth of the chemin-de-ronde (sentry vent) during the British regime (Brown 1973) (Figure 8.4).

After 1761 British commanders steadily sought to buy out privately owned plots in order to build military facilities to accommodate an expanded presence at the site. Expansion of civilian population was confined to the area surrounding the fort (Maxwell and Binford 1961).

The new burden placed upon the fort led to expansion allowing the permanent residences that traders and other service personnel would require. It is probably not accidental that sometime before 1743 the church was moved from its location among the Indian population to serve the more demanding European parishioners living at the fort (Maxwell and Binford 1961, 33–34). Among the support personnel specifically mentioned is a blacksmith who was evidently under exclusive contract with the Jesuit priests for both White and Indian clients (Armour 1976).

Building Permanence

Housing types responded indirectly to transportation efficiency through the capacity to support a larger permanent population. Michilimackinac was well known as having miserable housing. Every visitor from 1749 to 1780 describes the domestic housing in the most disparaging terms. Only

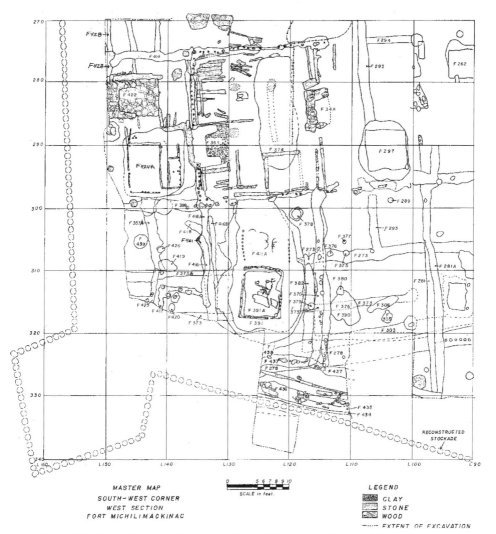

Figure 8.4 Master Map of the Southwest Corner, West Section, Fort Michilimackinac

with the fourth stockade do the number of structures with floors elevated above the ground surface increase. But not until the fifth stockade does this trend become striking. When the British had the capability to invest in facilities meant to last longer than a mere decade, habitations shifted primarily to poteaux-sur-sole (posts-on-sill), and several British military structures incorporated limestone into their foundations. Even more structures incorporated this building material in other ways. When the post was moved to the island in 1781, permanent military and trading facilities were incorporated into the plan from the outset (Armour and Widder 1978).

It is significant that Fort Michilimackinac was constructed with curtain walls of wooden posts driven without preparation into the sand. Although archaeological post holes scarcely reach 0.5m below the present-day ground surface, Lotbinière stated that "This fort is built of Cedar posts 12 feet high [13.2 Br. ft.= 4m] above the ground" (Gerin-Lajoie 1976, 4, 6). The resulting construction was destined to last about a dozen years before serious post failure threatened the stockade. Investment was minimal, thereby in keeping with the flexibility that the distance effect imposed. Such construction techniques were no commentary on French engineering skills, since the well-built stone constructions at Fortress Louisbourg and Fort de Chartres testify to the architectural achievements to which they were capable, provided their will to invest (Keene 1991). Whereas both Louisbourg and Fort de Chartres were deemed of prime strategic importance, posts such as Fort Michilimackinac were regarded as of decidedly lesser value to a financially stretched colonial administration.

The same minimal investment was brought to the construction of military, commercial, and private housing at the fort. Up to the post enlargement of the 1730s, all structures were of the inherently impermanent kind, that is, poteaux-en-terre (posts-in-ground) (Heldman 1991). Walls built by seating posts directly into the ground were as impermanent as they were cheap. Little commitment to place was inherent in this type of construction. Starting with the third stockade, the distinctive pilaster pits marking the foundations for the main support uprights of poteaux-sur-sole construction are present. The 1749 map of Lotbinière keys out seventeen of forty structures as plank-covered with the "planche" notation (Heldman 1991). Notable exceptions were the church and the missionary's house, which were built of stacked and dressed log construction (piece-sur-piece). These two structures were unusual for the permanence of their construction. Indeed, they were deemed solid enough to be among the structures the British transported to Mackinac Island on the winter ice of 1780–1781. More permanent construction would await the investment that a more financially solvent British administration could provide (Binford 1961). The military invested in freestone foundations of limestone to support the soldiers' barracks (F3) and the provisions storehouse (F21) that were constructed in 1769 and 1772/1773 respectively (Maxwell and Binford 1961; Stone 1974). Among the domestic dwellings during this period, the third and last rebuilding of SSW House 1 had a limestone flag floor (Brown 1973). Investment at the fort took place first with use of elevating buildings on pilasters and later on foundations of limestone.

Subsistence Trends

Archaeological measures of building construction, subsistence trends, and artifact trends provide material confirmation for the trends delineated by documentary evidence. Canoe load increases account for a rise in imported goods after 1730 and find their trace in the number of trade goods in archaeological context (e.g., glass seed beads). Improvements in the transportation of foodstuffs in bulk has an impact on the shift away from the consumption of locally available meat, particularly fish, and toward increased use of domesticated animals. Pressure on the availability of a sufficient variety of food is related to on-site agricultural improvements in the form of the investment in manured gardens and the number of edible plant remains after 1760.

In his forward-looking "Comparison of the Faunal Remains from French and British Refuse Pits at Fort Michilimackinac: A Study in Changing Subsistence Patterns," Charles Cleland (1970) pointed out the similarities of early French subsistence practices to Native American ones and also the degree that both differed from British ones (see also Cleland 1988; Noble 1983; Scott 1985; Shapiro 1979). Although earlier research focused on the effect of national identity or ethnicity (see Binford 1961; Maxwell and Binford 1961; Stone 1974), subsequent analysis has shown the ethnic connection to be inconclusive (Scott 1985). Trends identified over time are secure. They mark the change away from fish-eating dependence and toward foodstuffs preferred in a European diet. Since these foodstuffs are either not grown locally or are raised only with difficulty, more effective transport had to be made. As transportation links strengthened beyond the limitations of the three-man canoe, provisioning patterns changed, with imported grains, domestic animals, sugar, and tea entering the system, albeit somewhat differentially.

A change in the character of the occupation is accompanied by the deposition of a heavy humic, clay-rich stratigraphic deposit that is strikingly different from the stained sand of preceding occupations. This change is reasonably attributed to the deliberate use of manure to enrich the garden soil. While a benefit to defense, the spit of sandy land at the south shore location was ill suited for agriculture, and this windy location sacrificed comfort to exigency (Gerin-Lajoie 1976, 8). Peter Pond reported that "the Land about Macenac is Varey Baren a mear Sand Bank But the Gareson By Nanure Rase Good Protaters and Sum Vegatabels," dismissing it as a sand bank that only came to yield crops after improvement through manuring (Gates 1965, 32). Even so improved, the location at the straits continued to have a history of being too mist-covered in the growing season for reliable maize production (Blake 1981; Blake and Cutler 2001). The maize cobs recovered from the garden of SSW House 2 were small in length in keeping with varieties that required few growing days. Clearly, the French counted on provisioning the post from the nearby region. Consequently, outside food sources had to be secured to sustain the entrepôt.

Much produce came from Cross Village, twenty miles down the Lake Michigan coast. Pond reported that "thare is Sum Injan Villeges twentey or thirtey Miles in ye from this Plase whare the Natives Improve Verey Go[o]d Ground thay rase Corn Beens and Meney artickels which thay youse in Part ftem Selves and Bring the Remainder to Marke[t]" (Gates 1965, 32). As this source became increasingly insufficient, additional food was secured by boat from Detroit and Fort Erie (Quaife 1928, 75). In preparation for the removal of Fort Michilimackinac in 1779, the commissary at the fort received substantial quantities of "rum, [wheat] flour, pork, pease, butter and oatmeal." These provisions were intended for the "Garrison & Navy at Michilimackinac, for artificers & others on the Island & for Indians" (Michigan Historical Collections 1877–1929, 9:655). During the American Revolution, the British shipped their cargoes on armed sloops (9:657).

The humic soil buildup of the Late Occupation Zone (Stone's [1974] "British Zone") was evidently initiated mainly after the British took over the fort. When ceramic and pipestem-bore date averages are used to estimate the median age span of occupational use, it can be assumed that as much time transpired before this median as elapsed up to abandonment in 1781. The lower range of the median falls shortly after the installation of the fourth stockade in 1744, but the garden land connected with SSW Houses 1 and 2 have inception dates fully a dozen years later in the early 1760s, according to the later dates for these ceramic assemblages (Table 8.2). Using a slightly different method, Heldman and Grange (1981, 148) report a ceramic date for this zone (their "Black Sandy Loam") of 1762 ± 11. However, the westernmost house of the southernmost tier of row houses was absent on the map of 1749. The end date is documented archaeologically by the deposit of an upper lens of the Late Occupation Zone that was found to overlay the initial trench of the fifth curtain wall on the south. The upshot of these differences highlights the uneven land-use development within the stockade as well as a stepped-up tempo of occupation with each successive decade.

Large-scale provisioning of the fort's garrison and its inhabitants appears to have grown during the British period to the point where it became

Table 8.2 Lower Age Estimates of the Late Occupation Zone Duration[*]

Sample	Ceramic Date[†]	Pipestem Date[‡]	Mean Date	Differences	Lower Date[§]
North Midden	1762.5	1763.9	1763.2	+1.4	1745.4
Late Occupation Zone					
South Midden	1772.6	1768.9	1770.8	–3.7	1760.6
Gardens of SSW Tier of Row Houses					
SSW House 1, combined floors	1760.7	1768.1	1764.4	+7.4	1746.8
SSW House 2, floor deposit	1763.6	1765.4	1764.5	–1.8	1747.0

[*] The lower age estimates relate to Ceramic Date, Pipestem Date, and Mean Date and are drawn from Brown's (1973) calculations of Mean Artifact Date Estimates from the 1967–1969 excavations.

[†] Based on South (1977).

[‡] Based on Binford (1972).

[§] Equal to the lower limit of the median with an upper range set at 1781.

a conspicuous operation. Documentary testimony is ample during this period, particularly in the last five years of the lower peninsula location. Garden spaces that produced much-needed vegetables are indicated on the Crown map (Stone 1974). Archaeologically, remains of domesticated plants (maize, squash, pea, cabbage, and other members of the mustard family) have been recovered from both French and British deposits (Blake 1981; Blake and Cutler 1978, 2001). But Scott (1985) points out correctly that only after 1760 did cold cellars for food storage become an important feature of each of the residences at the site.

Secondary Craft Products

Lyle Stone (1974, 350–351) concluded from his evaluation of the first ten years of archaeological work that the number of trade goods increased with the third period of French occupation, now dated to the early 1730s, reflecting the growth of trade at the site. Contrary to White's (1991) conclusion, native technology did not persist in the vicinity of the post.[5] Items of primarily native use had already incorporated European materials, such as iron and sheet-brass arrowheads and brass tinkling cones. In addition,

---

5. White (1991, 138–139) accepts the dating of aboriginal artifacts at Fort Michilimackinac made by Maxwell (1964) and Stone (1970, 1:60). Most of the assemblage they cite fits the precontact Mackinac Phase, and, in any case, it is from disturbed deposits. In 1967–1969 an occupation of this phase was recovered in a sealed context beneath SSW House 2 (Brown 1973; Mainfort and Lovis n.d.).

large numbers of goods catering to an Indian market were strongly in evidence. Excavation in 1867 revealed in the floor deposits of the adjacent house (SSW House 2) large numbers of glass seed beads in linear concentrations where evidently they had dropped through the overlying puncheon floor boards. To account for such large numbers, it is likely that bulk packages of glass beads were probably stored in this dwelling.

With permanent civilian occupation came the appearance of cottage workshops for the production of items for sale to Indian clients. Craft working in catlinite is documented by the 1968 excavation. A concentration of fine residue of this mineral was discovered on the clay apron of SSW House 1.

Not only were firearms stored at the fort, but Crown policy placed at the disposal of Indians and others blacksmith facilities for the repair of arms (White 1991). Although such repair facilities were important to Indian clientage, the implementation of this policy was given over as a monopoly to the Jesuits, who funded the shops and supported the blacksmiths in return for fees. Michilimackinac was no exception (Armour 1976). Access to the forge was controlled by resident clerics with a gate behind the priests' house to regulate access. Treaty rights secured the same arrangement under British administration. The major concentration of firearm parts lay north of the priests' house in the vicinity of a blacksmithing work area. In the excavations of 1967–1969, almost all of the identifiable iron parts (many were partly reworked into unrecognizable shapes) belonged to private hunting or sporting arms. Only one Brown Bess part was found despite the arsenal of British issue annually inventoried at the post. In contrast, the lead ball ammunition was disproportionately distributed in the large calibers of the military-size range (Brown n.d.).

Conclusion

Distance parity theory provides us with a powerful framework in which to interpret the documentary and material record of the fur trade. Both system-wide studies as well as place-specific ones can be fruitfully examined in light of this theory. The focus above has been on the Straits of Mackinac during the mid-eighteenth century. The site has an advantage in examining distance effects because it has always been limited agriculturally. Thus, its population depended on contributed food to an extent that was in direct proportion to the density of population. When imperial powers were able effectively to launch a larger and more complex trade network,

Michilimackinac was directly affected by becoming a distribution center (entrepôt) after years of being little more than a fortified mission and trading post. Although Michilimackinac retained the material signature of a trading post, its size and diversity of occupation expanded considerably under these new conditions. In keeping with the minimal investment in imperial ventures, the formal shell of an entrepôt that was instituted around 1733 was slow to be fully achieved. It took many decades before support facilities grew significantly to effect the fort layout, the construction of specialized military and commercial structures, and the buildup of local responses to provisioning problems. This growth signature remains a significant pattern after the effects of defensive emergencies (viz., in 1716, 1744, 1781) are taken into account.

In the past, changes in material culture here and elsewhere have been described in terms of national identity, native acculturation, and classic economizing (e.g., Jackson 1930). A more useful approach is to examine change in such things as building construction, subsistence, and artifacts as responses to action at a distance, with the colonial stances diminishing with distance.

Europeans were increasingly called to the frontier to invest their individual labor and capitol to make the mercantile system operate. This investment was forced by the pattern of expanding regional exploitation to operate at increasingly more extended distances. The involvement of the metropolitan center in a system that increasingly looked to the bottom line was always minimally funded. This kept the system fragile with repeated shutdowns in the flows of gifts to native Americans, who saw the trade in entirely different terms from how Europeans and Americans viewed it. The latter increasingly placed capital investments on beefing up the logistics rather than the endless gifting to increase marginal returns. This applies equally to French, British, and American alike.

They also off-loaded the responsibility for direct negotiations to a local population dominated by métis. Colonial interests grew significantly by the end of the eighteenth century. At the same time, a land-hungry colonial-American population pushed over the Appalachian mountain barrier to disrupt the delicate balance in the exchange relationships provided by the métis. The accelerated growth of the Americans was critical toward tipping the evolutionary balance away from potential métis domination.

A distance parity theoretical perspective toward the eighteenth-century history of the Upper Great Lakes allows for the creation of parallel accounts for the European and Indian sides. One fruitful insight into this trade is the lessons learned from outcomes in other cultural encounters in which the protagonists vary greatly in their economic, technological, and demographic advantages. The specific histories of change varied by region, and it is here that the archaeology stands to contribute to the delineation of those histories.

All of this can be wrapped up by calling for renewed attention to larger processes than mere events and for a studied application of anthropological archaeology in the charting of the history of one of the major sectors of the world system, that of the fur trade, and the activities of this mercantile system in a transportation gateway, the Great Lakes.

Acknowledgments

I wish to thank my colleagues Tim Earle, Bill Lovis, and Gil Stein for the helpful comments they have offered. In particular, Bill Lovis provided critical help in reorganizing an earlier version of the article.

9

Subsistence Under Siege

Animal Remains from 11ML6, the Suspected Site of the 1730
Mesquakie Fort

Terrance J. Martin

For twenty-three days during the late summer of 1730, fourteen
hundred French and Indian allies laid siege to more than nine
hundred Mesquakie who were en route to west central Indiana.
Historians and archaeologists have long debated the precise location of this event. Field schools from Parkland College, Cham-
paign, Illinois, investigated site 11ML6 in east-central Illinois,
where they discovered traces of semi-subterranean structures and
early eighteenth-century artifacts. The uniqueness of the site's
faunal assemblage is considered in light of historical information
on the Mesquakies' dire situation.

CHARLES CLELAND IS renowned for his contributions to ecological anthropology, historical archaeology, and Great Lakes Native American studies. Chuck introduced me to the archaeology of the French Colonial period in 1977 when he invited me to undertake a study, conducted
in cooperation with the Tippecanoe County Historical Association, of the
subsistence practices at Fort Ouiatenon, an eighteenth-century French
fur trade post in the central Wabash Valley. The site of Fort Ouiatenon
was the subject of a six-year-long field investigation during the 1970s that
culminated in much information and data about the site and Ph.D. dissertations by Judy Tordoff, Vergil Noble, and me. Since that initial foray,
I have retained a particular fondness for (or addiction to) studies of eighteenth-century animal exploitation patterns in the Midwest and Great
Lakes region.

I first learned of the Fox Fort in 1988 at the Midwest Archaeological

Conference hosted by the University of Illinois at Champaign-Urbana. At that meeting, Lenville Stelle presented a first-year progress report on his Parkland College field school project—revisiting a site in McLean County, Illinois, that had been the object of archaeological surveys and historical investigations over the years (Brigham 1936; Burnham 1908; see also Faye 1935). Not only was the Fox Fort investigation interesting to me because of its connections to ongoing studies in the Illinois Country and to the Wea Indians to the east in the Wabash Valley, but I was intrigued by the nature of the materials that were being found there. The unusual situation of a group under siege seemed to be reflected by the site's artifact assemblage. Surely, dietary remains under conditions of severe hostility should present a signature quite different from what we would find at a typical habitation site.

Everyone acquainted with Chuck Cleland knows how he enjoys the occasional atypical research topic; for example, Late Pleistocene caribou phalanges, Jesuit finger rings, Ojibwa symbolism on shale discs, and alleged astronomical stone circles on islands in northern Lake Michigan (Cleland 1965, 1972, 1985; Prahl et al. 1990). As a consequence, Chuck's festschrift provided the perfect incentive to initiate an analysis of the faunal assemblage that accrued over four years of excavation at site 11ML6. The project also recalls a theme that Chuck preaches to his archaeology students when they first become involved with historical materials. To quote Chuck from his 1988 article in *Historical Archaeology,* "Questions of Substance, Questions that Count," unlike prehistoric archaeology, historical archaeology

> has the potential to provide independent tests of propositions using two distinct and fairly reliable data sets, that is written/oral as well as archaeological data. Scientific methodology calls for hypotheses drawn from one data set to be tested by another. (Cleland 1988, 15)

Historical Background

The historical confrontation between New France and the Mesquakie (alias, the Fox or Renards) known as the Fox Wars (ca. 1710–1740) has been discussed and summarized in several accounts and texts (Hauser 1966; Kellogg 1908, 1925; Peyser 1980, 1987; Stelle 1989), the most recent being the comprehensive book by David Edmunds and Joseph Peyser (1993). Also recommended is an article by Stelle (1992a).

Briefly summarized, in early June of 1730 the Mesquakies sought safety from the French by sending runners—both to the east to appeal to the Senecas and to the Wabash Valley to secure safe passage through the lands of the Weas and Miamis. Some nine hundred Mesquakies (three hundred warriors, six hundred women and children) departed southern Wisconsin. According to three primary accounts—the official report filed by Lt. de Villiers, commandant at the St. Joseph River; a narrative by an unnamed person from Fort de Chartres under the direction of Lt. Robert Groston de St. Anges; and the narrative of Jean-Baptiste Reaume, the interpreter for the Indians living along the River St. Joseph—a confrontation near Starved Rock between several Cahokias and Mesquakies resulted in the discovery of the Mesquakie's plan (Stelle 1992a, 301–304; Thwaites 1906, 109–118). The alarm was sent out to the Kickapoos and Mascoutens as well as to the French at Fort de Chartres and to the French and their Indian allies along the St. Joseph River. The Mesquakies set off onto the Grand Prairie and continued moving to the east in hope of alluding their enemies. In early August, Cahokia warriors again encountered the Mesquakies, who were camped in a small grove of trees. By the tenth of August, approximately fourteen hundred men at arms surrounded the Mesquakie camp, which had been loosely fortified by this time. A siege continued into September, with the allied forces now including warriors from some of the Illini tribes as well as from the Mascoutens, Kickapoos, Sauk, Potawatomi, Miamis, Piankashaws, Weas, and even the Hurons. As the siege wore on, some Indian allies began sympathizing with the Mesquakies and smuggled food to them, while some others left the battle altogether. On the eighth of September the Mesquakies took advantage of a severe thunderstorm to escape their fort during the night. Although children's crying alerted the French sentries, pursuit was postponed until daylight. At dawn, the French and their allies caught up with the Mesquakies some "8 leagues" (ca. nineteen miles) from the fort (Stelle 1992a, 270). The Fort de Chartres narrative reported that only fifty to sixty unarmed Mesquakie men escaped.

The Search for the Fox Fort

At least ten possible locations for the Fox Fort have been discussed in the historical literature, but claims for each are ambiguous and speculative regarding distances, directions, and landmarks (Stelle 1992a, 272). The Arrowsmith site in McLean County is located in the headwaters of the Sangamon River, approximately eighty statute miles east and south of

Starved Rock (Figure 9.1). Although this site was investigated in 1897 and during the 1930s, the earlier collection is lost and the later collections (reportedly at the McLean County Historical Museum) are incomplete and may include artifacts with no recorded provenance from other sites (see Stelle 1992a, 276–278).

The Fort de Chartres narrative describes the Mesquakie fort as being in a small grove of trees on a gentle slope on the west and northwest side of a small river. "Their cabins were very small and excavated in the earth like the burrows of the foxes from which they take their name" (Thwaites 1906, 111, quoted by Stelle 1992a, 269). The Reaume narrative provides more details of the fort itself with descriptions of internal and external

Figure 9.1 Location of Site 11ML6 in Illinois

ditches, subterranean cabins, and covered pathways. At the Arrowsmith site, Stelle (1992a, 274) points out, "The presumed location of the fort is upon the crest of a small knoll [5m above the floodplain], 250m east of the confluence of an unnamed tributary" to the Sangamon River. The drainage and slope of this knoll is generally northwest to southeast.

At least six maps of the 1730 Mesquakie siege have survived. The Fort de Chartres narrative is associated with a map titled *Carte du Fort* that was produced in New Orleans seven months after the event. Two additional maps found in the National Library in Paris were drawn by members of the St. Joseph River contingent (Peyser 1987). Stelle (1992a, 271) suggests that the *Fort des Renards* map may have been drawn at the site and that it may have served as a model for the *Sauvages Renards attaqués* map.

Recent Archaeological Investigations

The Parkland College field schools from 1988 through 1991 employed infrared aerial survey, an uncontrolled surface collection of cultivated farmlands, a follow-up controlled surface collection, a shovel probe survey over the top of the knoll, a metal detector survey, and excavation of forty-seven trenches and test units totaling 104m² (Stelle 1992b). The excavations exposed fifteen semi-subterranean structures, eight connecting ditches, and five unusual subsurface features (see Figure 9.2). Pieces of cattail matting were found preserved in two structures, which, along with rafters and

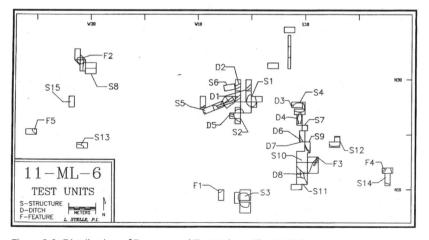

Figure 9.2 Distribution of Features and Test Units at Site 11ML6

banked earth, seemed to have been part of the roofing system. The ditches were 50cm wide and extended to 50cm below the ground surface. No clear evidence of a perimeter ditch or palisade was found, but the area of occupation seems to be approximately 50m by 70m, which corresponds quite well with the just under 58.5m² (= 1 arpent) size indicated by the *Sauvages Renards attaques* map.

More than two hundred artifacts were recovered, but perhaps most impressive are the fifty-eight spent musket balls comprising 28 percent of the artifact assemblage, along with gunflints, gun parts, iron knives, and, from French Louisiana, a brass military button. European glass beads suggest a time range of 1719 to 1731. Objects of Native American manufacture include fourteen sherds featuring a Bell type I rim sherd, a stone pipe, three pieces of catlinite, eighteen chipped stone hafted bifaces including arrow points and some Late Archaic–Early Woodland projectiles, three brass arrowheads, and eleven brass tinkling cones. An Indian presence dating to the first half of the eighteenth century is clearly indicated, and the artifacts and architectural features are also consistent with the site of a battle. Although it is most difficult to conclusively demonstrate the presence of French and Mesquakie combatants, it is important to remember that the French contingent consisted of fewer than two hundred habitants and coureur de bois, and their encampment was more than a half-mile from the fort (Stelle 1992b).

Dietary Considerations

Historical Accounts

When contemplating what the Mesquakie diet was like under such a dire situation as the 1730 siege, we can look to the various narratives along with other historical accounts. When the Mesquakies established their camp in the tree grove, "hunters scoured the surrounding prairies, hunting meat for their trek to the Wea villages along the Wabash" (Edmunds and Peyser 1993, 137), and returned with several bison and white-tailed deer (141). It was while stalking bison on the prairie southeast of their camp that they encountered Cahokia hunting parties (137). During the siege that followed, the Mesquakies held secret meetings with the Sauk and Weas and persuaded them to share some of their surplus food. Despite this, the Mesquakies' food supplies diminished (146–147). So, minimally we would expect to find bones from bison and white-tailed deer in the 11ML6 refuse. The Mesquakies might have also been opportunistic and consumed animal species that they would not ordinarily consider as a source of meat under less trying situations.

Archaeozoological Remains

Soil conditions at the site are not conducive for the preservation of animal remains, and the hard clay rendered many smaller bones into "stains" that could not be easily extracted from their matrix. Many of the large mammal bones were highly fragmented. Because of their fragile condition, most concentrations of bones or teeth were taken out in clay blocks and wrapped in aluminum foil. In order to analyze the faunal assemblage, it was necessary to soften the hard clay nodules by slowly squirting drops of water on the matrix and then carefully removing bones and teeth with probes or tweezers. As a result, the total volume of animal remains following the extraction and analysis was reduced from .311m³ (11 sq. ft.) to .056m³ (2 sq. ft.).

The faunal assemblage consists of 1,084 animal remains having a total weight of just over 3,600g (Table 9.1). Mammals contributed 98 percent by specimen count and 99.6 percent by specimen weight. Some remains of modern animals were intrusive into the eighteenth-century deposit. Recent animals include sheep or goat, opossum, eastern cottontail, and ring-neck pheasant. Archaeologists also encountered poorly preserved concentrations of bones from at least two juvenile pigs. The intrasite distribution of the faunal assemblage is presented in Table 9.2.

The most conspicuous species in the assemblage is bison (which includes fifteen definite bison specimens, five "cf. bison" remains, and twenty-one fragmentary "*Bison/Bos*" bones and teeth). A minimum of two adult individuals are indicated by left distal tibiae, right distal tibiae, and right distal humeri. At least one subadult individual is represented by a deciduous premolar and a proximal radius. Due to their large size, eight additional tooth fragments and two long-bone shaft pieces could *conceivably* be from either bison, cattle, or elk, but the assemblage did not have any bones or teeth that were positively identified as elk. These remains are referred to as "Unidentified Artiodactyl" in the species composition tables. Although no cranial bones were identified, nearly 40 percent of the bison (or large bovid) specimens are isolated teeth. All other skeletal portions are represented, however (Table 9.3). One of the thoracic vertebra spines has knife cuts, and one of the rib fragments was chopped.

Canid remains are slightly more plentiful with forty-seven specimens.

Table 9.1 Species Composition of Animal Remains from 11ML6

	NISP*	MNI†	NISP Wt (g)	Comments
MAMMALS				
Opossum, *Didelphis virginianus*	2	1	11.4	Modern intrusive
Eastern cottontail, *Sylvilagus floridanus*	1	1	.6	Modern intrusive
Beaver, *Castor canadensis*	10	1	20.0	
Unidentified medium rodent	1	1	.2	
cf. Wolf, *Canis* cf. *lupus*	2	1	3.4	
Dog/coyote/wolf, *Canis* sp.	45	4	69.8	
Raccoon, *Procyon lotor*	1	1	2.5	
Swine, *Sus scrofa*	22	2	615.0	Modern intrusive
White-tailed deer, *Odocoileus virginianus*	3	1	6.6	
Sheep/goat, *Ovis/Capra*	2	1	22.7	Modern intrusive
cf. Cattle, *Bos taurus*	1	1	41.5	Modern?
Bison, *Bison bison*	15	2	937.8	
cf. Bison, *Bison bison*	5	—	82.3	
Bison/cattle, *Bison/Bos*	21	—	274.5	
Unidentified artiodactyl	10	—	13.8	
Unidentified very large mammal	141	—	742.7	
Unidentified large mammal	546	—	665.5	
Unidentified medium/large mammal	237	—	79.9	
Unidentified small mammal	1	—	.1	
BIRDS				
Great blue heron, *Ardea herodias*	1	1	2.2	
Ring-necked pheasant, *Phasianus colchicus*	2	1	2.7	Modern intrusive
FISH				
Freshwater drum, *Aplodinotus grunniens*	11	1	.8	
UNIDENTIFIED VERTEBRATA	1	—	.3	
BIVALVES				
Fatmucket, *Lampsilis siliquoidea*	1	1	7.4	
Unidentified mussel	2	—	1.6	
Totals	1,084	21	3,605.3	

*NISP, number of identified specimens.

†Minimum minimum number of individuals estimates (MNI[min]) based on assemblage as a whole, ignoring features designations.

Table 9.2 Distribution of Animal Remains (Number of Identified Specimens) from 11ML6

	Structures													
	2	3	4	5	6	7	8	9	10	11	12	13	14	15
MAMMALS														
Opossum	—	—	—	—	—	—	—	—	—	—	—	—	—	—
Eastern cottontail	—	—	—	—	—	—	—	—	—	—	—	—	—	—
Beaver	—	10	—	—	—	—	—	—	—	—	—	—	—	—
Unidentified medium rodent	—	—	—	—	—	—	1	—	—	—	—	—	—	—
cf. Wolf	—	2	—	—	—	—	—	—	—	—	—	—	—	—
Dog/coyote/wolf	5	5	3	—	21	—	2	—	—	—	1	1	2	—
Raccoon	—	—	—	—	—	—	—	—	—	—	—	—	—	—
Swine	—	—	—	—	—	—	—	—	—	—	—	—	—	—
White-tailed deer	—	—	—	—	—	—	1	—	—	—	1	—	1	—
Sheep/goat	—	—	—	—	—	—	—	—	—	—	—	—	—	—
cf. Cattle	—	—	—	—	—	—	—	—	1	—	—	—	—	—
Bison	—	7	—	—	3	—	1	—	—	1	—	—	—	—
cf. Bison	—	1	—	1	—	—	1	—	—	—	—	1	—	1
Bison/cattle	—	2	—	—	—	1	2	—	4	4	1	1	1	1
Unidentified artiodacty	1	—	—	—	—	—	—	1	—	2	3	—	—	1
Unidentified very large mammal	—	15	—	2	2	2	13	—	8	17	—	2	6	3
Unidentified large mammal	—	108	15	3	17	6	35	—	58	66	4	39	59	2
Unidentified medium/large mammal	26	18	1	2	111	1	5	—	17	9	1	—	1	—
Unidentified small mammal	—	—	—	—	—	—	—	—	1	—	—	—	—	—
BIRDS														
Great blue heron	—	—	—	—	—	—	—	—	—	—	—	—	—	—
Ring-necked pheasant	—	—	—	—	—	—	—	—	—	—	—	—	—	—
FISH														
Freshwater drum	—	11	—	—	—	—	—	—	—	—	—	—	—	—
Unidentified vertebrata	—	—	—	—	—	—	—	—	—	—	—	—	—	—
BIVALVES														
Fatmucket	—	—	—	—	—	—	—	—	—	—	—	—	—	—
Unidentified mussel	—	—	—	—	—	—	—	—	—	1	—	—	—	—
Totals: NISP	32	181	19	8	154	10	62	1	91	99	11	44	70	8
Totals: NISP Wt (g)	23.0	558.4	14.1	55.0	81.9	28.1	261.5	14.0	259.1	581.1	11.6	110.8	269.3	71.1

Table 9.2 Distribution of Animal Remains (Number of Identified Specimens) from 11ML6 (continued)

	Ditches			Features		All Other Areas	Grand Totals
	1	2	4	2	3		
MAMMALS							
Opossum	—	—	—	—	—	2	2
Eastern cottontail	—	—	—	—	—	1	1
Beaver	—	—	—	—	—	—	10
Unidentified medium rodent	—	—	—	—	—	—	1
cf. Wolf	—	—	—	—	—	—	2
Dog/coyote/wolf	—	—	—	—	5	—	45
Raccoon	—	—	—	—	—	1	1
Swine	—	—	—	—	—	22	22
White-tailed deer	—	—	—	—	—	—	3
Sheep/goat	—	—	—	—	—	2	2
cf. Cattle	—	—	—	—	—	—	1
Bison	—	—	—	—	—	3	15
cf. Bison	—	—	—	—	—	—	5
Bison/cattle	—	—	—	—	—	4	21
Unidentified artiodactyl	—	—	—	—	—	—	10
Unidentified very large mammal	1	—	—	—	5	64	141
Unidentified large mammal	1	1	2	1	2	125	546
Unidentified medium/large mammal	—	—	—	11	—	34	237
Unidentified small mammal	—	—	—	—	—	—	1
BIRDS							
Great blue heron	—	—	—	—	—	1	1
Ring-necked pheasant	—	—	—	—	—	2	2
FISH							
Freshwater drum	—	—	—	—	—	—	11
Unidentified vertebrata	—	—	—	—	—	1	1
BIVALVES							
Fatmucket	—	—	—	—	—	1	1
Unidentified mussel	—	—	—	—	—	1	2
Totals: NISP	1	1	2	12	12	264	1,084
Totals: NISP Wt (g)	2.8	2.8	16.7	2.9	20.9	1,220.2	3,605.3

Table 9.3 Skeletal Portions of Bison, cf. Bison, Bison/cattle, and Artiodactyl (Number of Identified Specimens) from 11ML6

Skeletal Portion	Structures											Misc. Areas	Total NISP	%
	3	5	6	7	8	10	11	12	13	14	15			
Cranial elements	—	—	—	—	—	—	—	—	—	—	—	—	0	—
Isolated teeth	2	—	2	1	3	2	—	4	1	1	1	3	20	39.2
Vertebrae	4	—	—	—	1	—	1	—	—	—	—	—	6	11.8
Ribs	2	—	—	—	—	2	—	—	—	—	—	—	4	7.8
Proximal forequarter	—	1	—	—	—	2	2	—	—	—	—	1	6	11.8
Innominate bone	1	—	—	—	—	—	—	—	—	—	—	—	1	2.0
Proximal hindquarter	3	—	—	—	—	—	3	—	1	—	1	1	9	17.6
Lower legs and feet	—	—	1	—	1	—	—	—	—	1	1	2	5	9.8
Totals	12	1	3	1	5	6	6	4	2	1	3	7	51	100.0

A mandibular fourth premolar and first molar, both from the left side and both from the same test unit within Structure 3, compare favorably to wolf in size and morphology. The remaining specimens are probably from domestic dogs with a minimum of four individuals indicated by right fourth upper premolars. Overall, teeth contribute 64 percent of all canid specimens, and foot bones add an additional 17 percent. The underrepresentation of cranial and postcranial bones may reflect soil conditions that are unfavorable for bone preservation. Stelle's discussion of the 11ML6 excavations includes mention of a black bear canine tooth (Stelle 1992a, 300). Inspection of this tooth in the laboratory after cleaning reveals that it is instead from a large canid—a large dog or possibly wolf.

Unusual for American Indian faunal assemblages in the Midwest, white-tailed deer remains are rare. Only three specimens were recovered, two teeth and a calcaneus, from three different structures. This seems to reflect the prairie habitat setting of 11ML6 and an apparent concentration on bison by the hunters from the site.

Beaver is represented by ten specimens, which include one cranial fragment, eight teeth, and an ilium. All of these are probably from the same individual, and all were found within Structure 3. While removing a beaver ilium from its clay matrix, I discovered eleven isolated freshwater drum pharangeal teeth. These are the only fish remains from the assemblage. Because of the context of these specimens, the association seems to be more than a mere coincidence.

The only other identified specimens consist of a raccoon ulna, a great blue heron dentary, and three freshwater mussel shells.

The assemblage also includes five modified animal remains. Two large mammal long-bone shaft fragments, probably from bison, came from the northwestern part of the site. A carved and whittled fragment was found within Structure 8, and a roughly carved diamond-shaped fragment was found within a roasting pit adjacent to Structure 8 (Figure 9.3). Two "counters," possibly made from antler, were found together in Structure 3. One is round in cross-section, the other is rectangular. Both were associated with a piece of sheet brass, animal hide, and cattail vegetable fiber, and both retain a green stain (Figure 9.4). An incomplete piece of thin, green-stained, cut bone was also found in the same structure. Fossil objects are sometimes called "spirit stones" by the Mesquakie (Lenville Stelle, personal communication, 1999), and a solitary fossil horn coral was unearthed from Structure 3 (Figure 9.5). If not intriguing enough, this is also the context in which the beaver pelvis and the drum teeth were discovered. In fact, all of the beaver

Figure 9.3 Modified large mammal bones from Structure 8 (left) and the adjacent roasting pit (right).

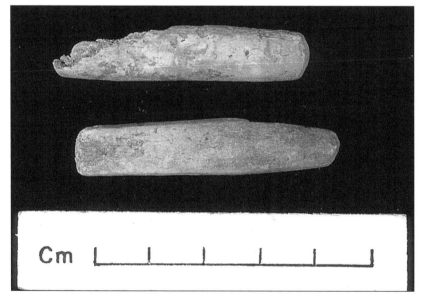

Figure 9.4 "Counters" from Structure 3

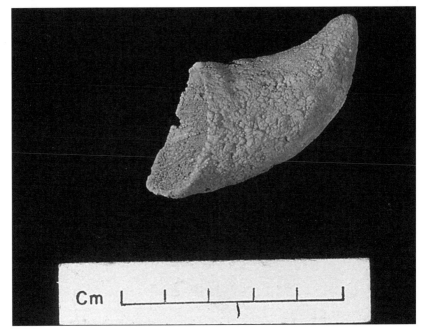

Figure 9.5 Fossil Horn Coral from Structure 3

remains, both of the wolf teeth, five dog elements, and several bison bones were found inside Structure 3 along with brass and chert arrow points, gunflints, tinkling cones, a galena cube, and seven musket balls.

The faunal assemblage from 11ML6 is not typical of a Native American habitation site of the Middle Historic period. If we refer to the Bell site in east-central Wisconsin, a major Mesquakie village only somewhat earlier in time than the 1730 siege, we see a much more complete picture of Mesquakie subsistence (Parmalee 1963). There, fishing for lake sturgeon and large catfish was important, along with the pursuit of beaver and white-tailed deer. Black bears and domestic dogs were afforded considerable ceremony, and dogs were occasionally eaten. Skulls of otter and fisher were apparently part of medicine bundles, and a variety of other bones were modified into tools, weapons, and gaming pieces.

Conclusion

When the Mesquakie made their desperate attempt to cross the vast prairie of the Illinois Country en route to the Wabash and farther east, the

French narratives state that they hunted bison and deer and attempted to accumulate meat to feed their families during the difficult trek. When intercepted and surrounded by their French and Indian enemies, they managed to obtain some meat from sympathetic Sauk and Weas.

Inspection of animal remains from 11ML6 provides a picture consistent with our expectations. Bison was the major prey item at this site, and dogs may have been used as an emergency food item during the siege. Modified bones in the way of counters and gaming pieces would also not be out of place at the Bell site in Wisconsin. Perhaps the beaver pelvis and freshwater drum teeth, fossil horn corral, wolf teeth, and beaver skull were part of one or more medicine bundles that were left inside a temporary semi-subterranean cabin within a makeshift palisade. No human remains were identified, and this also seems consistent with what we know about the events that morning following the severe thunderstorm when the Mesquakies made their desperate escape, only to be pursued and caught some miles away from the little grove of trees.

In a brief review of the Middle Historic period, Carol Mason wrote:

> The Bell site is a moment in the lives of the Fox, frozen in time, and one of the major anchors for an understanding of them in the Historic period. Other moments, of just as great significance, have yet to be identified. . . .
>
> Literally and figuratively, archaeologists have just begun to scratch the surface of the history of the people called "Fox." (Mason 1998, 314–315)

Site 11ML6 remains a serious candidate for the so-called Fox Fort in Illinois. The faunal assemblage joins with the cartographic and artifact data sets in providing additional support for the proposition that 11ML6 is, in fact, the location of the 1730 Mesquakie siege.

Acknowledgments

I would like to thank Lenville Stelle (Parkland College) for allowing me to analyze the faunal assemblage from 11ML6 and for freely sharing maps and other information of his findings during and since his fieldwork. Subsequent to the analysis and inventory of the field school collection at Parkland College, all artifacts and records from 11ML6 were donated in 1996 by Mr. and Mrs. Wayne Smith, the property owners of the site, to the Illinois State Museum for curation. We are indebted to the Smiths for their conscientiousness. The map that constitutes Figure 9.2 was drafted by Len Stelle, and the photographs in Figures 9.3 through 9.5 were produced by Gary Andrashko of the Illinois State Museum. And last, but not least, thanks to Chuck Cleland for encouraging students to pursue not only "questions of substance" and "questions that count," but also for urging us to appreciate the "thrills and satisfactions of discovery" that contribute to "the romance of archaeology" (Cleland 1994).

10

Guess Who Sat Down to Dinner?

Archaeology-In-Laws

Neal Ferris

RECENT DECADES have done much to take archaeology beyond the domain of academic research and avocational pursuit in North America. Notably, lawmakers have recognized the need to conserve sites threatened with development impact, and as a result cultural resource management (CRM) is now arguably the most active form of archaeology in North America, largely funded directly by public or private developers. The participation of Native Americans in archaeology has also increased as a result of burial issues, land and resource claim research, etc. Of course, this creates a wider constituency of interests and makes archaeology a policy issue, leading lawmakers to respond to these additional constituents (e.g., demands of accountability from those who pay for CRM, demands for input and access by those whose heritage is archaeologically significant, etc.). And as a policy issue additional questions arise, such as who owns (as in controls) archaeology? And if it is the state, on what basis is that ownership asserted? In Canada, recent case law and Supreme Court decisions regarding aboriginal rights are indirectly speaking to this issue. The picture emerging is that ownership and management of archaeology may have less to do with preserving the past and more to do with the state's fiduciary responsibility for aboriginal vestige interests. This essay will review some of the implications this trend may have on the future of archaeology in North America.

When I was asked to participate in the session at the 1999 Midwest Archaeological Conference in East Lansing honoring Charles Cleland, I first thought to present some of my recent historic Native American research, since it was through earlier such work that I first came to know Chuck (Ferris 1989). However, as I thought about it, I realized that over the last decade when we met, we rarely talked about research but rather talked more about the various issues arising from our respective involvement in what could broadly be termed applied archaeology—ranging from land and resource claims to archaeology in government policy. Of course, as an archaeologist working for the province of Ontario, I operate daily in this kind of intertidal zone where archaeology meets the wider world, a place where Chuck also regularly visits as a result of some of his diverse applied research interests. And it is in this zone where change occurs so rapidly and ramifications for archaeology are first realized. As such, I thought it might be more appropriate to speak about this shared dimension of our respective pursuits, since it really is in this so dominant part of my world that Chuck's broad interests are clearly reflected in my approach to professional life. So I offer the following take—albeit personal—on recent trends and future implications happening out here in the zone.

My tenure as a civil servant dates back more than fifteen years, and in that time I've seen many of the changes that are occurring elsewhere in North America manifest themselves in the practice and management of archaeology in Ontario. Indeed, when I first became involved in archaeology, that community consisted of academics, students, and avocationals and was a time, for instance, when newly hired archaeologists in the Ontario government mostly grappled with issues such as where to survey and do research to expand knowledge, or how to integrate the professional and avocational worlds, and wondered what to do about the alarming loss of sites to development pressures.

In fact, this latter issue of trying to ensure effective conservation has been the almost single-minded focus of my department over the last twenty years, so like elsewhere across North America, the trend toward responsible conservation in legislation has been a long one (see Ferris 1998; Fowler 1991; Green and Doershuk 1998). But at least in Ontario—and at least for the moment—the 1990s saw the successful completion of efforts to integrate relatively prescriptive archaeological conservation requirements in all major regulated land-use development activity in the province (Ontario Ministry of Tourism, Culture and Recreation 1997). This success is noteworthy since it means that development proponents as wide-ranging as government agencies, natural resource harvesters, private housing developers, and even individual landowners subdividing land into residential lots all are expected to address possible threats to archaeological sites. And significantly, addressing these requirements is considered a legitimate cost of developing land or harvesting resources, and as such is subject to the basic principle of proponent-pay. In short, these various pieces of land-use legislation require that the public interest in conserving the past be addressed directly by anyone threatening that interest, even if the threat occurs on lands privately owned—a direction several other Canadian jurisdictions also have taken, but only a few American jurisdictions, especially municipalities, have been prepared to venture into (but see Kearns and Kirkorian 1991).

Not surprisingly, this marriage of a conservation ethic to the practice of archaeology has had tremendous impacts. While CRM-based archaeology was unknown in Ontario two decades ago, today more than 250 individuals are employed in CRM, leading to the discovery of five hundred to seven hundred sites a year and more than one hundred large-scale site excavations each year. In all, the industry is generating millions of dollars of archaeological activity in Ontario each year. Of course, this has generated a wealth of data and created meaningful and viable employment opportunities for most archaeological students leaving university. But for both practitioners and civil servants such as myself, this explosion has also left us reeling, as it is all we can do to keep on top of the demands of the industry, often at the expense of the more traditional research and avocational sectors of the archaeological community.

And at the same time, this explosion has brought forward and spotlighted many of the internal flaws and inadequacies of the discipline. We wring hands and have angst-filled debates over the ethics and professionalism, or lack thereof, of CRM. Storage facilities bulge at the mass of collections waiting for someone to fulfill the potential of their contribution to understanding the past. And so on. While many of these issues are common from state to state or province to province, and were in part anticipated by the earlier efforts toward professionalization on the part of Chuck and others, the systemic changes needed to remedy these problems are only beginning to emerge and have been greeted with cynicism and pessimism. (For a fuller discussion of the issue of ethics in CRM, see Ferris 2000.)

Another impact of CRM is that archaeology is slowly rising above the radar of public perception. In Ontario, consultant crews can be found in every corner of the province addressing statutory conservation requirements on behalf of their clients. This exposure is generally a good thing for providing a sense of the legitimacy and relevancy of archaeology within today's society. However, all these crews are out across the province because they are being paid by others to undertake this work.

Thus, the most significant increase in the profile of archaeology in society has occurred within public and private development sectors. And these proponents, then, are the people who now generally fund most if not all archaeological activity in Ontario—as is also the case now for most other jurisdictions in North America.

In my experience, the development sector rarely welcomes its role as financial backer, and its lack of expertise and often a personal sentiment of "Who cares?" leave this group suspicious of the whole enterprise. This sentiment is further exacerbated when archaeologists justify the need for the expense of archaeology in terms of the research value of the undertaking—of fulfilling a scientific prerogative, if you will—that often can sound to many nonarchaeologists as self-serving rationalization to justify a personal interest in playing with archaeological materials at someone else's expense. That these archaeologists also tend to use obscure and highly technical jargon to explain concepts such as potential or site significance (i.e., the basis from which money decisions are ultimately made) just makes the proponent even more insecure and suspicious of the profession (Ferris 1999). While this can lead to accusations of it all being a waste of money and a boondoggle for unemployed archaeologists, the development sector increasingly, and more legitimately, is demanding that archaeologists demonstrate relevance and accountability in terms and measurements understandable to and supportable by a broader sector of society than just professional archaeologists.

Now, in a regulated environment such as land-use development, these demands eventually lead directly back to the government and lawmakers who originally placed the provisions for conserving archaeology in legislation. This, in turn, raises the profile of archaeology internally in government, which can also be problematic for archaeologists. We live in a time when political and legislative decision-making across much of North America is driven by a sustained conservatism that views process and accountability as red tape interfering with the free reign of capitalist enterprise. This makes the complaints from the development sector as much a political consideration as a program or statutory issue. As such, in most instances when senior-level managers in government think about archaeology, it is inevitably in a negative context, when someone is screaming at them or their political masters about cost and interference of business. Additionally, decision makers at this level are also predisposed to being sympathetic toward the complainant because they themselves are not archaeologists and find archaeology's arcane language and terminology just as inaccessible as the developer does. Also, these people share many of the developer's same societal preconceptions and values and thus, at some level, the same suspicion as to what the value of archaeology is in society. And finally, as a simple reality of archaeology being managed in government, there is always pressure to favor backing away from whatever issue has been brought forward, as this will most expediently diffuse the politically charged environment. Ironically, the result can be that government perceives these issues as being due to "unreasonable archaeologists" and archaeological sites of "dubious value," rather than due to a developer trying to cut costs or avoid statutory responsibility. And though simply addressing the conservation ethic established in law, the archaeologist is often perceived of as the party with the vested interest, and thus given less credibility. That archaeologists seemingly can't communicate in terms and values easily understandable to nonspecialists is simply viewed as the archaeologists' problem—a demonstration of their inability to see the "bigger" picture—and so further compromises their credibility and objectivity.

So, what generally can emerge and pervade the political core where the jurisdiction has adopted strong conservation legislation is a sense that somehow the archaeological community is taking advantage of a reasonable societal impulse to do some "good." In other words, while lawmakers and government decision makers have been convinced that preserving the past and avoiding the destruction of archaeological treasures are good things to do—and understandable concepts to support—it is a much more difficult task to convince these same people that this then requires millions of dollars to be spent on things that aren't popularly thought of as treasures, or on continuing to dig up the seemingly same kinds of rocks, animal bones, and mud pottery over and over again.

Of course, whatever the doubts at the political core, it isn't actually easy, and neither is there the willingness, to change a regulation or statute simply to make the development proponent happier. Rather, there is a great deal of pressure put on archaeologists to be "reasonable," which archaeologists in CRM often translate as meaning to compromise the quality of their work. This, then, further fosters the sentiment in archaeology of angst and inevitable decline. But precisely because the status quo offers only a pessimistic future, especially in CRM, the archaeological community needs to respond to both the implied and the direct criticism of the practice by tackling the hard issues brought on by early success. Indeed, stripped away from all other agendas, what archaeologists are in fact being asked to do by development proponents and political bureaucrats is simply to demonstrate that the value of the whole enterprise has lived up to the advance billing archaeologists made when first arguing twenty to forty years ago that the horrible loss of the record had to be stopped.

And this should not be such a daunting task, after all, but it has to occur in a context of archaeologists participating in and balancing the needs of the broader society we are a part of. To me, this is essential both to confirm that the knowledge potential is worthy of the cost the state[1] imposes on proponents for recovering that data and to demonstrate the necessity of archaeologists continuing to play a primary role in the education and promotion of why the past is of value and relevant to today's world. In part, this is because it isn't just developers and senior levels of bureaucracy who now sit at the table with us making decisions about the practice and future of archaeology.

While aggressive developers and demanding archaeologists clearly make government decision makers overworked and under siege, what gets government's attention even more are the vocal demands of Native Americans to be more actively involved in archaeology. Curiously, though, while these demands question the archaeological community's exclusive ownership to the resource and are rapidly becoming the next "central" focus of my working world, I think it also may provide a relevancy to archaeological conservation that more directly responds to the challenges of the development sector and the political core.

The demands of Native Americans to control what happens to their heritage originate from a number of significant though divergent paths. Certainly, investigation of burial and sacred sites is significant, as this has long been accompanied by outrage over the believed desecration by archaeologists of these places (Ferguson 1996; Zimmerman 1989). And archaeologists have been generally slow to acknowledge these concerns and have tended to cite the scientific prerogative and their right as scholars and researchers to justify what they do (Downer 1997; Goldstein and Kintigh 1990)—a not dissimilar argument made to developers to justify spending money in order to conserve the scientific value of the data being recovered from sites. But defending the scientific prerogative without including meaningful involvement of those clearly associated with the subject matter, beyond being aggressively challenged as self-serving (e.g., Deloria 1995), has curried little

---

1. My use of the term "state" in this essay is in reference to the collective jurisdictional authority held by government, be it federal or state/provincial.

sympathy from the public and lawmakers. Ultimately in the United States, the response to this tension was adoption of the Native American Graves Protection and Repatriation Act (NAGPRA), which requires the treatment of all intentional burials found on federal or tribal land to be determined by the wishes of Native Americans. It also requires all federally funded institutions to list their holdings of skeletal remains, funerary objects, sacred items, and objects of cultural patrimony, and to seek repatriation of these materials to the appropriate Native American community. This has given rise to an unprecedented level of interaction between archaeologists and Native Americans, not all of which has been in the negative (Zimmerman 1997). And, while there has been much discussion and criticism of and even legal challenge to NAGPRA, clearly some form of interaction will remain entrenched, thus ensuring that archaeology retains a high profile among Native Americans.

Likewise, while there is no NAGPRA in Canada, most jurisdictions recognize a role for First Nations when dealing with burial discoveries. In Ontario, the provincial Cemeteries Act excludes archaeologists from any direct say in the disposition of skeletal remains and associated grave goods—disposition being an issue exclusively between landowner and First Nation acting as a de facto next of kin. Heavy on negotiation and equal weight of interests, the Cemeteries Act ensures that archaeologists will need to develop extensive and ongoing relationships with First Nation councils and traditionalists.

Less common to increasing the profile of archaeology among Native Americans but no less important has been the occasional role of archaeologist as ethnohistorian and expert witness in assisting communities with land or resource claims. Archaeology in particular can be an important expansion of the written record when that record is mute or vague on such issues as the ancestry of subsistence practices, land tenure, and territoriality. Certainly, Chuck's role in making historic native archaeology relevant and of importance to various aboriginal communities in their legal battles has had the additional benefit of demonstrating, in a real and practical way, how archaeology works and what stories it can tell (e.g., Cleland 1992, 1993). Finally, there is also a growing number of archaeologists who, as a matter of course, simply consult with Native Americans, sharing the results of their research and seeking input into analyses and findings. Recognition of this relationship has been captured both informally and formally by a number of archaeological organizations, most notably the Canadian Archaeological Association (1997).

But this direct interaction with First Nations by archaeologists, be it burials issues, sharing research, or sitting side by side in a courtroom, inevitably leads to a wider discussion about the role of archaeology in documenting the history of Native Americans. After all, the archaeological record is the heritage of existing Native American communities, and as individual groups are made aware of fieldwork and site findings, they begin to ask not illegitimate questions, such as why shouldn't they have a say in how their past is being managed and interpreted, and who owns this past (e.g., Anyon 1991; Asch 1997; Jemison 1997; Ravesloot 1997)? There is little legislation in Canada or the United States that speaks directly to these questions, and few heritage acts specifically recognize ownership of or even special status in regard to archaeological heritage for Native Americans. At best, in some jurisdictions there is overt recognition of public ownership or at least control of the material remains of the past, while elsewhere provisions are either vague or, by default through common law, ownership falls to the landowner. But then, with the exception perhaps of site looters, questions regarding who owns the vast majority of the material archaeologists collect—the compiled detritus of material remains left behind as a result of daily activities at a fixed locale over the course of occupation at that place—have not attracted as much attention as have questions about the ownership of mortuary remains and ceremonial/sacred objects. Indeed, for this part of the archaeological record, "owning" the past is really only secondarily about the physical possession of endless boxes of lithics, animal bones, or ceramic pot sherds. Much more so, it is about owning the ability to reconstruct and tell stories about the past, and owning the authority to make decisions about the archaeological record (Tsosie 1997).

The distinction I am making here between sacred or mortuary archaeological remains (human remains, grave goods, ceremonial artifacts, etc.) and the cultural material remains of day-to-day life is itself debatable. Nonetheless, this is consistent with the way legislation has viewed aboriginal archaeological heritage, with the material things from habitation sites generally assumed in legislation to refer to property, while legislation around the treatment of human remains and associated grave goods tends to arise out of human rights principles of fair and equal treatment (Higginbotham 1982; Tsosie 1997). But it should be recognized that such a distinction imposes a rather Eurocentric conception of "religious" values onto the issue without consideration of Native American views (e.g., Bell 1992a, 516; Bell 1992b; Clements 1991). Indeed, the distinction between sacred items and cultural property neatly removes the latter from legislative provisions that otherwise provide aboriginal groups access to the remains of their heritage, leaving control with others who have a vested interest, be they archaeologists or importers/exporters of cultural property (see Anaya 1996; Asch 1997; Coombe 1993; Tsosie 1997). I suspect that regardless of current practice, given that legislation such as NAGPRA actually captures terms such as "objects of cultural patrimony," future legal tests will be needed to clarify the application and definition of such terminology in relation to the full scope of the archaeological record and thus clarify how "real," in law anyway, the distinction between sacred objects and cultural objects is.

But for the moment, and in the absence of clear legislation, claims of ownership—of authority and access—to cultural remains of a nonsacred nature is generally vested with and asserted by archaeologists. Traditionally, these assertions are based on demonstrated formal training and a commitment to preserving the past for the betterment of a common good. Thus, through licensing or permitting provisions in heritage statutes, archaeologists become the caretakers if not the owners on behalf of the state of the things recovered from archaeological sites. Certainly these assertions are in effect a legal claim of ownership (Tsosie 1997, 66), and most heritage conservation statutes in North America implicitly support this claim by excluding "unqualified" individuals from being eligible to obtain archaeological permits or licenses, and in many cases making it a penalty for such people to "loot" sites. Here, then, is recognition in statute that the state acknowledges some higher claim of ownership by archaeologists over looters and the public in preserving a "public" trust in the conservation of archaeological remains. But such a basis of claim sits in isolation to direct claims of ownership by descendants, and indeed marginalizes existing First Nations from their heritage by making archaeological remains primarily scientific material to be studied, rather than objects of cultural patrimony.

In terms of nonmortuary archaeological remains, the implementation of conservation statutes such as the U.S. federal Archaeological Protection Act of 1979, and provincial or state statutes such as the Ontario Heritage Act of 1975, can be seen as the relatively recent recognition of the state's responsibility in caring for these resources. The assignment of primary control of archaeological remains to archaeologists that arose with these statutes tended to coincide with the growth in the discipline during the 1960s and 1970s (Ferris 1998). These statutes were developed generally without any meaningful Native American consultation. They also reflect commonly held attitudes of the time about archaeological remains and First Nations—essentially, that these resources were the forgotten and obscure remains of dead people and an ancient past (McGuire 1997; Trigger 1980). As such, these were things that, once gone, would be "sad" to have lost, denying today's society the knowledge of that all-but-forgotten past. And thus the need exists for trained experts—archaeologists—to care for these fragile fragments, and also needed is the imposition of a conservation ethic in order to protect those remains. It is telling, in light of this, that for at least some states and provinces the protection provisions of Native American heritage exist in statute alongside protection provisions for fossils and other paleontological remains.

Clearly, though, popular attitudes about Native Americans, even if it is just a simple recognition that they are indeed alive and vibrant communities, are shifting, and so it is not unreasonable to assume that the state will begin to "think" beyond the logic of existing statutes. And since the exclusivity of authority currently ascribed to archaeologists essentially arises from these statutes, any decline in this authority ultimately will come from the state, as it did in the case of NAGPRA where both law and the public debate required state insertion of a different form of ownership than what had existed previously. And there is nothing, of course, that precludes the state from deciding to remove the exclusivity of access that heritage conservation legislation currently assigns the archaeological community, or revising statutes to accommodate other voices—except for the same structural constraints that preclude the political core from changing conservation legislation the first time a powerful developer objects to having to pay for archaeology. Indeed, what is interesting to me, from the perspective of being within government looking out at these issues, is that the challenges Native Americans make to archaeological claims of ownership are similar to the challenges developers make of the basic value of archaeology; both question the traditional acceptance that archaeologists can best care for, speak for, and evaluate what is best for archaeological remains. So these challenges ultimately are requiring the state to reexamine the conceptual framework it had imposed over archaeological heritage. Indeed, it will ultimately be up to the state to determine whether these challenges require removal or reconfirmation of the legislative authorities archaeologists currently have through permitting and licensing, or if that control should be vested elsewhere, or if there should no longer be restrictions on access to and use of the resource (i.e., if conservation requirements should be removed).

The general direction state management of archaeology follows, then, rests on archaeologists continuing to effectively make their case, the degree of political influence other sectors can impose on the state, and ultimately the willingness of the state to continue to assert control over the past. However, I see emerging a broader context that I believe will greatly constrain the state's ability to either walk away from the conservation of archaeological resources or protect archaeologists' exclusivity in this area. Specifically, an intriguing trend in recent court decisions around both aboriginal rights and the obligations of the state may ultimately exert the greatest influence on future directions in the management of aboriginal archaeology. As such, we should be familiar with this trend, since there may come a day when conserving archaeology is seen as having less to do with preserving the past and more to do with meeting the state's fiduciary obligation to care for that heritage on behalf of First Nations (Ferris and Leclair 1999).

To examine this issue, first it is important to recognize that, in Canada, the majority of archaeological sites east of the Rockies are on land that has been covered by some kind of formal land surrender—in other words, on lands that have come into private hands through treaty between one or more First Nations and the Crown. Moreover, in the United States, it is also the case that lands in the Midwest and eastern United States largely became American sovereign territory through negotiated treaties between the U.S. government and Native American nations. While the Indian Appropriation Act of 1871 effectively removed American requirements to continue to negotiate treaties with Native American tribes, that act also recognized the more than three hundred treaties that had been negotiated by the state with Native Americans as of 1871 and left them in effect (Fairbanks 1995; Wilkins 1997). These treaties were negotiated with First Nations first by British and then by American and Canadian powers because these colonial powers recognized that, under even colonial law, Native Americans did hold title to the lands they resided on and thus the surrender of these lands had to arise from a nation-to-nation negotiated treaty (e.g., Foster 1993; Ordon 1985, 60).

Basically, under both national and international law, when two sovereign nations co-sign a treaty that will lead to one of the nations being subsumed by the other, as in the case of North American states and First Nations, the remaining sovereign (Canada or the United States) has accepted a trust relationship between itself and the other sovereign and inherits a fiduciary responsibility for continuing to protect the interests and rights of that other nation (Donohue 1989; Rotman 1996). In Canada and the United States, the British Royal Proclamation of 1763 first defined this trust relationship between Native Americans and the Crown. The proclamation recognized that aboriginal people held a sovereign right of use and occupancy to their land, and as such any Crown assertion of title had to arise from the voluntary surrender of these rights through negotiation (Cohen 1947; Donohue 1989, 370). Given this, it is important then to understand exactly what treaty rights represent: such rights, negotiated and enshrined in the formal surrender, are rights *retained* and unsurrendered by the subsumed sovereign (and not privileges granted to that group by the remaining sovereign, as is often popularly assumed).

The basic assumption of the Crown at the time, that it was the supreme legal authority and thus could impose British law over the land, is certainly fodder of much debate. It is also true that the courts largely fail to recognize this as an issue, citing the doctrine of discovery as basis for the Crown's assertion of absolute title—in other words, affirming a kind of Social Darwinian hierarchy to the concept of aboriginal and European sovereign rights and titles in which the discovering nation, by weight of complexity and western sensibilities, scores higher and thus is attributed more rights (Ferris 1999). Nonetheless, it is also true that the British Crown did impose, through the British Royal Proclamation of 1763, rules of law that the Crown itself had to follow in its relationship with First Nations. So the proclamation at least established a level of expected responsibility and liability on the part of the Crown that all its subsequent actions can be measured against.

Unfortunately, it is also a fact of subsequent history that the state's recognition of its fiduciary obligation waned over the next two centuries, with the U.S. Congress in 1871 ultimately abandoning the principle of negotiated surrender, while Canada simply stopped entering into nation-to-nation negotiations for large areas in the western and northern parts of the country. Moreover, in the late nineteenth and early twentieth centuries, Supreme Court decisions in both Canada and the United States tended to further erode Native American rights and the protection of aboriginal title (e.g., Bell and Asch 1997; Cohen 1947; Donohue 1989; Wilkins 1994, 1997).

However, more recent court rulings have begun to reaffirm the principle of fiduciary responsibility, especially in Canada (Bell and Asch 1997; Donohue 1989), and it is in this trend where I see fiduciary responsibility ultimately reaching toward archaeology. Of Canadian court decisions that are noteworthy, the 1984 ruling in *Guerin v. Canada* described aboriginal land rights as "inalienable" and ruled that "the Crown is under an obligation to deal with the land on the Indians' behalf when the interest is surrendered." The justices also found that the fiduciary obligation owed to the Indians by the Crown is sui generis, or unique, by noting the special character both of the Indians' interest in the land and of their historical relationship with the Crown.

Adopted in 1982, Section 35 of the Canadian Constitution recognized the existence of aboriginal and treaty rights. A subsequent Supreme Court of Canada decision, known as *R. v. Sparrow,* upheld Section 35 to protect the cultural identity of aboriginal peoples. Also, it identified the relationship between the government and native people as being "trust-like, rather than adversarial" (Bell and Asch 1997). Although the case involved aboriginal fishing rights, it isn't unreasonable to suggest that aboriginal archaeological heritage is also part of the cultural identity of aboriginal peoples and thus needs protection. Most recently, Supreme Court decisions over the obligations of the Crown to treaty obligations (e.g., the 1999 Marshall ruling) or with regard to definitions of First Nation rights and the inextinguishable nature of cultural rights and privilege (as in the Delgamuukw ruling; see Persky 1998) further expand First Nation interests and constrain governments from acting independent of those interests.

It is also worth noting that contemporary treaty negotiations in Canada now expressly identify First Nations' interests in and jurisdiction over their heritage. This obviously has implications for archaeology, because if contemporary treaty negotiations identify heritage as an aboriginal interest and Crown responsibility on lands is surrendered, this suggests that aboriginal heritage is an underlying right and interest that aboriginal communities had at the time of the Royal Proclamation of 1763; otherwise, the Canadian government would not have to recognize the issue today. So even if First Nations' interest in their cultural heritage and burials is absent from the text of eighteenth- and nineteenth-century treaties, there is a good argument to be made that the interest and thus underlying title for aboriginal heritage was nonetheless present. This, then, would be the basis for arguing that the Crown has a fiduciary responsibility to care for aboriginal heritage on lands under its control as a result of surrender. This doesn't, of course, affirm a First Nation's ownership to archaeology, but it does suggest that failure on the part of the Crown to care for and protect that heritage could be read as a failure of fiduciary responsibility and perhaps make the original surrender null and void. This presumably is a good justification for the Crown to uphold archaeological conservation statutes.

While this argument is based on mounting judicial precedent in Canada, it is also worth considering if an argument can be made for a fiduciary responsibility toward the conservation of Native American heritage in the United States. Certainly, many of the same underlying principles exist where American sovereignty followed treaty and land surrender, and the principle of nation-to-nation treaty status has been affirmed in both the courts and Congress (Cohen 1947). And the exclusive authority of the American sovereign to alienate land from aboriginal title has been long acknowledged as establishing a fiduciary relationship with aboriginal peoples, embodying the sovereign with the responsibility to act in the Native Americans' best interests (Cohen 1947; Donohue 1989; Ordon 1985). Indeed, it could be argued that an act such as NAGPRA is a very real manifestation of the American sovereign's recognition of its fiduciary responsibility toward an obvious aboriginal vestige interests.

Also, it is significant that the position taken by the Canadian Supreme Court in the Marshall ruling, and recognition of unextinguished treaty rights, is considered to have largely adopted the thinking behind the U.S. Supreme Court decision in the Lac Courte Oreilles ruling against Wisconsin (McEvoy 2000). That ruling, as well as the more recent Mille Lacs Band decision against Minnesota (see McClurken 2000), reaffirmed Native American treaty rights as existing unless otherwise *expressly* extinguished by executive order, and constrains any state action that would lead to a degradation of those rights. The consistency of the Canadian and U.S. Supreme Courts in their current reckoning of treaty rights isn't so surprising, given the common basis from which these concepts arose in law, and suggests that the interpretive basis for extending principles of fiduciary responsibility to native heritage applies for each country.

However, it is also true that recent Canadian Supreme Court decisions, especially as seen in the Guerin, Sparrow, and Delgamuukw cases, go much further in defining aboriginal rights and state fiduciary obligations than the American judiciary are traditionally comfortable with (e.g., Claiborne 1997/1998; Donohue 1989, 372). Asserting a Native American vestige interest beyond federal or reservation lands, for example, challenges a much more strongly entrenched principle of the exclusivity of private landowner rights than found in Canadian society, not to mention creating jurisdictional conflicts between federal and state levels of government. And while the Lac Courte Orielles and Mille Lacs decisions are part of a good body of U.S. rulings affirming unextinguished aboriginal treaty rights, particularly for hunting and fishing beyond reservations, nonetheless these rights continually come under attack. Indeed, individual state authorities often take very aggressive legal positions against even the most basic tenets of aboriginal rights and challenge the basis of any federal jurisdiction in these areas (e.g., Bergman 1993; Loew 1997; McClurken 2000; Turcheneske 1993). More so in the United States than in Canada (at least recently), the broad historical trend in court decisions reflects the court's function as a tool of the absolute sovereignty of the state to erode and limit aboriginal rights, and thus will prove to be a much more daunting forum for assertion of rights by Native Americans.

In effect, heritage conservation beyond federally controlled lands will only occur by the will of the individual state, and if the state is unprepared to adopt conservation provisions, then aboriginal heritage resources not otherwise under jurisdiction of federal statutes will be allowed to be destroyed in the normal course of land-use changes and development growth. Could such scenarios be challenged as failure of the state to meet a treaty-originating fiduciary responsibility? Certainly the human rights principles of fair and equal treatment for human remains and sacred sites captured in NAGPRA suggest that, for cemeteries and the like, failure on the part of an individual state to protect such places could be actionable. Indeed, the creation of NAGPRA opens the door to explore more fully the U.S. fiduciary responsibility toward aboriginal heritage. For example, it might not be inconceivable to envision a day when a Native American community brings forward a legal suit against a state (either directly with the participation of third parties, or indirectly through a suit against the federal government for failing to ensure state compliance with inherited fiduciary responsibilities). The argument, presumably, would cite the state's inaction or legislative void as the reason an obvious sacred site or burial ground was destroyed due to development or looting. The argument could also be made that the principle of NAGPRA should extend to state responsibility. Such a suit, I think, would easily open a Pandora's box of issues, testing and perhaps defining exactly what treaty and inherent rights the state inherited from the federal government at the time of formation. Indeed, such a court action around the specific issue of a failure to respect or protect obvious aboriginal heritage could serve as a pivot for many of the broader key debates in American Indian law today and quickly place the United States on a path similar to that seen emerging from Canadian court rulings. I suspect that if this were to happen, archae-ologists would find something much more pervasive than NAGPRA and unethical consulting practices to think about.

But I would also suggest that it is in none of our interests to wait for legisla-tors or the judiciary to decide what changes happen next to archaeology. While court decisions tend to reaffirm rights, they often leave the implementation and application to negotiation between the state and the affected parties. But why wait to be dragged to the table to negotiate with our "in-laws"? Rather, as archaeologists we are in a position to both recognize the broad direction that our own success is taking us and speak directly to those whose interests in archaeology are not necessarily incompatible with our own. And a solution reached through discussion and a development of mutual understanding will be far better than anything imposed by the political or legal world.

So to conclude, and at the risk of flogging a metaphor well past death, I'd like to suggest that the marriage of archaeology and the conservation ethic has brought us face to face with a larger family of interests. And these interests, in-laws by marriage if you will, have very different views and positions, sometimes incompatible with ours and sometimes not. But when we all sit down to the table, we ultimately will need to figure out how to get along. And to me, what Chuck Cleland's achievements in both the academic and applied worlds of archaeology have demonstrated is that his skill and effort in bridging these worlds, and ultimately getting along with at least some of these in-laws, makes his resulting research both a superior product and relevant to more than just basic research interests. Its certainly an important lesson I've learned, and one I can only try to adhere to in my own day-to-day world—um, my professional world, that is. I still have issues at a personal level with my familial in-laws!

Acknowledgments

Earlier versions of this paper benefited from discussions with several colleagues, especially Laurie Leclair, John Van West, Dean Jacobs, Alison Wylie, and Michael Johnson. Nonetheless, these observations are my own, and any deficiencies in them are my doing. Likewise, the views expressed here represent my professional and personal opinions, and are not neces-sarily shared by my employer. Finally, as everyone else in this volume has done, I wish to extend my thanks and appreciation for the importance of Chuck's personal input and professional output in my work. I fully expect that to continue for many years to come.

References Cited

Abler, T. S. 1992. "Beavers and Muskets: Iroquois Military Fortunes in the Face of European Colonization." In *War in the Tribal Zone,* ed. R. B. Ferguson and N. L. Whitehead, 151–174. Santa Fe, N.M.: School of American Research Press.

Albert, D. A., S. R. Denton, and B. V. Barnes. 1986. *Regional Landscape Ecosystems of Michigan.* Ann Arbor: School of Natural Resources, University of Michigan.

American Monument Association, Inc. 1947. *Memorial Symbolism, Epitaphs, and Design Types.* Boston: American Monument Association, Inc.

Anaya, J. 1996. *Indigenous Peoples in International Law.* New York: Oxford University Press.

Anderson, D. L. 1991. "Variability in Trade at Eighteenth-Century French Outposts." In *French Colonial Archaeology: The Illinois Country and the Western Great Lakes,* ed. J. A. Walthall, 218–236. Urbana: University of Illinois Press.

Anderson, F. 2000. *Crucible of War: The Seven Years War and the Fate of Empire in British North America, 1754–1766.* New York: Alfred A. Knopf.

Anderton, J. B., and D. J. Weir. 1991. *1990 Cultural Resource Survey, Hiawatha National Forest.* Report No. R-0082. Commonwealth Cultural Resources Group, Jackson, Michigan.

Anonymous. n.d. *Smiley History.* Mimeographed family history presented to Freeman United Coal Mining Company. Copy on file, Department of Anthropology, Michigan State University.

Anyon, R. 1991. "Protecting the Past, Protecting the Present: Cultural Resources and American Indians." In *Protecting the Past,* ed. G. Smith and J. Ehrenhard. Baton Rouge: CRC Press. Available online at www.cr.nps.gov/seac/protectg.htm.

Armour, D. A. 1976. "Jean-Baptiste Amiot." In *Firearms on the Frontier,* T. M. Hamilton, 25–26. Reports in Mackinac History and Archaeology No. 5. Lansing, Mich.: Mackinac Island State Park Commission.

Armour, D. A., and K. R. Widder. 1978. *At the Crossroads: Michilimackinac during the American Revolution.* Lansing, Mich.: Mackinac Island State Park Commission.

Asch, D. L., K. B. Farnsworth, and N. B. Asch. 1979. "Woodland Subsistence and Settlement in West Central Illinois." In *Hopewell Archaeology: The Chillicothe Conference,* ed. D. S. Brose and N. Greber, 80–85. Kent, Ohio: Kent State University Press.

Asch, M. 1997. "Cultural Property and the Question of Underlying Title." In *At a Crossroads: Archaeology and First Peoples in Canada,* ed. G. Nichols and T. Andrews, 266–271. Archaeology Press Publication No. 24. Vancouver: Simon Fraser University.

Axtell, J. 1992. *Beyond 1492: Encounters in Colonial North America.* New York: University of Oxford Press.

Baerreis, D., and J. Freeman. 1958. "Late Woodland Pottery in Wisconsin as Seen from Aztalan." *Wisconsin Archeologist* 39: 35–61.

Bell, C. 1992a. "Aboriginal Claims to Cultural Property in Canada: A Comparative Legal Analysis of the Repatriation Debate." *American Indian Law Review* 17(2): 457–521.

———. 1992b. "Repatriation of Cultural Property and Aboriginal Rights: A Survey of Contemporary Legal Issues." *Prairie Forum* 17(2): 313–334.

Bell, C., and M. Asch. 1997. "Challenging Assumptions: The Impact of Precedent in Aboriginal Rights Litigation." In *Aboriginal and Treaty Rights in Canada,* ed. M. Asch, 38–74. Vancouver: UBC Press.

Bell, E. L. 1990. "The Historical Archaeology of Mortuary Behavior: Coffin Hardware from Uxbridge, Massachusetts." *Historical Archaeology* 24(3): 54–78.

Bergman, G. 1993. "Defying Precedent: Can Abenaki Aboriginal Title Be Extinguished by the 'Weight of History'?" *American Indian Law Review* 18(2): 447–485.

Binford, Lewis R. 1961. "A Discussion of the Contrasts in the Development of the Settlement at Fort Michilimackinac under British and French Rule." *Southeastern Archaeological Conference Newsletter* 9(1): 50–52.

———. 1972. "The 'Binford' Pipe Stem Formula: A Return from the Grave." *The Conference on Historic Site Archaeology Papers 1971* 9(Part 1): 230–253.

Blake, L. W. 1981. "Floral Remains from the 1978–1979 Excavations along the Rue de la Babillarde." In *Excavations at Fort Michilimackinac, 1978–1979: The Rue de la Babillarde,* D. P. Heldman and R. T. Grange, Jr., 366–375. Archaeological Completion Report Series, No. 3. Mackinac Island, Mich.: Mackinac Island State Park Commission.

Blake, L. W., and H. C. Cutler. 1978. "Floral Remains from House 1 of the South Southeast Row House Excavation of 1977." In *Excavations at Fort Michilimackinac, 1977: House One of the South Southeast Row House,* D. P. Heldman, 155–160. Archaeological Completion Report Series, No. 2. Mackinac Island, Mich.: Mackinac Island State Park Commission.

———. 2001. "Corn from Fort Michilimackinac, A.D. 1770–1780." In *Plants from the Past,* L. W. Blake and H. C. Cutler, 59–65. Tuscaloosa: University of Alabama Press.

Branstner, M. C. 2001. *Columbus Avenue Neighborhood Park, Bay City, Michigan: A Survey and Evaluation of Cultural Resources.* Great Lakes Research Report 2001-1. Williamston, Mich.: Great Lakes Research.

Branstner, M. C., and T. M. Branstner. 1993. "Part 2, Cultural Resource Sensitivity Model: Historic Period Archaeological and Architectural Properties, Marquette Avenue Realignment Project, Bay City, Michigan." In *A Phase I Archaeological Survey of the Marquette Viaduct Replacement, City of Bay City, Michigan,* compiled by M. B. Holman and W. A. Lovis, i–v, 1–75. Archaeological Survey Report No. 129. East Lansing: Michigan State University Museum.

Brashler, J. G. 1998. *1996–97 Excavations at the Prison Farm Site.* Paper presented at the 1998 Midwest Archaeological Conference, Muncie, Indiana.

Brashler, J. G., and E. B. Garland. 1993. *The Zemaitis Site (20OT68): A Stratified Woodland Occupation on the Grand River in Michigan.* Paper presented at the Midwest Archaeological Conference, Milwaukee, Wisconsin.

Brashler, J. G., T. J. Martin, K. E. Parker, J. A. Robertson, and M. J. Hambacher. 2000. *Middle Woodland Occupation in the Grand River Basin of Michigan.* Paper presented at the Middle Woodland in the Millennium Conference, Kampsville, Illinois.

Brashler, J. G., and B. E. Mead. 1996. "Woodland Archaeology in the Grand River Basin." In *Investigating the Archaeological Record of the Great Lake State: Essays in Honor of Elizabeth Baldwin Garland,* ed. M. B. Holman, J. G. Brashler, and K. Parker, 181–250. Kalamazoo: New Issues Press.

Brigham, W. 1936. "The Arrowsmith Battlefield." *Transactions of the McLean County Historical Society* 4: 33–43.

Brose, D. S. 1968. "The Backlund Mound Group." *Wisconsin Archeologist* 49: 34–51.

———. 1970. *Archaeology of Summer Island: Changing Settlement Systems in Northern Lake Michigan.* Anthropological Papers No. 41, Museum of Anthropology. Ann Arbor: University of Michigan.

———. 1975. "The Fisher Lake Site (20LU21): Multicomponent Occupations in Northwest Michigan." *Michigan Archaeologist* 21(2): 71–90.

Brose, D. S., and M. J. Hambacher. 1999. "The Middle Woodland in Northern Michigan." In *Retrieving Michigan's Buried Past: The Archaeology of the Great Lakes State,* ed. J. R. Halsey with M. D. Stafford, 173–192. Bulletin 64. Bloomfield Hills, Mich.: Cranbrook Institute of Science.

Brown, C. 1925. "Fifth Addition to the Record of Wisconsin Antiquities, A to M." *Wisconsin Archeologist* 4: 9–78.

Brown, J. A. 1973. *Final Report of the Excavations at Fort Michilimackinac, Emmet County, Michigan, Conducted by the Department of Anthropology and Museum, Michigan State University, 1967, 1968, 1969.* Manuscript on file, Mackinac Island State Park Commission, Mackinac City, Mich.

———, ed. n.d. *From Depot to Entrepot: Archaeological Dimensions of Settlement Growth on the Western Fur Trade Frontier. Report of the Excavations at Fort Michilimackinac, Emmet County, Michigan.* Conducted by the Department of Anthropology and Museum, Michigan State University, 1967, 1968, and 1969. Manuscript.

Buckmaster, M. 1979. *Woodland and Oneota Settlement and Subsistence Systems in the Menominee River Watershed.* Ph.D. diss., Department of Anthropology, Michigan State University, East Lansing.

Buikstra, J. E. 2000. "Historical Bioarcheology and the Beautification of Death." In *Never Anything So Solemn: An Archeological, Biological, and Historical Investigation of the Nineteenth-Century Grafton Cemetery,* ed. J. Buikstra et al., 15–20. Kampsville Studies in Archeology and History, No. 3. Kampsville, Ill.: Center for American Archeology.

Buikstra, J. E., and D. Ubelaker, eds. 1994. *Standards for Data Collection from Human Skeletal Remains.* Arkansas Archaeological Survey Research Series 44. Fayetteville: Arkansas Archaeological Survey.

Buikstra, J. E., J. A. O'Gorman, and C. Sutton, eds. 2000. *Never Anything So Solemn: An Archeological, Biological, and Historical Investigation of the Nineteenth-Century Grafton Cemetery.* Kampsville Studies in Archeology and History, No. 3. Kampsville, Ill.: Center for American Archeology.

Burnham, Capt. John. 1908. "Mysterious Indian Battle Grounds in McLean County, Illinois." *Transactions of the Illinois State Historical Society* 13: 186–191.

Butterfield, Sir Herbert. 1931. *The Whig Interpretation of History.* London: G. Bell.

Canadian Archaeological Association. 1997. "Canadian Archaeological Association: Statement of Principles for Ethical Conduct Pertaining to Aboriginal Peoples." *Canadian Journal of Archaeology* 21: 5–6.

Cannon, A. 1989. "The Historical Dimension in Mortuary Expressions of Status and Sentiment." *Current Anthropology* 30(4): 437–458.

Cardinal, E. A. 1974. "Faunal Remains." In *The Beyer Site,* ed. J. E. Fitting and W. S. Clarke. Special issue. *Michigan Archaeologist* 20(3–4): 265–267.

——. 1978. "Faunal Remains." In *The Gyftakis and McGregor Sites: Middle Woodland Occupations in St. Ignace, Michigan,* ed. J. E. Fitting, 97–111. Manuscript on file, Office of the State Archaeologist, Michigan Historical Center, Lansing, Michigan.

Carlander, K. D. 1970. *Handbook of Freshwater Fish Biology.* Vol. 1. Ames: Iowa State University Press.

Chenoweth, R., and S. W. Semonis. 1992. *The History of McDonough County, Illinois, Volume 1.* The McDonough County Genealogical Society, Macomb. Dallas: Curtis Media Corp.

Claiborne, L. 1997/1998. "The Trend of Supreme Court Decisions in Indian Cases." *American Indian Law Review* 22(2): 585–599.

Clarke, S. J. 1878. *History of McDonough County, Illinois: Its Cities, Towns, and Villages.* Springfield, Ill.: D. W. Lusk, State Printer and Binder.

Cleland, C. E. 1964. "Faunal Remains from Bluff Shelters in Northwest Arkansas." *Bulletin of the Arkansas Archaeological Society* 6(2–3): 39–62.

——. 1965. "Barren Ground Caribou (*Rangifer arcticus*) from an Early Man Site in Southeastern Michigan." *American Antiquity* 30: 350–351.

——. 1966. *Prehistoric Animal Ecology and Ethnozoology of the Upper Great Lakes.* Anthropological Papers No. 29, Museum of Anthropology. Ann Arbor: University of Michigan.

——. 1967. *Traverse Corridor: A Study of Prehistoric Culture Contact.* Proposal submitted to the National Science Foundation, Washington, D.C., on file at the Michigan State University Museum, East Lansing.

——. 1970. "Comparison of the Faunal Remains from French and British Refuse Pits at Fort Michilimackinac: A Study in Changing Subsistence Patterns." *Canadian Historic Sites: Occasional Papers in Archaeology and History,* 3: 8–23.

——. 1972. "From Sacred to Profane: Style Drift in the Decoration of Jesuit Finger Rings." *American Antiquity* 37: 202–210.

——. 1973. "The Pi-wang-go-ning Prehistoric District at Norwood, Michigan." In *The Environment: Man, Earth and Nature in Northwestern Lower Michigan,* 85–87. Michigan Basin Geological Society Annual Field Conference, 1973.

——. 1982. "The Inland Shore Fishery of the Northern Great Lakes: Its Development and Importance in Prehistory." *American Antiquity* 47(4): 761–784.

——. 1985. "Naub-cow-zo-win Discs and Some Observations on the Origin and Development of Ojibwa Iconography." *Arctic Anthropology* 22: 131–140.

——. 1988. "Questions of Substance, Questions that Count." *Historical Archaeology* 22(1): 13–17.

——. 1989. "Comments on 'A Reconsideration of Aboriginal Fishing Strategies in the Northern Great Lakes Region' by Susan R. Martin." *American Antiquity* 54(3): 605–609.

——. 1992. *Rites of Conquest: The History and Culture of Michigan's Native Americans.* Ann Arbor: University of Michigan Press.

——. 1993. "Economic and Adaptive Change among the Lake Superior Chippewa of the Nineteenth Century." In *Approaches to Cultural Contact: Ethnohistorical and Archaeological Perspectives on Change,* ed. J. Rodgers and S. Wilson, 111–122. New York: Plenum Press.

——. 1994. "Confessions of an Archaeologist." In *Linkages,* 5, 7. East Lansing: Michigan State University College of Social Sciences.

——. 2000. *And One Thing Led to Another . . .* Paper presented at the 2000 Meeting of the Society for Historical Archaeology, Quebec, Canada.

——. *The Place of the Pike (Groozhekaaning): A History of the Bay Mills Indian Community.* Ann Arbor: University of Michigan Press.

Clements, R. 1991. "Misconceptions of Culture: Native Peoples and Cultural Property under Canadian Law." *University of Toronto Faculty of Law Review* 49(1): 1–26.

Cohen, F. 1947. "Original Indian Title." *Minnesota Law Review* 32: 28–59.

Coir-Hambacher, D. E. 1993. "Land Use History of the Third Street Bridge Right-of-Way, Bay City, Michigan." In *The Archaic, Woodland, and Historic Period Occupations of the Liberty Bridge Locale, Bay City, Michigan,* ed. W. Lovis, 20–34. Michigan Cultural Resource Investigation Series Volume 1. Lansing: Michigan Department of State.

Colburn, M. L., and T. J. Martin. 1989. "P-Flat Site, 47AS47, Manitou Island, Wisconsin: Faunal Remains from the 1984 Excavations. Appendix A." In *1984 Excavations at Site 47AS47: A Fishing Camp on Manitou Island, Wisconsin,* comp. J. J. Richner, 100–124. U.S. Department of the Interior, National Park Service, Midwest Archaeological Center, Lincoln, Nebraska.

Coombe, R. 1993. "The Properties of Culture and the Politics of Possessing Identity: Native Claims in the Cultural Appropriation Controversy." *Canadian Journal of Law and Jurisprudence* 6(2): 249–285.

Deloria, V. 1995. *Red Earth, White Lies, Native Americans and the Myth of Scientific Fact.* New York: Scribner.

Demeter, S. C., J. A. Robertson, and K. C. Egan. 1994. *Phase I/II Archaeological Investigations of the Environmental Protection Agency Center for Ecology Research and Training, Bay City, Michigan.* Report R-0175, Commonwealth Cultural Resources Group, Jackson, Michigan.

Dickens, R. S., Jr. 1982. *Archaeology of Urban America: The Search for Pattern and Process.* New York: Academic Press.

Dirst, V. 1987. *Archaeological Research at Whitefish Dunes State Park, Door County, Wisconsin.* Madison: Wisconsin Department of Natural Resources.

——. 1993. *The People of the Dunes.* Madison: Wisconsin Department of Natural Resources.

——. 1995a. *Shanty Bay.* Madison: Wisconsin Department of Natural Resources.

——. 1995b. *Stockbridge Harbor: A Late Woodland Village on Lake Winnebago.* Madison: Wisconsin Department of Natural Resources.

Donohue, M. 1989. "Aboriginal Land Rights in Canada: A Historical Perspective in the Fiduciary Relationship." *American Indian Law Review* 15(2): 369–389.

Douglass, J., M. Holman, and J. Stephenson. 1998. "Paleoindian, Archaic and Woodland Artifacts from a Site at Green Lake, Grand Traverse County, Michigan." *Michigan Archaeologist* 44(4): 151–192.

Downer, A. 1997. "Archaeologists–Native American Relations." In *Native Americans and Archaeologists: Stepping Stones to Common Ground,* ed. N. Swidler, K. Dongoske, R. Anyon, and A. Downer, 57–63. Walnut Creek, Calif.: AltaMira Press.

Dunbar, W. F. 1980. *Michigan: A History of the Wolverine State.* Grand Rapids: Eerdman.

Eccles, W. J. 1974. *The Canadian Frontier, 1534–1760.* Rev. ed. Albuquerque: University of New Mexico Press.

——. 1979. "A Belated Review of Harold Adams Innis's 'The Fur Trade in Canada.'" *Canadian Historical Review* 60: 419–441.

——. 1983. "The Fur Trade and Eighteenth-Century Imperialism." *William and Mary Quarterly,* 3d ser., 40: 341–362.

——. 1984. "La Mer de l'Ouest: Outpost of Empire." In *Rendezvous: Selected Papers of the Fourth North American Fur Trade Conference 1981,* ed. T. C. Buckley, 1–14. St. Paul, Minn.: Fourth North American Fur Trade Conference.

——. 1988. "The Fur Trade in the Colonial Northeast." In *Handbook of North American Indians, Volume 4: History of Indian-White Relations,* ed. W. E. Washburn, 334–334. Washington, D.C.: Smithsonian Institution.

Edmunds, R. D., and J. L. Peyser. 1993. *The Fox Wars: The Mesquakie Challenge to New France.* Norman: University of Oklahoma Press.

Ehrhardt, K. L. 2002. *European Materials in Native American Contexts: Rethinking Technological Change.* Ph.D. diss., Department of Anthropology, New York University.

Fairbanks, R. 1995. "Native American Sovereignty and Treaty Rights: Are They Historical Illusions?" *American Indian Law Review* 20(1): 141–149.

Farmer, S. 1969. *History of Detroit and Wayne County and Early Michigan.* Detroit: Gale Research Company.

Farnsworth, K., and T. Emerson, eds. 1986. *Early Woodland Archaeology.* Kampsville Seminars in Archaeology 2, Center for American Archaeology, Kampsville, Illinois.

Faye, S. 1935. "The Foxes' Fort—1730." *Journal of the Illinois State Historical Society* 28(3): 123–163.

Feinman, G. A. 1997. "Thoughts on New Approaches to Combining the Archaeological and Historical Records." *Journal of Archaeological Method and Theory* 4(3–4): 367–377.

Ferguson, N. 2001. *The Cash Nexus: Money and Power in the Modern World, 1700–2000.* New York: Basic Books.

Ferguson, T. 1996. "Native Americans and the Practice of Archaeology." *Annual Review of Anthropology* 25: 63–79.

Ferris, N. 1989. *Continuity within Change: Settlement-Subsistence Strategies and Artifact Patterns of the Southwestern Ontario Ojibwa,* A.D. 1780–1861. Unpublished master's thesis, Department of Geography, York University, Downsview, Ontario.

———. 1998. "'I Don't Think We're in Kansas Anymore...': The Rise of the Archaeological Consulting Industry in Ontario." In *Bringing Back the Past Historical Perspectives on Canadian Archaeology,* ed. P. Smith and D. Mitchell, 225-247. Mercury Series Paper 158, Museum of Civilization, Archaeological Survey of Canada, Ottawa.

———. 1999. "What's in a Name? The Implications of Archaeological Terminology Used in Nonarchaeological Contexts." In *Taming the Taxonomy: Towards a New Understanding of Great Lakes Archaeology,* ed. R. Williamson and C. Watts, 111-121. Toronto: Eastendbooks.

———. 2000. "Current Issues in the Governance of Archaeology in Canada." *Canadian Journal of Archaeology* 24(2): 164-170.

Ferris, N., and L. Leclair. 1999. *Archaeology as Possession: Who Owns the Past in Ontario?* Paper presented at the 1999 Chacmool Conference, Calgary.

Fischer, F. W. 1972. "Schultz Site Ceramics." In *The Schultz Site at Green Point: A Stratified Occupation Area in the Saginaw Valley of Michigan,* ed. J. E. Fitting, 137-190. Memoir No. 4, Museum of Anthropology. Ann Arbor: University of Michigan.

Fitting, J. E. 1966. "Archaeological Investigations of the Carolinian-Canadian Edge Area in Michigan." In *Edge Area Archaeology,* ed. J. E. Fitting. Special issue. *Michigan Archaeologist* 12(4): 143-149.

———. 1972. "Lithic Industries of the Schultz Site." In *The Schultz Site at Green Point: A Stratified Occupation Area in the Saginaw Valley of Michigan,* ed. J. E. Fitting, 191-224. Memoir No. 4, Museum of Anthropology. Ann Arbor: University of Michigan.

———. 1976. "Patterns of Acculturation at the Straits of Mackinac." In *Cultural Change and Continuity: Essays in Honor of James Bennett Griffin,* ed. C. E. Cleland, 321-334. New York: Academic Press.

———. 1979. "Middle Woodland Cultural Development in the Straits of Mackinac Region: Beyond the Hopewell Frontier." In *Hopewell Archaeology,* ed. D. S. Brose and N. Greber, 109-112. Kent, Ohio: Kent State University Press.

Fitting, J. E., and W. S. Clarke. 1974. "The Beyer Sites (SIS-20)." In *Contributions to the Archaeology of the St. Ignace Area,* ed. James E. Fitting. Special issue. *Michigan Archaeologist* 20(3-4): 227-277.

Fitting, J. E., and C. E. Cleland. 1968. "The Crisis of Identity: Theory in Historic Sites Archaeology." *Conference on Historic Site Archaeology Papers 1967* 2(2): 124-138.

Flanders, R. E. 1977. "Some Observations on the Goodall Focus." In *For the Director: Research Essays In Honor of James B. Griffin,* ed. C. E. Cleland, 144-151. Anthropological Papers No. 61, Museum of Anthropology. Ann Arbor: University of Michigan.

Foster, H. 1993. "Forgotten Arguments: Aboriginal Title and Sovereignty." *Manitoba Law Journal* 21: 343-389.

Fowler, J. 1991. "The Legal Structure for the Protection of Archaeological Resources." In *Protecting the Past,* ed. G. Smith and J. Ehrenhard, 21-26. Baton Rouge: CRC Press. Available online at www.cr.nps.gov/seac/protectg.htm.

Fox, G. R. 1959. "Distribution of Garden Beds in Wisconsin and Michigan." *Wisconsin Archeologist* 40: 1-19.

Franzen, J. 1987. *Test Excavation and Locational Analysis of Prehistoric Sites in the Hiawatha National Forest, Michigan: 1985.* Cultural Resource Management Report No. 5, Hiawatha National Forest, Escanaba, Michigan.

Fuller, G. N. 1939. *Michigan: A Centennial History of the State and Its People.* Chicago: Lewis Publishing Company.

Gallagher, J. P., R. F. Boszhardt, R. F. Sasso, and K. Stevenson. 1985. "Oneota Ridged Field Agriculture in Southwestern Wisconsin." *American Antiquity* 50(3): 605–612.

———. 1987. "Floodplain Agriculture in the Driftless Area: A Reply to Overstreet." *American Antiquity* 52(2): 398–404.

Gallagher, J. P., and R. F. Sasso. 1987. "Investigations into Oneota Ridged Field Agriculture on the Northern Margin of the Prairie Peninsula." *Plains Anthropologist* 32(16): 141–151.

Gartner, W. G. 1999. "Late Woodland Landscapes of Wisconsin: Ridged Fields, Effigy Mounds and Territoriality." *Antiquity* 73(281): 671–683.

Gates, C. M., ed. 1965. "The Narrative of Peter Pond." In *Five Fur Traders of the Northwest,* 18–55. St. Paul: Minnesota Historical Society.

Gerin-Lajoie, M. 1976. "Fort Michilimackinac in 1749: Lotbinière's Plan and Description." *Mackinac History.* Vol. 2, Leaflet No. 5. Mackinac State Park Commission, Mackinac Island, Michigan.

Gillis, E. V. 1964. "The Round Lake Site: Antrim County, Michigan." *Coffinberry News Bulletin* 11: 26–31.

Gilman, C. 1982. *Where Two Worlds Meet: The Great Lakes Fur Trade.* St. Paul: Minnesota Historical Society.

Godfrey, W. E. 1986. *The Birds of Canada.* Rev. ed. Ottawa: National Museum of Natural Sciences, National Museum of Canada.

Goldstein, L., and K. Kintigh. 1990. "Ethics and the Reburial Controversy." *American Antiquity* 55(3): 585–591.

Grayson, D. K. 1984. *Quantitative Zooarchaeology: Topics in the Analysis of Archaeological Fauna.* Academic Press. New York.

Green, W., and J. Doershuk. 1998. "Cultural Resource Management and American Archaeology." *Journal of Archaeological Research* 6(2): 121–167.

Greenman, E. F. 1957. "The Garden Beds around Lake Michigan." *Michigan Archaeologist* 3(2): 12–27.

Griffin, J. B., R. E. Flanders, and P. F. Titterington. 1970. *The Burial Complexes of the Knight and Norton Mounds in Illinois and Michigan.* Memoir No. 2, Museum of Anthropology. Ann Arbor: University of Michigan.

Haberstein, R. W., and W. M. Lamers. 1962. *The History of American Funeral Directing.* 2d ed. Milwaukee: Bulfin Printers.

Halsey, J., ed. 1999. *Retrieving Michigan's Buried Past: The Archaeology of the Great Lakes State.* Bulletin 64. Bloomfield Hills, Mich.: Cranbrook Institute of Science.

Hambacher, M. J. 1988. "The Point Arcadia Site (20MT120), Manistee County, Michigan: A Preliminary Consideration of the Williams Collection." *Michigan Archaeologist* 34(4): 81–102.

Hambacher, M. J., S. B. Dunham, M. C. Branstner. 1994. *Phase 3 Cultural Resource Mitigation: 20GT58, Grand Traverse County, Michigan.* Great Lakes Research Associates, Inc. GLRA Report No. 93-06, Williamston. Submitted to Michigan Department of Transportation and Michigan Department of State.

———. 1995. *Cultural Resource Investigations of the Broadway/Washington Avenue Corridor Project Area, Bay City, Michigan.* Submitted to HNTB Michigan, Inc., Okemos,

Michigan, and the Michigan Department of Transportation, Lansing. Report No. 95-21, Great Lakes Research Associates, Inc., Williamston, Michigan.

Hambacher, M. J., and J. A. Robertson. 2000. *Data Recovery Field Work Completion Report US-131 S-Curve Bridge Replacement Project.* Report prepared for Michigan Department of Transportation by Commonwealth Cultural Resources Group, Jackson, Michigan.

Hamilton, T. M. 1976. *Firearms on the Frontier: Guns at Fort Michilimackinac, 1715–1781.* Reports in Mackinac History and Archaeology No. 5, Mackinac Island State Park Commission.

Harris, M. 1984. *Old Cemetery, Macomb, Illinois.* Manuscript on file, McDonough County Genealogical Society, Macomb.

Hauser, R. E. 1966. *An Ethnohistorical Approach to the Study of the Fox Wars, 1712–1735.* Master's thesis, Northern Illinois University, DeKalb.

Heldman, D. P. 1991. "The French in Michigan and Beyond: An Archaeological View from Fort Michilimackinac toward the West." In *French Colonial Archaeology: The Illinois Country and the Western Great Lakes,* ed. John A. Walthall, 201–217. Urbana: University of Illinois Press.

Heldman, D. P., and R. T. Grange, Jr. 1981. *Excavations at Fort Michilimackinac, 1978– 1979: The Rue de la Babillarde.* Archaeological Completion Report Series, No. 3, Mackinac Island State Park Commission, Mackinac Island, Michigan.

Henry, A. 1969. *Travels and Adventure in Canada and the Indian Territories between the Years 1760 and 1776,* ed. J. Bain. Rutland, Vt.: Charles E. Tuttle Co.

Hickerson, H. 1973. "Fur Trade Colonialism and the North American Indians." *Journal of Ethnic Studies* 1: 15–44.

Higginbotham, C. 1982. "Native Americans Versus Archaeologists: The Legal Issues." *American Indian Law Review.* 10: 91–115.

Hinsdale, W. B. 1931. *An Archaeological Atlas of Michigan.* Ann Arbor: University of Michigan Press.

Holman, M. B. 1978. *The Settlement System of the Mackinac Phase.* Ph.D. diss., Department of Anthropology, Michigan State University, East Lansing.

Holman, M., and J. Brashler. 1999. "Economics, Material Culture, and Trade in the Late Woodland Lower Peninsula of Michigan." In *Retrieving Michigan's Buried Past: The Archaeology of the Great Lakes State,* ed. John R. Halsey, 212–220. Bulletin 64. Bloomfield Hills, Mich.: Cranbrook Institute of Science.

Hubbard, B. 1878. "Ancient Garden Beds in Michigan." *American Antiquarian* 1: 1–19.

Hunt, G. T. 1940. *The Wars of the Iroquois: A Study in Inter-tribal Trade Relations.* Madison: University of Wisconsin Press.

Innis, H. A. 1962. *The Fur Trade in Canada.* Reprint of 1956 rev. ed. New Haven, Conn.: Yale University Press.

Jackson, M. G. 1930. "The Beginnings of British Trade at Michilimackinac." *Minnesota History* 11: 231–270.

Jemison, G. 1997. "Who Owns the Past?" In *Native Americans and Archaeologists: Stepping Stones to Common Ground,* ed. N. Swidler, K. Dongoske, R. Anyon, and A. Downer, 57–63. Walnut Creek, Calif.: AltaMira Press.

Jennings, F. 1984. *Ambiguous Iroquois Empire.* New York: W. W. Norton.

Kearns, B., and C. Kirkorian. 1991. "Protecting Sites at the Local Level: The Responsibility and the Legal Authority Towns Have to Protect Their

Archaeological Resources." In *Protecting the Past*, ed. G. Smith and J. Ehrenhard, 247–252. Baton Rouge: CRC Press. Available online at www.cr.nps.gov/seac/protectg.htm.

Keene, D. 1991. "Fort de Chartres: Archaeology in the Illinois Country." In *French Colonial Archaeology: The Illinois Country and the Western Great Lakes*, ed. John A. Walthall, 29–41. Urbana: University of Illinois Press.

Kellogg, L. P. 1908. "The Fox Indians during the French Regime." In *Proceedings of the State Historical Society of Wisconsin at Its 55th Annual Meeting*, 147–178. Madison.

——. 1925. *The French Regime in Wisconsin and the Northwest*. Madison: State Historical Society of Wisconsin.

Kennedy, P. 1987. *Economic Change and Military Conflict from 1500 to 2000*. New York: Random House.

Kent, T. J. 1997. *Birchbark Canoes of the Fur Trade*. 2 vols. Ossineke, Mich.: Silver Fox Enterprises.

Kingsley, R. G. 1981. "Hopewell Middle Woodland Settlement Systems and Cultural Dynamics in Southern Michigan." *Midcontinental Journal of Archaeology* 6(2): 131–178.

Kreisa, P. 1992. "Excavations at the Island Village Site (47MN101): A Heins Creek Occupation in Manitowoc County, Wisconsin." *Wisconsin Archeologist* 73: 118–159.

Larsen, C. E. 1985a. "Geoarchaeological Interpretation of Great Lakes Coastal Environments." In *Archeological Sediments in Context*, ed. J. K. Stein and W. R. Farrand, 91–110. Orono, Maine: Center for the Study of Early Man.

——. 1985b. *A Stratigraphic Study of Beach Features on the Southwestern Shore of Lake Michigan: New Evidence of Holocene Lake Level Fluctuations*. Illinois State Geological Survey, Environmental Geology Notes 112, Illinois State Geological Survey, Urbana.

Larsen, C. E., and S. Demeter. 1979. Archaeological Investigations of the Proposed West River Drive, Bay City. Commonwealth Associates, Inc., Report R-2090, Jackson, Michigan.

Lawrence County, Ohio. n.d. *Land and Property Deed Index, 1818–1864, for Grantee/Grantors*.

Lawson, M. G. 1943. *Fur: A Study in English Mercantilism, 1700–1775*. Toronto: University of Toronto Press.

Leone, M. P., and P. B. Potter, Jr. 1988. "Introduction: Issues in Historic Archaeology." In *The Recovery of Meaning: Historical Archaeology in the Eastern United States*, ed. M. P. Leone and P. B. Potter, Jr., 1–22. Washington, D.C.: Smithsonian Institution.

Lester, D. n.d. *Rural Cemeteries of McDonough County, Illinois*. Volume 2, Bethel-Industry. Schuyler, Ill.: Schuyler-Brown Historical and Genealogical Society and the Schuyler Jail Museum.

Little, B., K. M. Lanphear, and D. W. Owsley. 1992. "Mortuary Display and Status in a Nineteenth-Century Anglo-American Cemetery in Manassas, Virginia." *American Antiquity* 57(3): 397–418.

Loew, P. 1997. "Hidden Transcripts in the Chippewa Treaty Rights Struggle: A Twice Told Story: Race, Resistance and the Politics of Power." *American Indian Quarterly* 21(4): 713–728.

Losey, T. C. 1967. "Toft Lake Village Site." *Michigan Archaeologist* 13(3): 129–134.

Lovis, W. A. 1971. "The Holtz Site (20AN26), Antrim County, Michigan: A Preliminary Report." *Michigan Archaeologist* 17(2): 49–64.

——. 1973. *Late Woodland Cultural Dynamics in the Northern Lower Peninsula of Michigan.* Ph.D. diss., Michigan State University. Xerox University Microfilms, Ann Arbor.

——. 1985. "The Role of the Fletcher Site and the Lower Basin in the Woodland Adaptations of the Saginaw Valley." *Arctic Anthropology,* 22(2): 1–5.

——. 1993a. *The Archaic, Woodland, and Historic Period Occupations of the Liberty Bridge Locale, Bay City, Michigan.* Michigan Cultural Resource Investigation Series Volume 1. Lansing: Michigan Department of State.

——. 1993b. "Discussion and Conclusions." In *The Archaic, Woodland, and Historic Period Occupations of the Liberty Bridge Locale, Bay City, Michigan,* ed. W. Lovis, 225–229. Michigan Cultural Resource Investigation Series Volume 1. Lansing: Michigan Department of State.

——. 2002. *A Bridge to the Past: The Post-Nipissing Archaeology of the Marquette Viaduct Replacement Sites 20BY28 and 20BY387, Bay City, Michigan.* Report submitted to the City of Bay City by Michigan State University, East Lansing.

Lovis, W. A., and J. O'Shea. 1994. "A Reconsideration of Archaeological Research Design in Michigan: 1993." *Michigan Archaeologist* 39(3–4): 107–126.

Lovis, W. A., K. Egan, G. W. Monaghan, B. Smith, and E. Prahl. 1996. "Environment and Subsistence at the Marquette Viaduct Locale of the Fletcher Site." In *Investigating the Archaeological Record of the Great Lakes State: Essays in Honor of Elizabeth Baldwin Garland,* ed. M. Holman, J. Brashler, and K. Parker, 251–305. Kalamazoo: New Issues Press.

Lovis, W. A., K. C. Egan, B. A. Smith, and G. W. Monaghan. 1994. *Origins of Horticulture in the Saginaw Valley: A New View from the Schultz Site.* Paper presented at the Southeastern Archaeological Conference, Lexington, Kentucky.

Lovis, W. A., and M. B. Holman. 1976. "Subsistence Strategies and Population: A Hypothetical Model for the Development of Late Woodland in the Mackinac Straits–Sault Ste. Marie Area." *Michigan Academician* 8(3): 267–276.

Lovis, W. A., G. Rajnovich, and A. Bartley. 1998. "Exploratory Cluster Analysis, Temporal Change, and the Woodland Ceramics of the Portage Site at L'Arbre Croche." In *From the Northern Tier: Papers in Honor of Ronald J. Mason,* ed. C. E. Cleland and R. A. Birmingham. Special issue. *Wisconsin Archaeologist* 79(1): 89–112.

Lubinski, P. M. 1996. "Fish Heads, Fish Heads: An Experiment on Di∑erential Bone Preservation in a Salmonid Fish." *Journal of Archaeological Science* 23: 175–181.

Macomb, J. N. 1856. *Lower Reach of the Saginaw River and Bar in Front.* Bureau of Topographical Engineers of the War Department. Copy on file, Michigan Historical Collections, Lansing.

Mainfort, R. C. 1979. *Indian Social Dynamics in the Period of European Contact, Fletcher Site Cemetery, Bay County.* Anthropological Series 1:4, Publications of the Museum, Michigan State University, East Lansing.

Mainfort, R. C., and W. A. Lovis. n.d. "Prehistoric Materials." In *From Depot to Entrepot: Archaeological Dimensions of Settlement Growth on the Western Fur Trade Frontier. Report of the Excavations at Fort Michilimackinac, Emmet County, Michigan,*

J. A. Brown. Conducted by the Department of Anthropology and Museum, Michigan State University, 1967, 1968, and 1969. Manuscript.

Martin, S. R. 1985. *Models of Change in Woodland Settlement in the Northern Great Lakes Region.* Ph.D. diss., Department of Anthropology, Michigan State University, East Lansing.

———. 1989. "A Reconsideration of Aboriginal Fishing Strategies in the Northern Great Lakes." *American Antiquity* 54(3): 594–604.

———. 1999. *Wonderful Power: The Story of Ancient Copper Working in the Lake Superior Basin.* Detroit: Wayne State University Press.

Martin, T. J. 1975. "Animal Remains from the Spoonville Site, 20-OT-1, Ottawa County, Michigan." *Michigan Archaeologist* 21(1): 1–8.

———. 1980. "Animal Remains from the Winter Site, a Middle Woodland Occupation in Delta County, Michigan." *Wisconsin Archeologist* 61: 91–99.

———. 1982. *Animal Remains from the Scott Point Site: Evidence for Changing Subsistence Strategies during the Late Woodland Period in Northern Michigan.* Paper presented at the Annual Meeting of the Michigan Academy of Science, Arts, and Letters, Kalamazoo, Michigan.

———. 1984. "Animal Remains from the Ten Mile Rapids Site (09-10-02-366)." Appendix B in *1983 Cultural Resource Survey of the Hiawatha National Forest,* D. C. Roper, D. J. Weir, and W. E. Rutter. Report No. R-2589, Commonwealth Associates, Inc., Jackson, Michigan.

———. 1995. *Animal Remains from the Fayette Cliffs Site, A Middle Woodland Mortuary at Burnt Bluff in Delta County, Michigan.* Technical Report 95-000-29, Illinois State Museum Society, Quaternary Studies Program, Springfield.

Mason, C. 1970. "The Oneota Component at the Porte des Morts Site, Door County, Wisconsin." *Wisconsin Archeologist* 51: 191–227.

———. 1998. "The Historic Period, Native Peoples." In *Wisconsin Archaeology,* ed. R. A. Birmingham, C. I. Mason, and J. B. Stoltman. Special issue. *Wisconsin Archeologist* 78(1–2): 298–319.

Mason, R. 1966. *Two Stratified Sites on the Door Peninsula of Wisconsin.* Anthropological Papers No. 26, Museum of Anthropology. Ann Arbor: University of Michigan.

———. 1976. *Rock Island: Historical Indian Archaeology in the Northern Lake Michigan Basin.* Midcontinental Journal of Archaeology Special Paper No. 6. Kent, Ohio: Kent State University Press.

———. 1981. *Great Lakes Archaeology.* New York: Academic Press.

———. 1990. "Late Woodland and Oneota Occupations on Rock Island, Wisconsin." *Wisconsin Archeologist* 71: 115–136.

———. 1991. "Rock Island and the Laurel Cultural Frontier in Northern Lake Michigan." *Midcontinental Journal of Archaeology* 16: 118–155.

———. 1992. "Compilation of Door County Radiocarbon Dates." *Wisconsin Archeologist* 73: 111–117.

Masulis, M. C., and T. J. Martin. 1987. "Animal and Plant Remains from Archaeological Sites in the Manistique District of the Hiawatha National Forest, Michigan." In *Test Excavation and Locational Analysis of Prehistoric Sites in the Hiawatha National Forest, Michigan: 1985 Season,* John G. Franzen. Appendix 2. Cultural Resource Management Report No. 5, Hiawatha National Forest, Escanaba.

Maxwell, M. S. 1964. "Indian Artifacts at Fort Michilimackinac, Mackinaw City, Michigan." *Michigan Archaeologist* 10: 23–30.

Maxwell, M. S., and L. R. Binford. 1961. *Excavations at Fort Michilimackinac, Mackinaw City, Michigan. 1959 Season.* Michigan State University, Publications of the Museum, Cultural Series, Vol. 1:1, East Lansing.

McClurken, J., ed. 2000. *Fish in the Lakes, Wild Rice, and Game in Abundance.* East Lansing: Michigan State University Press.

McCombie, A. M., and F. E. Fry. 1960. "Selectivity of Gill Nets for Lake Whitefish, Coregonus Clupeaformis." *Transactions of the American Fisheries Society,* 89(2): 176–184.

McDonough County Genealogical Society. 1996. "War of 1812 Bounty Map." *McDonough County Genealogical Society Newsletter* 17(2): 33.

McEvoy, J. 2000. *Treaty Rights Renovation or Modernisation?* Unpublished paper presented at the Canadian Law Society Conference on Native Rights, Moncton.

McGuire, R. H. 1997. "Why Have Archaeologists Thought the Real Indians Were Dead and What Can We Do about It?" In *Indians and Anthropologists,* ed. T. Biolsi and L. Zimmerman, 63–91. Tucson: University of Arizona Press.

——. 1988. "Dialogues with the Dead: Ideology and the Cemetery." In *The Recovery of Meaning: Historical Archaeology in the Eastern United States,* ed. M. P. Leone and P. B. Potter, Jr., 435–480. Washington, D.C.: Smithsonian Institution.

McPherron, A. L. 1967. *The Juntunen Site and the Late Woodland Prehistory of the Upper Great Lakes Area.* Anthropological Papers No. 30, Museum of Anthropology, University of Michigan, Ann Arbor.

Mead, B. 1979. *The Airport Sites—Manistee County.* Site file report on file at the Division of Archaeology, Michigan Historical Center, Lansing.

Meekhof, E., and T. J. Martin. 1998. *Middle Woodland Animal Exploitation in the Middle Grand River Valley, Michigan: Impressions from the Prison Farm Site (20IA58).* Paper presented at the Midwest Archaeological Conference, Muncie, Indiana.

Michigan Historical Collections. 1877–1929. *Michigan Pioneer Historical Society: Collections and Researches.* Lansing, Michigan.

Micozzi, M. S. 1991. *Postmortem Change in Human and Animal Remains: A Systematic Approach.* Springfield, Ill.: Charles C. Thomas.

Miller, J.J., II, and L. M. Stone. 1970. *Eighteenth-Century Ceramics from Fort Michilimackinac, A Study in Historical Archaeology.* Smithsonian Studies in History and Technology, No. 4. Washington, D.C.: Smithsonian Institution.

Monaghan, G. W., and W. A. Lovis. 2002. *Exploration for Buried Archaeological Sites in the Great Lakes Region: Michigan as a Case Study.* Report submitted to the Michigan Department of Transportation by Michigan State University, East Lansing.

Morse, E. W. 1979. *Fur Trade Canoe Routes of Canada/Then and Now.* 2d ed. Toronto: University of Toronto Press.

Mueller, Eileen. 1976. *Two Hundred Years of Memorialization.* Evanston, Ill.: Monument Builders of North America.

Murnahan, V. M. 1987. *Earliest Marriage Records of Lawrence County, Ohio, Volumes* I-II-III. April 11, 1817, to July 23, 1843. Indexed Male & Female Surnames. Typescript.

Needs-Howarth, S. J. 1999. *Native Fishing in the Great Lakes—A Multi-disciplinary Approach to Zooarchaeological Remains from Precontact Iroquoian Villages near Lake Simcoe, Ontario.* Ph.D. diss., Rijksuniversiteit Groningen, The Netherlands.

Nicholson, R. A. 1992. "An Assessment of the Value of Density Measurements to Archaeological Fish Bone Studies." *International Journal of Osteoarchaeology* 2(2): 139-154.

Noble, V. E. 1983. "In Dire Straits: Subsistence Patterns at Mackinac." *Michigan Archaeologist* 29: 29-48.

Ohio Family Historians. 1964. *1830 Federal Population Census: Ohio*. Index, Volume 11, Part 1. Columbus: Ohio Library Foundation.

Ontario Ministry of Tourism, Culture and Recreation. 1997. *Conserving a Future for Our Past: An Educational Primer and Comprehensive Guide for Non-Specialists*. Toronto: Ontario Ministry of Tourism, Culture, and Recreation.

Ordon, K. 1985. "Aboriginal Title: The Trails of Aboriginal Indian Title and Rights—An Overview of Recent Case Law." *American Indian Law Review* 13(2): 59-78.

Overstreet, D. F. 1976. *The Grand River Lake Koshkonong, Green Bay and Lake Winnebago Phases—Eight Hundred Years of Oneota Prehistory*. Ph.D. diss., Department of Anthropology, University of Wisconsin—Milwaukee.

———. 1981. "Investigations at the Pipe Site (47-Fd-10) and Some Perspectives on Eastern Wisconsin Oneota Prehistory." *Wisconsin Archeologist* 62: 365-525.

Parker, K. E. 1992. *Plant Remains from Archaeological Excavations at Site 20SA1034 in the Saginaw Valley of Michigan*. Report submitted to the Institute for Minnesota Archaeology by Great Lakes Ecosystems, Inc., Indian River, Michigan.

———. 1996. "Three Corn Kernels and a Hill of Beans: The Evidence for Prehistoric Agriculture in Michigan." In *Investigating the Archaeological Record of the Great Lakes State: Essays in Honor of Elizabeth Baldwin Garland*, ed. M. B. Holman, J. G. Brashler, and K. E. Parker, 307-339. Kalamazoo: New Issues Press.

———. 2000. *Plant Remains from Archaeological Excavations at the Prison Farm Site (20IA58): Final Report*. Indian River, Mich.: Great Lakes Ecosystems.

Parkins, A. E. 1918. *The Historical Geography of Detroit*. Lansing: Michigan Historical Commission.

Parmalee, P. W. 1963. "Vertebrate Remains from the Bell Site, Winnebago County, Wisconsin." *Wisconsin Archeologist* 44(1): 58-69.

Peckham, H. A. 1938. *Old Fort Michilimackinac at Mackinaw City, Mich*. Ann Arbor: University of Michigan Press.

Persky, S. 1998. *Delgamuukw—The Supreme Court of Canada Decision on Aboriginal Title*. Vancouver: Greystone Books.

Peske, G. R. 1966. "Oneota Settlement Patterns and Agricultural Patterns in Winnebago County." *Wisconsin Archeologist* 47: 188-195.

Peter, V. S., and M. B. Hotchkiss. 1996. *Churches of McDonough County, Illinois*. Macomb, Ill.: McDonough County Genealogical Society.

Peters, B. 1980. "Comments on the Distribution of Garden Beds in Kalamazoo County." *Ecumene* 12: 31-39.

Peyser, J. L. 1980. "1730 Fox Fort." *Journal of the Illinois State Historical Society* 63: 201-213.

———. 1987. "The 1730 Siege of the Foxes: Two Maps by Canadian Participants Provide Additional Information on the Fort and Its Location." *Illinois Historical Journal* 80: 147-154.

Pleger, T., and N. Lowrey. 1994. *A Preliminary Report of the 1994 Field Research at the Chautauqua Grounds Site (47-Mt-71).* Paper presented at the 40th Midwest Archaeological Conference, Beloit, Wisconsin.

Prahl, E. J. 1987. *Preliminary Land Use History, Fletcher Property, Bay City, Michigan, Section 16, T14N, R5E.* Report submitted to Roese-Shaw Development Corporation by Caminos Associates, Inc. Manuscript on file, Michigan State University Museum, East Lansing.

———. 1990. "Excavations at the Trombley House (20BY70): A Settlement Period House Site in Bay City, Michigan." *Michigan Archaeologist* 35(3–4).

———. 1991. "The Mounds of the Muskegon." In *Pilot of the Grand: Papers in Tribute to Richard E. Flanders, Part II,* ed. T. J. Martin and C. E. Cleland. Special issue. *Michigan Archaeologist* 37(2): 59–125.

Prahl, E. J., C. E. Cleland, J. Prahl, and J. Cleland. 1990. "The Making of the Mysterious Beaver Island Sun Circle (20CX65)." *Michigan Archaeologist* 36(3–4): 253–276.

Prevec, R. 1988. *The Shawana Site BkHk-1 Faunal Report.* Unpublished manuscript in possession of author.

———. 1991. *Hunter's Point BfHg-3 Faunal Report.* Manuscript on file, Ontario Ministry of Culture and Communication, Toronto, Canada.

Quaife, M. M. 1928. *The John Askin Papers, 1747–1795.* Vol. 1. Burton Historical Records, Detroit Library Commission, Detroit, Michigan.

Quimby, G. I. 1941. "The Goodall Focus: An Analysis of Ten Hopewellian Components in Michigan." *Indiana Historical Society* 2(2): 63–161.

Ravesloot, J. 1997. "Changing Native American Perceptions of Archaeology and Archaeologists." In *Native Americans and Archaeologists: Stepping Stones to Common Ground,* ed. N. Swidler, K. Dongoske, R. Anyon, and A. Downer, 172–177. Walnut Creek, Calif.: AltaMira Press.

Ray, A. J. 1980. "Indians as Consumers in the Eighteenth Century." In *Old Trails and New Directions: Papers of the Third North American Fur Trade Conference,* ed. C. M. Judd and A. J. Ray, 255–271. Toronto: University of Toronto Press.

———. 1988. "The Hudson Bay's Company and Native People." In *Handbook of North American Indians, Volume 4: History of Indian-White Relations,* ed. W. E. Washburn, 335–350. Washington, D.C.: Smithsonian Institution.

———. 1996. "The Northern Interior, 1600 to Modern Times." In *The Cambridge History of the Native Peoples of the Americas, Volume 1: North America, Part 2,* ed. B. G. Trigger and W. E. Washburn, 259–327. Cambridge: Cambridge University Press.

Regier, H. A., and D. S. Robson. 1966. "Selectivity of Gill Nets, Especially to Lake White Fish." *Journal of the Fisheries Research Board of Canada* 23(3): 423–454.

Richner, J. J. 1991. *Archeological Excavations at the Platte River Campground Site (20BZ16), Sleeping Bear Dunes National Lakeshore 1987.* Technical Report No. 10, United States Department of Interior, National Park Service, Midwest Archeological Center, Lincoln, Nebraska.

Riley, T., and G. Freimuth. 1979. "Field Systems and Frost Drainage in the Prehistoric Agriculture of the Upper Great Lakes." *American Antiquity* 44(2): 271–285.

Rogers, J. D. 1990. *Objects of Change: The Archaeology and History of Arikara Contact with Europeans.* Washington, D.C.: Smithsonian Institution.

Roper, D. 1979. "Archaeological Survey and Settlement Pattern Models in Central

Illinois." *Illinois State Museum Scientific Papers, Vol. XVI, Midcontinental Journal of Archaeology Special Paper No. 2.* Illinois State Museum, Springfield.

Roper, D. C., D. J. Weir, and W. E. Rutter. 1984. *1983 Cultural Resource Survey of the Hiawatha National Forest.* Report No. R-2589. Commonwealth Associates, Inc., Jackson, Michigan.

Rotman, L. 1996. *Parallel Paths: Fiduciary Doctrine and the Crown-Native Relationship in Canada.* Toronto: University of Toronto Press.

Ruger, A. 1867. *Bird's-Eye View of Bay City, Portsmouth, Wenona, and Salzburg, Bay Co., Michigan.* Chicago: Chicago Lithographing Company.

———. 1879. *Panoramic View of the City of Bay City, Bay County, Michigan.* Madison, Wis.: J. J. Stoner.

Russell, N. V. 1939. *The British Regime in Michigan and the Old Northwest, 1760–1796.* Northfield, Minn.: Carleton College.

Sanborn Map Company. 1912. *Insurance Maps of Bay City, Michigan.* New York: Sanborn Map Company.

Sasso, R. F., R. F. Boszhardt, J. C. Knox, J. L. Theler, K. P. Stevenson, J. P. Gallagher, and C. Stiles-Hanson. 1985. *Prehistoric Ridged Field Agriculture in the Upper Mississippi Valley.* Report of Investigations No. 38, Mississippi Valley Archaeology Center, LaCrosse, Wisconsin.

Schoolcraft, H. R. 1860. *Archives of Aboriginal Knowledge. Containing All the Original Papers Laid before Congress Respecting the History, Antiquities, Language, Ethnology, Pictography, Rites, Superstitions, and Mythology of the Indian Tribes of the United States.* Volume I. Philadelphia: J. B. Lippincott & Company.

Scott, E. M. 1985. *French Subsistence at Fort Michilimackinac, 1715–1781: The Clergy and the Traders.* Archaeological Completion Report Series, No. 9. Mackinac Island State Park Commission, Mackinac Island, Michigan.

Scott, W. B., and E. J. Crossman. 1973. *Freshwater Fishes of Canada.* Bulletin 184, Fisheries Research Board of Canada, Ottawa.

Schumacher, J. 1918. "Indian Remains in Door County." *Wisconsin Archeologist* 16: 125–145.

Shapiro, G. 1979. "Early British Subsistence Strategy at Michilimackinac: A Case Study in Systemic Particularism." *Conference on Historic Site Archaeology Papers 1978* 13: 315–356.

Smith, B. A. 1983. *Analysis of the Faunal Remains from Seven Northern Michigan Archaeological Sites.* Manuscript on file, Archaeology Laboratory, Michigan Technological University, Houghton, Michigan.

———. 1985. "The Use of Animals at the 17th Century Mission of St. Ignace." *Michigan Archaeologist* 31(4): 97–122.

———. 1988. *Faunal Remains from the Point Arcadia Site (20MT120), Michigan.* Manuscript on file, Division of Anthropology, The MSU Museum, Michigan State University, East Lansing.

———. 1989. *Protohistoric Odawa Fishing at the Providence Bay Site, Manitoulin Island: Further Evidence of the Inland Shore Fishery of the Upper Great Lakes?* Paper presented at the Annual Meeting of the Canadian Archaeological Association, Fredericton, New Brunswick.

———. 1993. "Faunal Remains." In *1992 Cultural Resource Surveys: Phase II Evaluations,*

Hiawatha National Forest, S. B. Dunham, M. J. Hambacher, and M. C. Branstner, 130–138. Report No. 93-04, Great Lakes Research Associates, Inc., Williamston, Michigan.

——. 2000a. *Fish Faunal Identifications from Late Woodland Component at the Summer Island Site.* Unpublished manuscript in possession of author.

——. 2000b. *Faunal Identifications from the Sturgeon River site, Delta Co., MI.* Unpublished manuscript in possession of author.

Smith, B. A., and C. E. Cleland. 1987. "Analysis of the Faunal Material from Test Unit 1 of the P-Flat Site." Appendix A in *Archaeological Investigations at Apostle Islands National Lakeshore, 1979–1980,* Jeffrey J. Richner. U.S. Department of the Interior, National Park Service, Midwest Archaeological Center, Lincoln, Nebraska.

Smith, B. A., K. C. Egan, W. A. Lovis, and G. W. Monaghan. 1994. *Targeting the Marsh: A Reanalysis of the Subsistence Patterns and Local Environments at the Schultz Site, Michigan.* Paper presented at the Symposium of the Ontario Archaeological Society, Toronto.

Smith, B. A., and R. Prevec. 2000. "Economic Strategies and Community Patterning at the Providence Bay Site (BkHn-3), Manitoulin Island." *Ontario Archaeology* 69: 76–91.

Smith, B. D. 1987. "Independent Domestication of Seed-bearing Plants in Eastern North America." In *Emergent Horticultural Economies of the Eastern Woodlands,* ed. W. F. Keegan, 3–47. Occasional Paper No. 7, Center for Archaeological Investigations, Southern Illinois University at Carbondale, Carbondale.

South, S. A. 1977. *Method and Theory in Historical Archeology.* New York: Academic Press.

State of Illinois. n.d. Illinois Statewide Marriage Index, 1763–1900. Illinois State Archives, www.cyberdriveillinois.com/GenealogyMWeb/marrsrch.html.

——. 1842. Illinois Public Domain Land Tract Sales Database. Illinois State Archives, www.cyberdriveillinois.com/GenealogyMWeb/landsrch.html.

Stein, G. J. 1999. *Rethinking World-Systems: Diasporas, Colonies, and Interaction in Uruk Mesopotamia.* Tucson: University of Arizona Press.

Stelle, L. J. 1989. "History, Archeology, and the 1730 Siege of the Foxes." *Journal of the Steward Anthropological Society* 18(1–2): 187–212.

——. 1992a. "History and Archaeology: The 1730 Mesquakie Fort." In *Calumet and Fleur-de-lys: Archaeology of Indian and French Contact in the Midcontinent,* ed. J. A. Walthall and T. E. Emerson, 265–307. Washington, D.C.: Smithsonian Institution.

——. 1992b. *The 1730 Fox Fort: Historical Debate and Archaeological Endeavor.* Paper presented at the 1992 SHA Conference on Historical and Underwater Archaeology, Kingston, Jamaica.

Stone, L. M. 1970. *Archaeological Research at Fort Michilimackinac, An Eighteenth Century Historic Site in Emmet County, Michigan: 1959–1966 Excavations.* 2 vols. Ph.D. diss., Michigan State University, East Lansing.

——. 1974. *Fort Michilimackinac, 1715–1781.* Publications of the Michigan State University Museum, Anthropological Series, Vol. 2, East Lansing.

Struever, S. 1964. "The Hopewell Interaction Sphere in Riverine-Western Great Lakes Culture History." In *Hopewellian Studies,* ed. J. R. Caldwell and R. L. Hall, 109–122. Illinois State Museum Scientific Papers, Vol. 12, Springfield.

Thwaites, R. G., ed. 1906. "The French Regime in Wisconsin—2, 1727–1748." *Collections of the State Historical Society of Wisconsin*, Vol. 17.

——. 1959. *The Jesuit Relations and Allied Documents: Travel and Explorations of the Jesuit Missionaries in New France, 1610–1791.* Vol. 55. New York: Pageant Books.

Tordoff, J. D. 1983. *An Archaeological Perspective on the Organization of the Fur Trade in Eighteenth-Century New France.* Ph.D. diss., Michigan State University, East Lansing.

Trigger, B. 1980. Archaeology and the Image of the American Indian. *American Antiquity* 45(4): 662–676.

——. 1985. *Natives and Newcomers: Canada's "Heroic Age" Reconsidered.* Montreal: McGill-Queen's University Press.

Tsosie, R. 1997. "Indigenous Rights and Archaeology." In *Native Americans and Archaeologists Stepping Stones to Common Ground,* ed. N. Swidler, K. Dongoske, R. Anyon and A. Downer, 64–76. Walnut Creek, Calif.: AltaMira Press.

Turcheneske, J., Jr. 1993. "Wisconsin's Attempt to Reach a Treaty Rights Settlement with Its Chippewa Indians." In *Papers of the Twenty-Fourth Algonquian Conference,* ed. W. Cowan, 381–401. Ottawa: Carleton University Press.

U.S. Bureau of the Census. 1850. *Federal Census Population Schedule, 1850, McDonough County, Illinois.*

——. 1870. *Federal Census Population Schedule, 1870, McDonough County, Illinois.*

——. 1880. *Federal Census Population Schedule, 1880, McDonough County, Illinois.*

U.S. Government. n.d. *Pay Rolls of Militia Entitled to Land Bounty Under the Act of Congress of Sept. 28, 1850,* and its supplement, *Muster Rolls of the Virginia Militia in the War of 1812.* The Library of Virginia, http://eagle.vsla.edu/war1812.

Volkel, L. 1980. *Transcription of 1860 Mortality Schedule for the State of Illinois.* Macomb, Ill.: McDonough County Genealogical Society.

Weir, D. J., and C. S. Demeter. 1991. *Historic Land Use Study: Ambassador Bridge Cargo Inspection Facility, Ambassador Bridge Border Station, Detroit, Wayne County, Michigan. Ellis, Naeyaert, Genheimer Associates, Inc., Troy, Michigan, and the General Services Administration, Public Buildings Services, Design and Construction Division 5PC, Chicago, Illinois.* Report R-0060, Commonwealth Cultural Resources Group, Jackson, Michigan.

Weir, D. J., C. S. Demeter, J. R. Kern, W. E. Rutter, and J. Schuldenrein. 1986. *Cultural Resource Assessment of Proposed Rehabilitation of the Platte River Campground and Limited Testing at Site 20BZ16, Benzie County, Michigan.* Report No. R-2792. Gilbert/Commonwealth, Inc., Jackson, Michigan. Submitted to National Park Service, Midwest Archeological Center, Lincoln, Nebraska.

Wells, E. 1969. "Additional Finds from Heins Creek." *Wisconsin Archeologist* 50: 1–25.

Wells, E. (Mrs.). 1964. "Another Toggle Head Harpoon from Door County." *Wisconsin Archeologist* 45: 99–101.

Wheeler, A., and A. K. G. Jones. 1989. *Fishes.* Cambridge: Cambridge University Press.

White, R. 1991. *The Middle Ground: Indians, Empires, and Republics in the Great Lakes Region, 1650–1815.* Cambridge: Cambridge University Press.

Wilkins, D. 1994. "The U.S. Supreme Court's Explication of 'Federal Plenary Power': An Analysis of Case Law Affecting Tribal Sovereignty, 1886–1914." *American Indian Quarterly* 18(3): 349–368.

———. 1997. *American Indian Sovereignty and the U.S. Supreme Court.* Austin: University of Texas Press.

Wisconsin Historical Collections. 1855–1911. *Collections of the State Historical Society of Wisconsin,* ed. L. C. Draper and R. G. Thwaites. Madison, Wis.: State Historical Society of Wisconsin.

Wolf, E. R. 1982. *Europe and the People without History.* Berkeley: University of California Press.

Yarnell, R. A. 1964. *Aboriginal Relationships between Culture and Plant Life in the Upper Great Lakes Region.* Anthropological Papers No. 23, Museum of Anthropology. Ann Arbor: University of Michigan.

Zimmerman, L. 1989. "Human Bones as Symbols of Power: Aboriginal American Belief Systems toward Bones and 'Grave Robbing' Archaeologists." In *Conflicts in the Archaeology of Living Traditions,* ed. R. Layton, 211–216. London: Unwin.

———. 1997. "Anthropology and Responses to the Burial Issue." In *Indians and Anthropologists,* ed. T. Biolsi and L. Zimmerman, 63–91. Tucson: University of Arizona Press.

Contributors

Janet G. Brashler is Professor and Curator of Anthropology at Grand Valley State University. She earned her B.A. from Northwestern University and her M.A. and Ph.D. from Michigan State University. Her primary research interests focus on the ecology and adaptive strategies of Great Lakes indigenous populations and on ceramic analysis, including stylistic, experimental, and technological studies. In addition to a continuing research agenda in western Michigan, she also works in Jordan on Nabatean and Roman period sites, most recently focusing on using archaeology to help model earthquake events in the Dead Sea Rift.

James A. Brown is Professor of Anthropology at Northwestern University. He earned his Ph.D. in 1965 at the University of Chicago. He is an archaeologist specializing in the cultural history of the mound-building peoples of the Mississippi River watershed with particular interest in the iconography of the Mississippian period (since 1000) as well as ritual and mortuary practices. Professor Brown's fieldwork has been devoted to the sites of Mound City (Hopewell) in Ohio, Michilimackinac (Contact period) in Michigan, and Koster (Archaic period), the Starved Rock area, and Cahokia in Illinois, as well as other locations. The Spiro site in eastern Oklahoma has been an area of intense interest as well.

Marla M. Buckmaster is Professor in the Department of Sociology, Anthropology, and Social Work at Northern Michigan University, where she has taught since 1971. She earned her Ph.D. in 1979 at Michigan State University with a dissertation focusing on Woodland and Oneota settlement in the Menominee River drainage. For more than three decades, her research into the precontact adaptations of Michigan's Upper Peninsula has spanned sites from the Late Paleo-Indian through European Contact periods. Her current work relates to the age and structure of ridged field agriculture in the northern Great Lakes.

Jane E. Buikstra, biological anthropologist and archaeologist, earned her Ph.D. from the University of Chicago. She is the Leslie Spier Distinguished Professor of Anthropology at the University of New Mexico and was formerly the Harold H. Swift Distinguished Service Professor of Anthropology at the University of Chicago. She was elected to the National Academy of Sciences in 1987. Her research interests include paleopathology, human skeletal biology, paleodemography, forensic anthropology, genetic relationships within and between paleopopulations, paleodiet, and funerary archaeology. She has edited or authored fourteen books and monographs, including *Prehistoric Tuberculosis in the Americas, Standards for Data Collection from Human Skeletal Remains* (with Douglas Ubelaker), and *Staging Ritual* (with Douglas Charles and Gordon Rakita). In addition, she has published more than a hundred articles or chapters on a variety of subjects, including bone chemistry in eastern North America, ancient treponematosis and tuberculosis in the Americas and in Egypt, leprosy in the Americas, diet and health of Argaric peoples (Bronze Age, Spain), australopithecine spinal pathology, trauma in Copan's founding dynasty (Maya), and coca-chewing, cranial deformation, tuberculosis, and funerary rituals of ancient Andeans.

Neal Ferris has worked for the past seventeen years for the Ontario provincial government as the regional archaeologist for southwestern Ontario, that part of the province surrounded by the Great Lakes of Huron, St. Clair, and Erie. He has worked on a wide array of archaeological sites, though his research has focused on the Late Woodland and seventeenth- through nineteenth-century Euro-Canadian and Native settlement of the region. Issues related to archaeologists and society, and Late Historic Native archaeology, have dominated his ongoing research. This work most recently has been tied to his Ph.D. research at McMaster University in Hamilton, thanks to a professional development opportunity provided by his employer.

Lynne G. Goldstein has been Professor and Chair of the Department of Anthropology at Michigan State University since 1996. Previously, she taught for many years at the University of Wisconsin–Milwaukee. She earned her B.A. in anthropology in 1971 from Beloit College and her Ph.D. in anthropology in 1976 from Northwestern University. Her work in Wisconsin has primarily focused on the late prehistoric Aztalan site. She has worked extensively with Native American tribes in Wisconsin and elsewhere, and in addition to her regionally based research program in southeastern Wisconsin, she has examined a variety of late prehistoric societies and their mortuary practices. Her mortuary analysis work includes prehistoric and historic sites, and Native American and European populations. She is active in regional and national professional organizations and has worked extensively with public programming.

Jim Harrison is a widely admired poet, novelist, essayist, and screenwriter who received B.A. and M.A. degrees in English and comparative literature from Michigan State University in 1960 and 1966, respectively. Born and raised in northern Michigan, he is the author of several acclaimed works of fiction, including *Wolf* (1971), *Legends of the Fall* (1979), *Dalva* (1988), *The Woman Lit by Fireflies* (1990), *The Road Home* (1999), and *The Beast God Forgot to Invent* (2000). His collections of poetry include *Plain Song* (1965), *Locations* (1968), *Letters to Yesenin* (1970), *The Theory and Practice of Rivers* (1989), *After Ikkyû* (1996), and *The Shape of the Journey* (1998). His first children's book, *The Boy Who Ran to the Woods* (2000), is a semiautobiographical account of his own childhood. His recently published *Off to the Side: A Memoir* (2002) is an autobiographical account of his upbringing in Michigan and his career. He now makes his home on a ranch in Montana.

Margaret B. Holman is an adjunct faculty member in the Department of Anthropology at Michigan State University and a research associate at the Michigan State University Museum. She teaches, does contract archaeology, and serves on graduate committees. She received her Ph.D. from Michigan State University under the direction of Charles E. Cleland. Her research focuses on the Great Lakes and centers on prehistoric hunters and gatherers, including subsistence-settlement, social organization, and mobility. Her interest in subsistence is reflected in several publications debating the question of whether Indians made maple sugar before they encountered Europeans. Other recent work examines Late Woodland social organization in relation to cooperative buffering between neighboring groups and addresses the use of storage in conjunction with strategies of Late Woodland mobility.

William A. Lovis is Associate Director for the Natural and Social Sciences and Curator of Anthropology at the MSU Museum, and Professor in the Department of Anthropology at Michigan State University. He is also the current editor of the *Midcontinental Journal of Archaeology*. His primary research interests are in hunter-gatherer adaptations, the transition to horticulture, and the relationship between paleoenvironmental and economic change in the Great Lakes and western Europe. He also has a continuing interest in analytic method and research design. His fieldwork in the Great Lakes and northern England during more than three decades has resulted in numerous research monographs, book chapters, and journal articles. He has also been active in national and state professional societies, particularly regarding issues of public policy and repatriation. He earned his B.S. in 1969 from New York University and both his M.A. in 1972 and Ph.D. in 1973 from Michigan State University.

Terrance J. Martin, a native of western Michigan, received his B.S. in anthropology in 1973 from Grand Valley State University, his M.A. in anthropology in 1976 from Western Michigan University, and his Ph.D. in anthropology in 1986 from Michigan State University. Currently a Curator of Anthropology at the Illinois State Museum in Springfield and an Adjunct Professor in the Sociology-Anthropology Program at the University of Illinois at Springfield, he has been involved in collaborative, interdisciplinary archaeological research projects for more than thirty years focusing on osteological evidence for animal exploitation in the greater Midwest. He is especially interested in the archaeozoology of late prehistoric and early historic Native American sites and in eighteenth-century French Colonial occupations.

Carol I. Mason is Adjunct Professor of Anthropology at Lawrence University, Appleton, Wisconsin, and Emerita Professor of Anthropology at the University of Wisconsin—Fox Valley. She earned both her M.A. and Ph.D. at the University of Michigan. Her major archaeological research interests cover northeastern Wisconsin prehistory and historic sites. She has been active in fieldwork on sites from the Paleo-Indian period through European settlement. Mason's most recent interests include the origins of maple sugaring and the use of Jesuit Rings for dating archaeological sites. Her publications include *Wisconsin Indians: Prehistory to Statehood* and *Anthropology through Science Fiction* as well as numerous papers in archaeological journals. A past president of the Wisconsin Archaeological Survey, she has been active in both state and regional archaeological affairs.

Vergil E. Noble, a native of suburban Detroit, received his B.S. in 1970, M.A. in 1979, and Ph.D. in anthropology in 1983 from Michigan

State University. Formerly on the faculty of Illinois State University (1984–1986), he has worked for the National Park Service, Midwest Archeological Center, Lincoln, Nebraska, since 1987. He provides oversight and technical assistance for seventy National Historic Landmark archaeological properties administered by nonfederal stewards and occasionally conducts field investigations in various National Park Service units within the thirteen-state Midwest region. His principal research interest centers on the archaeology of the eighteenth-century French fur trade, and he has long been involved with the interplay of archaeological research and heritage tourism. He is a past president of the Society for Historical Archaeology and has authored nearly one hundred publications.

Beverley A. Smith is an Associate Professor of Anthropology at the University of Michigan—Flint. She received her B.A. from the University of Toronto, Canada, and her M.A. and Ph.D. from Michigan State University, where she studied with Charles E. Cleland. Her research specialization is zooarchaeology, and she has analyzed animal bone collections from precontact and historic period sites throughout the Great Lakes and upper Midwest regions. She is particularly interested in human-animal relationships as they reflect subsistence strategies, exchange systems, and ritual. Her research has employed nutritional data to assist in reconstructing local and regional subsistence patterns.

Index